My Life with Christ

SPIRITUAL MEDITATIONS

FOR THE MODERN READER

BY

ANTHONY J. PAONE, S.J.

Author of MY DAILY BREAD

IMAGE BOOKS

A Division of Doubleday & Company, Inc.
Garden City, New York

Image Books Edition 1965
by special arrangement with Doubleday & Company, Inc.

Image Books Edition published February 1965

The New Testament quotations herein are from the Confraternity version, used with the permission of the Confraternity
of Christian Doctrine.

Dedicated to those whose practical human problems inspired the writing of this book.

CONTENTS

Contents

My Life with Christ

Contents

My Life with Christ

AN IMPORTANT MESSAGE TO THE READER

At best our earthly life is an imperfect performance. In spite of our best intentions and sincerest efforts, we are constantly subject to unintended mistakes, unwanted weaknesses, and occasional sins. On the one hand we believe that God understands our weaknesses, sees our sincerity, and accepts our good will. On the other hand, we feel that we may be deceiving ourselves, should try harder to please God, and deserve punishment for not being better than we are. Though Christ promised peace to His followers, we sometimes feel far from peaceful. In our self-doubts, we tend to fear that this situation is somehow our fault.

The truth is that most people have some mistaken ideas intermingled with their religious beliefs. Ignorance and misunderstandings color, distort, or hinder our view of God, religion, and daily human living. In time our mental and emotional errors become so much a part of us that we believe they represent the truth. A more objective view of God, ourselves, and others, would help us come closer to the ideals which Christ presented to us and the peace He promised.

Since God has made Himself known to us not only through His supernatural revelation, but also through the workings of nature, a balanced religious outlook depends not only on an adequate knowledge of revealed truth, but also on a proper understanding of human nature. This book is an attempt to help the reader toward this double goal. However, self-knowledge includes the awareness of one's own defects. This can sometimes be disagreeable, and even discouraging, if taken in large doses. The reader is therefore advised to read and reflect on *one chapter a day*.

Through the grace of God and his own daily efforts, the reader can gradually achieve a fuller emotional development and spiritual formation. As his self-appreciation grows, his external life will become more gratifying to himself and to those around him. At the same time, he will know God more intimately, through his deepening friendship with Jesus, the God-man. He will eventually possess a larger share of Christ's peace, and will learn to share it with his fellow men. All this can be accomplished by those who are willing to work for it day by day, with trust in God's help, confidence in their own sincerity, and a realistic acceptance of their God-given limitations.

MY LIFE WITH CHRIST

1. MY DIVINE SAVIOR

READ In the beginning was the Word . . . And the Word was God. . . . And the Word was made flesh. (John 1:1, 14)

REFLECT In his opening words, St. John gives us the theme of his entire gospel: Jesus is God, and He became Man to show us, in a human way how much God understands and loves us. Though His chosen people would reject their long-awaited Redeemer, Jesus would still follow out His divine plan of working, suffering, praying, and dying for them and for all men.

REVIEW Jesus is my God and Savior. By His earthly life He showed me His deep personal concern for me. In Him I find no stern Master who has no feeling for my natural weaknesses and human limitations. For my sake He endured most of the human experiences that weigh me down and discourage me at times. His human nature knew the bitter taste of misunderstandings, ingratitude, and disappointment. In His prayers, labors, frustrations, and sorrows He embraced the burdens, difficulties, and problems of my daily life, and asked me to bear them with Him.

No matter how far I may feel from Him at times, Jesus made Himself the closest, most constant, most faithful Companion of my daily life. I am no stranger to Him. He knows my innermost likes and dislikes, my hopes, my deepest desires and my most hidden fears. He is far more understanding and accepting toward me than I am toward myself. The better I become acquainted with Jesus, the more shall I find that His yoke is sweet and His burden light. He is much more reasonable with me than I am with myself. Though I may sometimes feel otherwise, He loves me more truly than I love myself. Regardless of what

I think of myself, He thought me worth redeeming by His personal labors, sufferings, and death. He invites me to make my daily life a true companionship with Him. He asks no more than an intelligent effort, based on His teachings and supported by His grace. He does not demand quick results nor perfect achievements, but only what little I can do this day in following His principles and imitating His holy example. Though I may fall short of His ideals, He will thank me for having tried.

RESPOND   My divine Savior, it is never too late to draw closer to You. During Your earthly life, You welcomed many people who came to You after a good part of their life was already spent. Let me not hesitate to follow their wise example. The gospels show that You want me as I am, and desire to help me make the most of what I have. Lord, I am willing to try with the help of Your grace. Amen.

2. ZACHARY AND ELIZABETH

READ   In the days of Herod, king of Judea, there was a certain priest named Zachary . . . and his wife was of the daughters of Aaron, and her name was Elizabeth. Both were just before God . . . But they had no son, for Elizabeth was barren; and they were both advanced in years. (Luke 1:5, 7)

REFLECT   These two good people had suffered a great disappointment in their married life. To be childless was disappointing enough. What made it more difficult to bear, was the fact that in their day a childless marriage was regarded as a cause for shame. Though Zachary and Elizabeth accepted God's will, they could not help feeling somewhat humiliated by the thinking of their neighbors.

REVIEW   If my earthly life were simply a matter between God and me, it would be difficult enough, due to the limitations and complexities of my fallen human nature. However, the personal problems and shortcomings of the people around me, complicate my life still further. These complications create pressures within me that often confuse my thinking and influence my conduct unfavorably.

Through knowledge, prayer, and daily practice, I can develop a stronger sense of God's nearness, a deeper understanding of those around me, and a mature respect for my personal needs and rights. With this richer interior life, I shall be more able and willing to live and let live. Though I shall have due consideration for the feelings and rights of others, I shall worry less about what others may think or say of me.

Strengthened by the friendship of Jesus, I shall be less dependent on the friendship of those who reject me; less alone when others neglect or overlook me; less afraid when required to defend myself against injustice. My personal love for Jesus will enable me to show good will toward those who seem to resent or despise me. In His friendship I shall find enough security and strength to overcome the self-doubts and natural fears which make me avoid some people and cater to others.

RESPOND   Jesus my Lord, the better I come to know You, the more easily shall I imitate the holy patience and resignation of Zachary and Elizabeth. Grant me some of Your divine understanding and good will toward those whose daily conduct is limited by earthly situations and controlled by worldly conditions. I shall strive to rise above the small-minded people around, and to base my conduct on Your wise principles and holy example. Even in defending my rights, let me do so with the clear thinking and calm decisions You manifested in Your public life. Amen.

3. ZACHARY'S DOUBT

READ   And there appeared to him an angel of the Lord
. . . But the angel said to him, "Do not be afraid, Zachary, for thy petition has been heard, and thy wife Elizabeth
shall bear thee a son" . . . And Zachary said to the angel,
"How shall I know this? For I am an old man and my wife
is advanced in years." (Luke 1:11, 13, 18)

REFLECT   This prophecy evidently shocked the aging
Zachary. He had prayed for years that God might bless his
home with children. Now, in his old age, he feared the angel's promise was too good to be true. Torn between these
emotions, Zachary's mind was overcome by doubt. He felt
impelled to request proof of the angel's words.

REVIEW   As long as I live in this earthly life, I too shall
have my personal desires, fears, and doubts. These emotions will arise within me with or without my awareness or
consent. What I do about them depends not only on my
supernatural faith and trust in God, but also on my emotional maturity. Emotional Childhood is not limited to the
early years of life. It endures as long as my emotions dominate my thinking, decisions, and external behavior. Such
immaturity is an obstacle to true spiritual progress. Many
human defects and shortcomings are due to this natural
weakness. The better I understand myself, the better prepared I shall be to direct my emotions toward a firm confidence in God's personal concern for me.
   Earthly living is very real. Sometimes I can change unpleasant circumstances to suit my desires, and at other
times I can make only partial changes. However, there will
always be some situations which are beyond my control.
I can face these situations as a child that refuses to accept

the facts; or I can look upon them with a supernatural outlook. If my supernatural outlook is strong, I shall find it easy to believe that God knows best and that He guides me with a fatherly hand through these disturbing circumstances.

At times I shall be torn between my natural inclinations and my supernatural desire to embrace God's holy Will in my present problems. I may even be burdened by yearnings, fears and doubts, strong enough to confuse my thinking and incline me to disregard right order. At such times, I must make an intention to please God, and believe that I want to mean it. If a decision is to be made, I must trust in my judgment as I see it at the moment. Through a manly self-confidence and a childlike trust in God, I shall prove myself a mature follower of Christ.

RESPOND   My Jesus, every man must endure some interior conflicts. Help me to understand my natural desires, fears and doubts without being unduly upset by them. Guide me aright when my mind is anxious or confused, and let me choose wisely in my efforts to follow Your principles. Amen.

4.   MARY OF NAZARETH

READ   Now in the sixth month the angel Gabriel was sent from God to a town of Galilee called Nazareth, to a virgin betrothed to a man named Joseph . . . and the virgin's name was Mary. (Luke 1:26, 27)

REFLECT   In the earthly life of Mary, we shall find a constant source of inspiration for our own daily life. In a number of ways Mary was "little"; little in her station as a simple Jewish maiden; little in her position as the betrothed of Joseph, the carpenter of Nazareth. Mary herself was quite aware of her "lowliness," but this did not depress her in the least. It did not make her feel unimportant. Rather, she was overwhelmed with gratitude as she counted her blessings. The magnitude and purity of her gratitude was proven by her constant readiness to embrace God's holy Will in all things.

REVIEW   In my own way, I share the "littleness" of Mary. On the other hand, I also share something of her greatness, since I, too, have my God-given purpose in life. Though I cannot always be sure what God expects of me, I can be certain that He guides me toward His purpose in His own mysterious ways. In my mistaken thinking, I tend to judge my daily life by its visible accomplishments and gratifying achievements. Yet, I find that Mary's greatness shone forth in the sincerity and simplicity with which she performed her most ordinary activities. Each moment of her life was a great moment because of her desire to please God in all things. Though I cannot hope to equal Mary's exalted holiness, I can endeavor to imitate her in my own limited way.

In imitating the greatness of Mary, no radical change is required of me. I need only be myself; learn God's truth as far as circumstances will permit; respect my personal dignity as a human being, redeemed by Christ; be grateful for the particular gifts which God has bestowed on me; be sorry for my sins; learn by my mistakes; do my limited human best to fulfill my earthly purpose in life; and enjoy with intelligent moderation the legitimate pleasures at my disposal. With time, grace, and practice, my spiritual yearnings and supernatural achievements will improve and multiply. I shall become more like Jesus as I imitate Mary, His most faithful reflection on earth.

RESPOND   My divine Savior, increase my understanding of Your mother. Help me to imitate her within the narrow limits of my personal powers. Since I can only use the gifts which You have granted to me, let me be content to develop the talents and graces within my grasp. Amen.

5. MARY'S VISIT TO ELIZABETH

READ Now in those days Mary arose and went with haste into the hill country, to a town of Juda. And she entered the house of Zachary and saluted Elizabeth. . . . And Mary remained with her about three months and returned to her own house. (Luke 1:39, 40, 56)

REFLECT Mary's soul was overflowing with gratitude to God for His numberless gifts. This gratitude raised her mind upward to God and outward to her neighbor. With this disposition, Mary set out to rejoice with her cousin, who had also received a great favor from God. When she found that God had revealed her divine motherhood to Elizabeth, Mary humbly gave thanks to God and poured forth her praises of the Divine Goodness, Power, and Majesty. She then remained to help Elizabeth until her child was born.

REVIEW Though I may not always feel grateful for God's generosity to me, the fact remains that I have received numerous gifts from Him. I take most of these gifts for granted because I have never been without them. Were I deprived of my sight or my hearing, or my health, I would quickly realize how precious these gifts are. Mary did not allow herself to forget that the things she had and used each day, were God's gifts. She constantly thanked Him not only in prayer but also by her disposition, intentions, and actions.

I must daily try to develop a keen awareness of God's fatherly generosity. Moreover, I must realize that I am never lost in a crowd, since God's concern for me is personal. He could not be more attentive to me if I were His only creation. Such an awareness will bring me a deep sense of my personal importance and supernatural dignity. If God takes such loving care of me, He must consider me worth His attention. True, my supernatural worth comes from the saving merits of Jesus, His divine Son. Nevertheless, this value has been granted to me, and I must respect myself for it.

Though my efforts to please God may be weak and faltering, though I may fail often in my attempts to imitate the wonderful virtues of Mary, I can be sure that my intentions and efforts are deeply appreciated by Jesus and pleasing to His heavenly Father. Secondly, true gratitude always inspires generosity. The more aware I become of God's many gifts to me, the more shall I be inclined to reach upward to Him through my praise, thanksgiving, and reparation. Finally, urged on by my heartfelt gratitude, I shall want to express good will to others by my attitudes, words, and actions. Like Mary, I shall feel a deep satisfaction in contributing to the happiness of others.

RESPOND   My God, I see in Mary an inspiring example of gratitude to You. Help me to imitate her by my prayers of praise, thanksgiving, and reparation, and by my readiness to help my neighbor in whatever way I can. May my daily disposition be one loud cry of thanks for your numerous gifts, which make my earthly life a steady journey toward heaven. Amen.

6.   BIRTH AND EARLY LIFE OF THE BAPTIST

READ   Now Elizabeth's time was fulfilled that she should be delivered and she brought forth a son. . . . And the child grew and became strong in spirit; and was in the deserts until the day of his manifestation to Israel. (Luke 1:57, 80)

REFLECT   The angel Gabriel had told Zachary that his child was to hold a special place in life. He was to prepare the Chosen People for their long-awaited Redeemer. At an early age John felt drawn to solitude, study, prayer, and self-discipline. At the appointed time, he came forth with a clear knowledge of God's truth, a deep understanding of human nature, and a strong appreciation of man's eternal destiny. His years in the deserts made him a living example of what he preached, and his words went to the very souls of the sincere people who heard him.

REVIEW   Every person born into this world has some opportunity to do good. Their greatest obstacle is often within themselves. Through ignorance, error, or sheer immaturity, they may find it difficult to be content with the opportunities at their disposal. They either expect more than their circumstances will permit, or they compare themselves unfavorably with others. In either case they become unduly ashamed of themselves. Though they sincerely desire to please God, they cannot quite shake off a sense of unworthiness. This makes them ill at ease with Him. Gradually, they feel less inspired by their initial ideals, less inclined to share their thoughts and desires with God, and less enthusiastic about doing good.

Through reflection and prayer, I must so absorb the truth, that it will influence the very depths of my soul. God has made my human nature as it is, and He has permitted it to develop as it has, for a good reason. Apart from my deliberate sins, He accepts me as I am, and sees some usefulness even in my less desirable habits. In order to improve my service of God, I must try to see myself as I really am, accept what I am, and strive for ideals which are within my reach. My efforts may be weak, faltering, and limited, but God will grant me the grace to make the most of what I have. Even when I feel unsure of my intentions or my efforts, I may be giving God as much of myself as I can. In my own little way, in my own little world, I may be another Baptist to those around me, because I have tried to know Christ better, imitate Him more, and show Him to others by my persevering effort to follow His teachings in my daily life.

RESPOND Jesus, my Savior, help me to think as You do. Let me think more of my higher intentions and efforts than of my unwanted defects and failures. If I can think positively, I shall be more disposed to keep trying, regardless of the limited results. Through knowledge, prayer, and persevering efforts, I hope to come closer to You each day, and to inspire others to do the same. Amen.

7. THE BIRTH OF THE SAVIOR

READ Now it came to pass in those days, that a decree went forth from Caesar Augustus that a census of the whole world should be taken. . . . And all were going, each to his own town, to register. And Joseph also went from Galilee . . . to the town of David, which is called Bethlehem, together with Mary his espoused wife, who was with child. And it came to pass while they were there, that the days for her to be delivered were fulfilled. And she brought forth her firstborn son, and wrapped him in swaddling clothes, and laid him in a manger, because there was no room for them in the inn. (Luke 2:1, 3–7)

REFLECT This decree of Caesar was no mere chance happening. It fitted perfectly into the eternal plans of God. He had inspired His prophet to predict the birth of the Savior in the town of David. The decree of the pagan Caesar provided the occasion for the fulfillment of this prophecy. All of the circumstances surrounding Christ's birth in a cave, were preordained by God. Thus many persons were involved, directly or indirectly, with the fulfillment of God's plan on that first Christmas night.

REVIEW In my effort to live in closer union with Jesus, I must beware of errors and misconceptions. Like Caesar and others on that first Christmas night, I often fulfill God's eternal purpose without knowing it. Though I may daily learn more of God's truth, I shall always have a number of unanswered questions. Though I do my best to practice the virtues of Jesus and His Saints, there will always be problems which I shall find difficult or impossible to manage.

I must not blame myself for my limited accomplishments, since I can only reaffirm my good intentions, do my human best under the circumstances, and leave the rest to God. Though I may see little or no good coming from the situation, I may rest assured that God is achieving His eternal purpose in His own mysterious ways. I must beware of demanding more of my human nature than God Himself requires. Surely, Joseph did not blame himself for the Savior's being born in a stable. He had done all he could to find suitable lodging. Joseph saw his failure as God's holy Will. And such it was, as the prophet had foretold long ago.

Though I may suspect the sincerity of my intentions, or doubt that I have done my best, I can only make a prudent judgment, and refuse to search endlessly for a sure answer to my uncertainties. In all my ignorance and doubts I shall need to exercise the great virtue of Christian hope, and save my energies for constructive planning for the future.

RESPOND Infant Jesus, I desire to make my mind Your abode and my heart Your throne. I wish to grow each day in Your knowledge and advance in Your way of thinking and living. At the same time, help me to correct the defects within my control and humbly accept my normal human limitations as God's holy Will. Amen.

8. THE SHEPHERDS

READ And there were shepherds in the same district living in the fields and keeping watch over their flock by night. And behold, an angel of the Lord stood by them and the glory of God shone round about them . . . And the angel said to them, "Do not be afraid, for behold, I bring you good news of great joy . . . for today in the town of David a Savior has been born to you, Who is Christ the Lord. And this shall be a sign to you: you will find an infant wrapped in swaddling clothes and lying in a manger." And suddenly there was with the angel a multitude of the heavenly host praising God and saying, "Glory to God in the highest and on earth peace among men of good will." (Luke 2:8–13)

REFLECT Why didn't the angels notify the leaders of God's chosen people? How are we to explain God's message to these simple men whose influence was confined to the fields in which they tended their flocks? Perhaps they were closest to the ideal of "good will" of which the angels sang. St. Luke tells us that the shepherds went with haste to pay their respects to the new-born Savior. And when they had seen, they understood what had been told them concerning this child.

REVIEW Good will is the first requirement for a lasting friendship with Jesus. Until I am ready to learn what God requires of me, and prepared to choose His holy Will, I shall not know the peace which Jesus promised to His true followers. The shepherds obeyed the angel's suggestion as quickly as they could make arrangements to have someone look after their sheep. Their good will was proven in their actions, and their reward was the gift of faith in Christ.

I may not have great talents. I may never achieve a high position or exceptional accomplishments in this earthly life. Yet, the most necessary disposition for eternal glory is always at my command. I can always express good will by my daily efforts to please God and help my neighbor. Good will is not a matter of feeling, nor even of visible success. Due to fixed habits of feeling, thinking, or external conduct, I may often fail to fulfill the good desires which God arouses within me. These failures do not disprove my good will. As long as they are due to inadvertence, or momentary weakness, I can still be a man of good will. My life may be one long chain of broken resolutions and resumed efforts toward self-improvement. My failures may far outnumber my successes. Yet God looks not upon the external accomplishments, but upon the internal disposition and continued effort. I must endeavor to think like Jesus. He never condemned human weakness, but only human malice, i.e., bad will.

RESPOND   My Infant Savior, kneeling in spirit with the shepherds at Your feet, I pledge myself to a life of good will. I shall try, with Your help, to prove my good will by my daily efforts to know You better and to follow Your teachings in my daily activities. May I never be discouraged by failures, or despair over my repeated sins. If I have nothing else to offer, I shall at least offer You the honor of my renewed efforts. Amen.

9. THE CIRCUMCISION

READ   And when eight days were fulfilled for his circumcision, his name was called Jesus, the name given him by the angel before he was conceived in the womb. (Luke 2:21)

REFLECT   Though this ceremony looked like just any other circumcision, it was far from that. This child was the God-man, Creator and Redeemer of the world. The slight pain and the few drops of blood involved in this ceremony were symbolic of the utter self-dedication which His early life would be. His very name was a message to the world. He was to be "Jesus," which means "Savior." For this did He come into this world; for this He lived His every moment; for this He worked, prayed, suffered, and died.

REVIEW   Even in His holy name, Jesus speaks to me. By this name He tells me that His concern for me will be as inseparable from Him as His name. He would spend a lifetime being my "Jesus," my Savior. I need not feel undeserving of such personal concern, since Jesus Himself made me worthy of it by the price He paid for my redemption. To deny my personal worth, would be to deny the value of His Blood, which He paid for my sins. Neither should I feel that I am merely one of the millions whom He saved, as though I were lost in the mass of humanity. His concern could not be more personal if I were the only one who needed His redemption.

Over and over again in His public life Jesus preached this truth. In the parables of the lost sheep, the lost coin, the doctor for the sick, the friend of the sinner, the prodigal son, God's providence over the grass of the fields and the birds of the air, and in other sermons, Jesus tried so hard to impress me with the "personal" quality of His redemptive work. I do Him a great injustice when I believe that He thinks of me as I think of myself. The mind and heart of Christ could never be so small as mine. His wisdom, love, and power are far beyond this confused, self-centered, weak nature of mine. As long as I remain doubtful of His personal concern for me, I shall be one of those who made it difficult for Jesus to give them all of the graces and blessings which He desired to give them. Of me too, He will say, "O foolish and slow of heart to believe!"

RESPOND   My Jesus, I shall never know the peace which You have offered to Your true followers unless I learn to see myself and others through Your eyes. Grant me the wisdom, patience, and strength to come each day a little closer to Your way of thinking and living. Then I shall gradually be convinced of Your personal love for me, and the supernatural value which You have given to my daily life. Free of anxiety and doubts, I shall find a holy contentment in my activities, and a supernatural joy in increasing my good works within the narrow limits of my daily possibilities. Amen.

10. THE MAGI

READ   Now when Jesus was born in Bethlehem of Judea, in the days of King Herod, behold the Magi came from the East to Jerusalem saying: "Where is he that is born king of the Jews? For we have seen his star in the East and have come to worship him." (Matt. 2:1–2)

REFLECT   The story of the Magi has a very important lesson for all men of good will. It tells of men who followed a life-long ideal. They were so intent on finding the newborn Savior that they refused to be deterred by the desert's midday heat and nightly cold, the perils of robbers, and the dangers of sandstorms. They simply refused to abandon their search until they had the joy of offering their personal gifts at the feet of the child-Redeemer.

REVIEW   In this story I can find a symbolic image of my own earthly life. I too can come daily closer to Jesus. I too have to surmount obstacles and face dangers that might well turn me back from the road leading to Him. I too have a gift to offer Him, a gift He desires of me, the gift of personal loyalty to His example and teachings. If, like

31

the Magi, I refuse to abandon my daily journey toward Jesus, human problems may confuse me for the moment, and human difficulties may deter me for a time, but the delays will only be temporary. Jesus will eventually reveal Himself to me.

How do I live this daily life of mine? Am I so preoccupied with the needs of the moment that I have no time to think, reflect, or pray? Have I become like so many in the town of Bethlehem on that first Christmas night, too busy to see the nearness of Christ? If so, I need not surrender to emotional feelings of guilt. It will be wiser and more pleasing to God if I strive for a fuller appreciation of my present graces and opportunities.

I can begin today a journey of my own, a journey lasting the rest of my life, to come daily closer to Christ through a quiet planned, daily effort. I can gradually come closer to Him in my way of thinking and living. I must not expect quick, or easy, or even visible results. I need only make a plan, based on sound knowledge and firm faith; an intelligent effort based on the facts and possibilities open to me in my present life-circumstances; a sustained endeavor that is not discouraged by my personal limitations, nor by undue self-blame for my unintended lapses into old faults.

RESPOND O Jesus, King and Redeemer of the world, fill my soul with an urge to seek You all through my earthly life. Give me an unquenchable thirst for Your truth, Your peace, and Your eternal friendship. However, in my daily endeavors to know You better and follow You more truly, let me not be unrealistic or unreasonable. Help me find You within the circumstances and opportunities that make up my daily life. Amen.

11. THE BOY JESUS

READ And his parents were wont to go every year to Jerusalem at the Feast of the Passover. And when he was twelve years old, they went up to Jerusalem according to the custom of the feast. . . . When they were returning, the boy Jesus remained in Jerusalem, and his parents did not know it. But thinking that he was in the caravan, they had come a day's journey before it occurred to them to look for him among their relatives and acquaintances. And not finding him, they returned to Jerusalem in search of him. And it came to pass after three days, that they found him in the temple . . . And his mother said to him, "Son, why hast thou done so to us? Behold, in sorrow thy father and I have been seeking thee." (Luke 2:41–48)

REFLECT In accordance with God's plan on this occasion, both Joseph and Mary made the mistake of presuming that Jesus was in the caravan. From what we know of them, we may be quite certain that neither Joseph nor Mary tried to blame the other for this mistake. They were mature enough to realize that this could happen to anyone. On finding the Boy, Mary exercised her authority by requesting an explanation. Though she and Joseph did not understand Jesus' answer, neither of them prolonged the matter with uncontrolled emotion or unnecessary reproaches.

REVIEW Am I one of those people who cannot tolerate mistakes in myself or in others? Am I mature enough to consider that it is human to err, or do I refuse to make due allowance for a normal margin of human error? People who demand a flawless performance in themselves or others live in constant fear of reproach or possible punishment, be it the reproach of their own self-disgust or the

33

punishment of external criticism and blame. These people see only one defense against these unpleasant consequences . . . namely, to be perfect in all things. If they avoid all mistakes, they cannot be blamed or punished. Usually these people are unaware of this emotional motive in their quest for perfection. They may actually believe that they are being moved solely by their conscious good intentions. The proof that such is not the case lies in their manner of living. They show uneasiness, tension, or rigid formality in their general behavior. When a mistake is made, they are inclined to exaggerate their mistake beyond its true proportions, or they explain it away. They often feel that someone must be at fault, so they will either blame themselves, someone else, or some circumstance. It never seems to occur to them that perhaps no one is to blame, since there was no forethought or malice.

RESPOND   Father of wisdom and understanding, grant me some small share in Your divine outlook on daily human living. Though I may advance in knowledge and virtue through the years, I shall always have my normal quota of human mistakes. Help me destroy the immature anxiety that makes me unduly annoyed at the innocent human errors committed by me or others. Grant me the light to see the difference between sin and human limitations, and teach me to live at peace with myself and all men of good will. Amen.

12. THE BAPTIST'S MESSAGE

READ   Now in the fifteenth year of the reign of Tiberius Caesar . . . the word of God came to John, the son of Zachary, in the desert. And he went into all the region about the Jordan, preaching a baptism of repentance for the forgiveness of sins. (Luke 3:1–3)

REFLECT   John urged his hearers to prepare for Christ's coming by reflecting on their daily life and re-evaluating themselves in the light of God's truth. He exhorted them to express sorrow for their sins and beg God's forgiveness. Those who followed the Baptist's advice, felt a growing confidence in God's mercy, a refreshing peace of mind, and an everlasting joy of heart. They lost their dread of God's justice and eagerly looked forward to the coming of their Redeemer.

REVIEW   In my effort to improve my relations with God, I must be realistic. In spite of my best intentions and sincerest efforts, there will always be some person, object, or situation capable of inciting me to an occasional sin of thought, word, deed, or omission. Without a very special grace from God, I simply cannot overcome all temptations. My sorrow for my sins will be proven best by an undiscouraged, unstraining, sincere renewal of effort.

The same temptations will arise again and again. The same sins will recur from time to time. Time and again, I shall have to face the same defects, the same faults, the same sins. Why? Because through the years I have learned to like some things too much. My natural inclinations have formed habits which often color my thinking and influence my decisions. Deep within me there stir emotions of which I am often unaware and against which I am sometimes helpless. In spite of my supernatural perceptions and deliberate intentions, I find myself moved by inclinations I do not want, and feelings I detest.

The more I understand myself, the less shall I be disturbed by these involuntary tendencies of my nature. I shall learn to tolerate them without shame or self-blame. I shall judge my moral worth by the intentions I make and by my deliberate efforts to follow the principles of Jesus in my thinking and conduct. No matter how confused I may become by this interior conflict, I shall believe that God judges neither the unwanted feelings, nor the involuntary thoughts but only the free choice I make to please Him in all things.

RESPOND My Jesus, my sorrow for my sins is often aroused by my fear of punishment and my desire for the eternal happiness of heaven. Though this sorrow is not the most excellent, it is still supernatural enough to bring me Your pardon in sacramental confession. However, I hope for the day when my motives will rise to a higher level. I shall then be less concerned with punishment or reward, and more concerned with the offended goodness of my heavenly Father. Amen.

13. THE BAPTISM OF JESUS

READ Then Jesus came from Galilee to John, at the Jordan, to be baptized by him. And John was for hindering him, and said, "It is I who ought to be baptized by thee, and dost thou come to me?" But Jesus answered and said to him, "Let it be so now, for so it becomes us to fulfill all justice." (Matt. 3:13–15)

REFLECT As man's Redeemer, Jesus came to "fulfill all justice," that is, to exercise all the virtues violated by the sins of men. In so doing, He would show each man the virtues he would need in daily life. On this present occasion, Jesus shows us the need for contrition. Without sorrow for our sins, we cannot profit by Christ's redemptive work. Though Jesus Himself was incapable of sin, He here expresses sorrow for my sins and the sins of the world.

REVIEW By this act of self-abasement, Jesus seeks to give inspiration and courage to those who find it difficult to confess, or even acknowledge their sins to themselves. Some people feel so ashamed, humiliated, or discouraged by their faults, that they automatically shun any consideration of them. In their ignorance they think that a new start requires a "feeling" of sorrow, or a "perfect" confession covering each and every sin ever committed, or a resolution strong enough to eliminate all sins in the future. Having tried and failed repeatedly in the past, they are now reluctant to try again.

I must beware of these errors in my own efforts to draw closer to God in my daily life. By His personal example Jesus shows me that His heavenly Father is pleased when I acknowledge my sins and express sorrow for them. This supernatural sorrow is not a matter of feeling. It is an intelligent admission that sin is evil, displeasing to God, and harmful to myself. My purpose of amendment does not mean that I shall never sin again, but only that I intend to do what I can to avoid sin in the future. As for my confessions, God does not expect me to remember "all" my sins nor to confess them with perfect clarity. I can only describe them as I remember them when they occurred, without going into needless details or repetition. Having expressed my sorrow and declared my intention to avoid them in the future, I must believe in my own sincerity. I must also believe that the heavenly Father forgives me for the sake of His divine Son, Who paid an infinite price for my redemption.

RESPOND   My Jesus, You have told me through the Scriptures that the just man falls seven times a day. Let me not demand an exemption from this common lot of men. Make me mature enough to acknowledge my sins, confident enough to trust in Your understanding and patience with my weaknesses; and hopeful enough to keep trying in spite of repeated failures. Though I may fail more often than I succeed, let me at least try more often than I fail. You will surely accept my efforts as proof of my sincerity and love. Amen.

14. CHRIST'S TEMPTATIONS IN THE DESERT

READ Then Jesus was led into the desert by the Spirit, to be tempted by the devil. (Matt. 4:1)

REFLECT Having given us an example of sorrow for sin, Jesus now proceeds to show us how to cope with temptations. After spending forty days and nights in solitude, meditation, prayer, and self-denial, He permits the devil to tempt Him. By His example, Jesus urges us to seek God in solitude from time to time. In prayerful reflection we can become better acquainted with God, ourselves, and with the deeper meaning of our daily life. Through an intelligent self-denial, we can gain a greater mastery over our unreasoning natural tendencies. Fortified with knowledge, understanding, grace, and practice, we shall be better prepared to deal with our daily temptations.

REVIEW No matter how carefully I may try to avoid occasions of sin, I cannot be entirely free of temptations in this life. Being partly material, partly animal, and partly spiritual, my nature is often torn between its natural instincts, emotional tendencies, acquired habits, and spiritual yearnings. This inner conflict between spontaneous appetites, emotional leanings, and supernatural desires is normal to every man. I need not be surprised at it, nor unduly afraid of it, nor needlessly ashamed of it. There is a world of difference between my temptations and my sins. Even when I find myself wanting what is wrong, I cannot sin until I have made a free and deliberate decision to choose it. True, I shall sometimes be in doubt about my free consent. At such times, I can only declare my doubt to God and express my desire to please Him in all things.

By His personal example, Jesus showed me how to prepare myself for the unavoidable temptations in my daily life. By prayerful reflection I can more easily see the good things of this world in their proper light. Through intelligent self-discipline I can gradually develop the supernatural prudence and strength to satisfy my needs and seek my advantages without violating God's commandments. The better I understand Jesus, the less troubled shall I be when unavoidable temptations draw me toward what is wrong, or away from what is right. I shall not be too ready to doubt the sincerity of my good intentions, nor shall I insist on blaming myself for what I could not foresee or control.

RESPOND My Jesus, help me to remain at peace when assailed by unavoidable temptations. Let me not magnify them into horrifying proportions, nor belittle them with a dangerous smugness. Having made my intention to please You, I will refuse to question my sincerity without sufficient reason. When unreasoning self-doubts confuse my mind and undue fears weaken my decisions, I shall declare my confidence in Your divine understanding, infinite mercy and personal concern for me. Amen.

15. THE BAPTIST'S MISSION

READ Now in the fifteenth year of the reign of Tiberius Caesar . . . the word of God came to John, the son of Zachary, in the desert. And he went into all the region about the Jordan, preaching a baptism of repentance for the forgiveness of sins. . . . And the crowds asked him, saying, "What then are we to do?" And he answered and said to them, "Let him who has two tunics share them with him who has none; and let him who has food do likewise." And the publicans also came to be baptized, and they said to him, "Master, what are we to do?" But he said to them, "Exact no more than has been appointed to you." And soldiers also asked him, saying, "And we—what are we to do?" But he said to them, "Plunder no one, accuse no one falsely, and be content with your pay." (Luke 3:1, 3, 10–14)

REFLECT   At the appointed time John came forth from his solitude to fulfill his life's mission. His message was simple and practical. God's chosen people should prepare for their Savior's coming by amending their lives. John's personal holiness made his words all the more impressive, and many turned to God with gratitude and repentance.

REVIEW   For all the differences between my life and that of the Baptist, there is, nevertheless, some resemblance between us. Like him, I am expected to do what I can to draw others to Christ. The Catholic doctrine of Christ's Mystical Body, places on me, as a member of His Church, the duty of promoting Christ's work as far as my life circumstances will permit. Having given me the gift of faith and the grace of supernatural union with Him, Jesus expects me to help Him in arousing the good will of others and directing it toward eternal life.

This God-given vocation does not involve obligations or time which I cannot afford, but is to be fulfilled within the framework of my present station in life. Without placing any impossible burden upon myself, I must do what I can to improve my understanding of Christ's truth, deepen my personal friendship with Him through sacraments and prayer, and strive to reflect His personal life in my daily activities. By doing so, I shall be an inspiration to those around me. At the same time I shall be obtaining actual graces for many people whom I shall never meet in this life. Many a person will turn his thoughts and desires toward God through the graces which Jesus will grant because of my daily intention and efforts to help others. This mission of cooperation with Christ is not a matter of feeling, but of faith. Like the Baptist, I must develop my faith and loyalty to Christ through whatever solitude, prayer, and self-denial I can attain without neglecting my ordinary obligations.

RESPOND My Jesus, help me to know You better, so that I may appreciate You more deeply and fulfill Your intention more faithfully in the future. I shall not look for any sudden changes or outstanding achievements, but I will do whatever I can to come closer to the inspiring example of the Baptist. May I never knowingly and willingly refuse to help others with the reasonable means at my command. Amen.

16. TESTIMONY OF THE BAPTIST

READ The next day John saw Jesus coming to him, and he said, "Behold the Lamb of God, who takes away the sin of the world! This is he of whom I said, 'After me there comes one who has been set above me, because he was before me' . . . Again the next day John was standing there with two of his disciples. And looking upon Jesus as he walked by, he said, "Behold the Lamb of God!" And the two disciples heard him speak, and they followed Jesus. (John 1:29, 30, 35–37)

REFLECT This attraction of the disciples to Jesus was not a sudden conversion. It was the result of the Baptist's training. However, though these disciples had completed the first stage of their spiritual development, they would not be ready for the marvelous graces of Pentecost for some time. They would require further training and growth under the direct guidance of Jesus.

REVIEW How often have I expected a complete transformation in my life, simply because I had experienced a new insight into the goodness of God or the horror of sin, or had changed some situation in my life? I made my resolution so ardently that my sincerity was beyond all doubt. Yet, as time passed, my ardor cooled, and I seemed to slide backward, as old habits reasserted themselves. In my ignorance of my human nature and of God's ways, I felt guilty of having rejected God's graces, and I considered myself unworthy of further help from God.

I must understand that, in His supernatural operations, God does not disregard the natural laws by which He governs this world. Just as a seed depends on the quality of the soil on which it falls and the amount of moisture and sunshine available to it, so does God's grace depend on the natural tendencies, habits, and conditions within my body and mind, and on the external circumstances influencing my thinking and my free choices.

Supernatural life, like natural life, requires nourishment, exercise, and time before it can arrive at the maturity of tested and proven virtues. My desire to be more pleasing to God is not insincere simply because my old ways persist in my daily life. Like a seed, my good desires are to be nourished by grace, sacraments, reading, reflection, and practice. In spite of my repeated relapses into old habits, Jesus is willing to wait for my spiritual development. All I can offer to Him this day, is my present effort, made intelligently, humbly and patiently. The improvement will come slowly, gradually and surely, in God's appointed time.

RESPOND   Lord Jesus, I may not have much to offer You. I may not even be able to offer it entirely, nor at once. However, I can offer to You my sincere desire to live in accordance with Your principles and ideals. At times my desire may seem hopeless or even insincere amid my feelings or acts of impatience, unkindness, laziness. Nevertheless, You offer me the grace to keep desiring, praying, and

trying until the day I die. This much at least I shall do
for You. Amen.

17. THE MARRIAGE AT CANA

READ   And on the third day a marriage took place at Cana
of Galilee, and the mother of Jesus was there. Now Jesus
too was invited to the marriage, and also his disciples.
And the wine having run short, the mother of Jesus said
to him, "They have no wine." (John 2:1–3)

REFLECT   Of the various lessons taught in this event, we
might do well to consider the attitude of Jesus and Mary
toward the merriment of their friends. Our Lord and His
mother could hardly have attended this affair without eating, drinking, and rejoicing with the people about them.
So much did they approve of this celebration that when
the wine ran short, Mary became concerned about the
imminent embarrassment of the newlyweds, and Jesus understood her motherly concern. After explicitly declaring
that this was neither the time nor the place for His first
public miracle, He proceeded to fulfill her unexpressed
request.

REVIEW   To live a life of virtue, I need not avoid or despise all legitimate enjoyments and pleasures. If I really
understand Jesus, I shall never believe that earthly pleasures are incompatible with true holiness. Virtue does not
consist in self-denial for its own sake. Some people give
this impression by their severe attitude toward any form
of self-indulgence, merriment or pleasure. Even though
they deny this attitude in theory, they affirm it in their
behavior. They are unable to enjoy the pleasures of this
world without some feeling of uneasiness or guilt. I, too,
can be a victim of this mistaken outlook.

In contemplating Jesus and Mary at Cana, I shall better understand the meaning of virtue. Virtue consists in the balanced use of things. It is violated by either excess or unreasonable self-denial. I am not necessarily less virtuous when I enjoy the good things of this life than when I deny myself this enjoyment. To eat when I am hungry or rest when I am tired, is usually an intelligent act, and therefore a virtuous act. To practice self-denial with a definite, intelligent purpose, is also an act of virtue. On the other hand, feeling obliged to deny myself when there is no obligation, or feeling guilty when no sin has been committed, is not virtuous. It indicates ignorance or immaturity.

RESPOND My Jesus, in imitation of Your holy example, I desire to use legitimate enjoyments and recreation for the real good which they can bring to my body and soul. May I never consider them evil, since they are Your gifts. On the other hand, may I never let them interfere with my duties or with my reasonable tendencies toward supernatural self-denial. You have so constituted this human nature of mine that it requires proper care and consideration. To disregard this need can hurt my bodily and spiritual life as much as any immature overindulgence. Teach me, Lord, to find that happy balance which belongs to every well-ordered life. Amen.

18. THE MERCHANTS IN THE TEMPLE

READ Now the Passover of the Jews was at hand, and Jesus went up to Jerusalem. And he found in the temple men selling oxen, sheep and doves, and money-changers at their tables. And making a kind of whip of cords, he drove them all out of the temple. (John 2:13–15)

REFLECT This custom of buying and selling in the temple had originated from sheer necessity. The holy season brought many devout Jews from distant lands. They needed to change their foreign money into the coin of Palestine. So too, they needed sheep and doves for their sacrificial offerings to God. However, with the passing of the time, the local merchants and money-changers had gotten permission to come farther into the temple grounds. They eventually became more concerned with their buying and selling than with reverence for this holy shrine of the one true God.

REVIEW Jesus was not condemning these merchants for pursuing their daily occupations, but only for allowing their earthly interests to blind them to the presence of God. The temple grounds were not a common marketplace, nor were these purchases an ordinary commerce. Both the place and the merchandise were closely related to the worship of God. The merchants should have been more aware of their part in that worship. Instead they had become too preoccupied with their earthly welfare to see the religious significance of their occupation.

There is a religious dignity and value in my own daily occupations, since God is very close to me in every activity of my daily life. As my Creator, He is my Partner every moment of my existence. He does not look upon my occupations as ordinary or common, since my life, energy, and grace proceed from His loving hand and fulfill His divine purpose. Though I readily admit this truth in theory, I tend, in practice, to lose sight of it. My emotions dull my reason and weaken my faith as I become aware of my personal shortcomings, the limitations of my achievements, the imperfections in my accomplishments, and the undesirable tendencies that sway my thinking and influence my decisions.

Yet, God sees more than these necessary conditions of my fallen human nature. He sees also the dignity bestowed on me through the redemption of His divine Son, the good will aroused in me by Christ's grace, and the sincere efforts I make in spite of my natural tendencies. God bids me look above my human surroundings and beyond my momentary failures or successes. He wishes me to become more aware of His presence in my daily life, and more impressed by the eternal value of my daily activities.

RESPOND My Jesus, let me never misunderstand the anger You showed toward the merchants in the temple. You do not have contempt for my daily activities and occupations, but a true respect for them. You Yourself embraced a carpenter's trade to earn Your daily bread, and You enjoyed Your recreations with Your friends. Following Your holy example, I shall have a deep respect for my person and my daily activities. I hope to become daily more aware of Your nearness to me in my labors and my legitimate pleasures. In this way I desire to bring my God more fully into my daily life. Amen.

19. NICODEMUS

READ Now there was a certain man among the Pharisees, Nicodemus by name, a ruler of the Jews. This man came to Jesus at night, and said to him, "Rabbi, we know that thou hast come a teacher from God, for no one can work these signs that thou workest unless God be with him." Jesus answered and said to him, "Amen, amen, I say to thee, unless a man be born again he cannot see the kingdom of God." (John 3:1–3)

REFLECT Nicodemus was not content with having good desires. He also felt a need to do what he could about fulfilling these desires. As a regard for his sincerity, Jesus revealed to him God's astounding plan of redemption: Through the merits of God's divine Son, man was to be "born again." Right here on earth, man was to receive a new life, a supernatural life, by which he would be able to share some of God's thoughts, desires, and actions. Without this new power, man's best intentions and efforts would be utterly inadequate to appease the Divine Justice and gain the eternal joys of heaven.

REVIEW I must never think or act as though my merits before God depend upon my unaided natural talents and endeavors. It is the supernatural life which Christ earned for me, that makes my good intentions and efforts meritorious for heaven. Unless I appreciate this fact, I shall never have that sense of worth that makes one content to be himself and live within the opportunities granted to him by God.

The only greatness and glory possible to me, lies within my present circumstances. I must not permit myself to be blinded by my human limitations and unintended personal defects in my prayers, efforts, and daily activities. God asks me to believe that the supernatural value of my life comes principally from the divine merits of Christ. My intentions and activities are to be evaluated not by the narrow limits of my human personality or the visible smallness of my circumstances, but by the priceless graces that elevate and inspire my daily intentions and actions. I must not permit myself to be so blinded by my many defects and shortcomings as to forget that every intention and endeavor of mine bears upon it the stamp of Christ's personal sacrifice for me.

RESPOND O, Jesus, let me never be so disgusted or discouraged with myself that I either give up trying to improve for Your sake, or strain beyond my natural or supernatural powers. I shall put my trust in Your divine merits, and learn to be content with the personal talents and graces You have granted to me. Let my sincerest efforts always be tempered with the humble acceptance of the limitations which You have placed upon my person and life. Amen.

20. RIVALRY AND DISPUTE

READ After these things Jesus and his disciples came into the land of Judea, and he stayed there with them and baptized . . . Now there arose a discussion about purification between some of John's disciples and the Jews. And they came to John and said to him, "Rabbi, he who was with thee beyond the Jordan, to whom thou hast borne witness, behold he baptizes, and all are coming to him." John answered and said, "No one can receive anything unless it is given to him from heaven. You yourselves bear me witness that I said, 'I am not the Christ but have been sent before him.' He who has the bride is the bridegroom; but the friend of the bridegroom, who stands and hears him, rejoices exceedingly at the voice of the bridegroom . . . He who comes from above is over all." (John 3:22, 24-29, 31)

REFLECT The disciples of John must have felt some threat to the prestige of their beloved Master. John, however, proceeds to teach them a precious lesson. He tells them that there is no reason to oppose Jesus, since He is unquestionably above everyone else. With peace of mind and freedom of heart John accepts his own position as a prophet and readily acknowledges the position of Jesus as his Lord and Master.

REVIEW In this meditation I find three precious principles of virtue, interior peace, and interpersonal harmony. First of all, John made it clear to his disciples that they must not expect him to claim or pretend to be more than he was. He could not be anyone except himself. He was not the Christ, but the forerunner of the Savior. Secondly, they must be ready to accept Jesus for what He really was . . . the bridegroom, i.e., the principal cause of their spiritual celebration and joy. They had no reason to resent His success with the people since He was truly above all others. Thirdly, John proclaimed himself the friend of Jesus, and he proved his friendship by an unreserved good will and service for the cause of Christ.

With these principles in my heart, I shall find my life changing slowly for the better. I shall enjoy a healthy peace of mind because of my self-acceptance. Amid my imperfect successes and recurring failures, I will be mature enough to give myself credit for good will when I have done what I could at the time. I shall be willing to let others be themselves within the normal limits of social living. I will never resent them for not following my personal tastes and preferences. Finally, I shall be more disposed to serve God within the limited circumstances of my daily life.

RESPOND   My divine Savior, most of the inner tensions and external frictions of daily living could be greatly alleviated by these wise and practical principles. Grant me the light to understand them, courage to apply them, and strength to continue my efforts in spite of repeated failures and a slow improvement. Amen.

21.   JESUS AT JACOB'S WELL

READ   Now he had to pass through Samaria. He came, accordingly, to a town of Samaria called Sichar, near the field that Jacob gave to his son Joseph. Now Jacob's well was there. Jesus therefore, wearied as he was from the journey, was sitting at the well. It was about the sixth hour. There came a Samaritan woman to draw water. Jesus said to her, "Give me to drink"; for his disciples had gone away into the town to buy food. The Samaritan woman therefore said to him, "How is it that thou, although thou art a Jew, dost ask drink of me, who am a Samaritan woman?" For Jews do not associate with Samaritans. Jesus answered and said to her, "If thou didst know the gift of God, and who it is who says to thee, 'Give me to drink,' thou, perhaps, wouldst have asked of him, and he would have given thee living water." (John 4:4–10)

REFLECT A prayerful reading of this incident will help me to appreciate more deeply the divine understanding, patience, and personal concern of Jesus for each individual. To a good number of Jews, this woman was someone despised. She was a Samaritan, a heretic, an outcast among the Jews. Moreover, in her conversation, she showed prejudice against all Jews, ignorance about God and religion, and a lack of regard for marital fidelity. And yet, in spite of these defects and faults, Jesus saw a basic sincerity and good will in her. In His concern for her spiritual welfare, He disregarded His fatigue, His hunger, His thirst, and possible scandal to His disciples.

REVIEW In His dealings with me, Jesus proceeds as He did with this woman. He sees me as I am, with my knowledge and my ignorance, my good will and my weaknesses, my efforts and my failures, my virtues and my faults, my good works and my sins. He judges me not only by my sins, but also by my sincere intentions and honest efforts to follow His teachings in my daily life.

In granting me His truth and grace, Jesus does not expect more of me than I can offer Him at any given moment. He is pleased with my good intentions, even when I am unable to carry them out. He appreciates my efforts even when I feel no enthusiasm in them. He understands my human frailty when I find it difficult to say, "Thy will be done." Jesus accepts my desire to love Him if that is all I can achieve just now. He is often more ready to believe in my sincerity than I am. He asks only that I do my reasonable best to follow His principles and imitate His example in my daily life.

RESPOND   My divine Savior, may I remember this precious lesson in my moments of disappointment, discouragement, or self-doubt. Enlighten my ignorance with Your truth. Strengthen my weakness with Your sacraments and grace. Inspire my good will with Your holy example. In my efforts to please You, let me never lose sight of Your infinite understanding, acceptance, and patience with the ignorant, the weak and the sinner. Amen.

22.   JESUS CLAIMS TO BE THE MESSIAS

READ   The woman said to him, "I know that Messias is coming (who is called Christ), and when he comes he will tell us all things." Jesus said to her, "I who speak with thee am he." . . . Meanwhile, his disciples besought him, saying, "Rabbi, eat." But he said to them, "I have food to eat of which you do not know. . . . My food is to do the will of him who sent me, to accomplish his work." (John 4:25–26, 31, 34)

REFLECT   So well-disposed was this woman that Jesus told her Who He was. She was deeply impressed by His person and utterly convinced of His truthfulness. This would not always be true of those who heard. Some would turn away from Him and return no more. On this occasion, Jesus shows His personal concern for each individual by neglecting His bodily needs to draw this solitary woman toward eternal life.

REVIEW   Jesus is just as eager to impress me as He was to convert this Samaritan woman. He often speaks to me through the books I read, the sermons I hear, the prayers I say, and the people I meet. I meet Him in every intelligent desire, hope, and intention that arises within me throughout the day. Unfortunately, I hold back or turn away from Him in a number of ways.

What hinders me from coming closer to Christ, is not necessarily a matter of sin. It may be due to misinformation or misunderstanding. I may feel that Jesus expects me to live with a perfect self-control at all times, free of all undesirable feelings or unwanted inclinations. In reading religious books, I may be aware that I fall far short of the principles and ideals they present. I may then blame myself for all my shortcomings, even those which are beyond my control. If I am to live at peace with myself, I must live in accordance with the facts. Some of my shortcomings are not easily controlled, and some are beyond my control. Because of this, I shall often be uncertain as to my culpability. The most I can do is to make a good intention and do what I can to diminish my defects and faults. When I am in doubt about myself, I can only present my doubts to God and leave the matter in His hands. Jesus saw all too clearly the shortcomings of the Samaritan woman. He also saw her good dispositions. He supplied His grace for her shortcomings, and built upon her good will. He desires to do the same with me. His greatest obstacle is my own self-doubt, or even my unreasonable self-discontent. I must learn to love myself with some of the love which Jesus has for me. If He thinks I am worth loving and helping, I must believe Him. With this sense of my own value, I shall be glad to be alive, glad to give my praises to God and my friendship to my fellow men.

RESPOND My Jesus, let me stop thinking myself unworthy of God's love or of human consideration. Let me accept my ignorance, weaknesses, and natural shortcomings as God's plan for me. Even when I recall my sins, I ought to profit by the memory and become a wiser and better person. Grant me the grace to be impressed not only by my natural limitations, but also, and especially, by Your wisdom, strength, and divine love for me. With eyes on You I shall more easily admit my faults, develop my talents and offer my friendship and help to those who need it. Amen.

23. THE NEED TO SEE SIGNS

READ   He came again, therefore, to Cana of Galilee, where he had made the water wine. And there was a certain royal official whose son was lying sick at Capharnaum. When he heard that Jesus had come from Judea into Galilee, he went to him and besought him to come down and heal his son, for he was at the point of death. Jesus therefore said to him, "Unless you see signs and wonders, you do not believe." (John 4:46 48)

REFLECT   In spite of the evident holiness and numerous miracles of Jesus, a number of those present on this occasion either could not or would not believe Him unless they themselves witnessed a miracle. Jesus expressed His disapproval of this kind of faith. He then proceeded to help this anxious father.

REVIEW   In spite of all that Jesus has said and done to win my trust and confidence, I too can have my occasional moments of doubt about Him. These doubts are not necessarily sinful. Being human, I occasionally experience within myself conflicting tendencies, desires, anxieties, and hostilities. In these interior conflicts, I cannot always be sure of my innocence or guilt. When my human nature inclines toward what is wrong, I am not always certain how freely I have consented to the inclination. In my self-doubt, I tend to fear that God will not view the matter in my favor, but will judge me guilty.

As a result of this uncertainty, I may find it difficult to place my trust in God's understanding and mercy. Since prayer could make me more aware of my uneasiness with God, I may become less inclined to prayer or more distracted in it. In my desire to forget my uneasiness with God, I may seek needless worldly distractions. With diminished prayer and increased distractions, I may gradually feel that God is far from me, or even that He does not exist at all. These latter doubts further increase my guilt-feelings and intensify my need to distract myself from religious thinking. Without dependable guidance, I shall find it extremely difficult, if not morally impossible, to escape the dread and despair that may develop from this situation.

RESPOND My Jesus, I must expect some spontaneous doubts as a normal part of human living. When I am uncertain about my part in these doubts, I shall seek advice from those qualified to give it. When unable to obtain this advice, I shall consider the matter in question, try to form an honest judgment, and then stand by my decision. Under the circumstances I must respect my own thinking. In Your earthly life You always respected the sincere man, even when he was wrong. With this mature self-respect and intelligent view of You, my normal human doubts will trouble me less, and I shall enjoy a greater peace with You. Grant me the grace to achieve this healthy growth. Amen.

24. THE MIRACULOUS CATCH OF FISH

READ But when he had ceased speaking, he said to Simon, "Put out into the deep and lower your nets for a catch." And Simon answered and said to him, "Master, the whole night through we have toiled and have taken nothing; but at thy word I will lower the net." And when they had done so they enclosed a great number of fishes . . . And they beckoned to their comrades in the other boat to come and help them. And they came and filled both the boats, so that they began to sink. But when Simon Peter saw this, he fell down at Jesus' knees, saying, "Depart from me, for I am a sinful man, O Lord." (Luke 5:4–8)

REFLECT   The miraculous catch so startled Peter that he became afraid. The supernatural power of Jesus made him intensely aware of his own human limitations and of his faults. Peter felt unworthy to be so close to Christ. He was seized with an urge to run, to get away from such exalted holiness and power. He spoke his words with genuine sincerity. Jesus, however, had other plans for Peter.

REVIEW   The urge to run from Christ is more common than I think. Different people turn away from Him in different ways. Some find it hard to keep their attention on Him when they are at prayer. Others find themselves becoming extremely tired or sleepy when attending church or listening to a sermon. Others feel time dragging when they are conscious of God. When these things occur repeatedly without an evident cause, it might be wise to suspect a hidden emotional cause.

Some of these causes are: (a) The mistaken notion that the only goodness is "perfect" goodness. This is not so. God accepts whatever degree of moral goodness I can achieve with my personal measure of graces, talents and opportunities. (b) The inability to acknowledge or confess my sins, or the lurking fear that God may refuse to forgive what I have confessed, or pardon what I have forgotten. If I humbly confess what I recall at that time, with a sincere intention to improve my life as far as I am able, God will forgive not only what I have confessed, but also what I have forgotten. (c) The fear that my limitations or defects are due to my own fault; that I might eliminate them if I tried harder. No matter how hard I try and how long I live, some defects will be with me until my dying day. (d) The fear that perhaps I am too ready to excuse myself of what is really my own fault. I can only trust in my good intentions and leave the rest to God. (e) Fear that I have not done enough penance for my sins. Every good work I perform this day can be offered as an act of reparation for my sins.

RESPOND O Jesus, true Son of God and King of eternal life, grant me the grace to understand myself in my moments of spiritual sluggishness. If I need a rest, grant me the prudence to take it. If, on the other hand, I am unreasonable in my immature expectations and demands upon myself, give me light to see my immaturity, strength to overcome it, and wisdom to begin again. Amen.

25. CHRIST THE TEACHER

READ And they entered Capharnaum. And immediately on the Sabbath he went into the synagogue and began to teach them. And they were astonished at his teaching, for he was teaching them as one having authority, and not as the Scribes . . . And they were all amazed, so that they inquired among themselves, saying, "What is this? What new doctrine is this? For with authority he commands even the unclean spirits, and they obey him." (Mark 1:21–22, 27)

REFLECT Having manifested His power over diseases of the body and those of the spirit, Jesus now reveals another power of His. He proceeds to teach without referring to the traditional interpreters of the law. He simply speaks on His own authority. So impressive was He that the people listened with amazement and awe. They did not quite know what to make of Him, but many rumors began to circulate. No doubt some of these rumors hinted at His being the long-awaited Messias.

REVIEW How impressed am I by Christ? How well do I really know Him? How much have I tried to know His mind and heart? These are vital questions, since they may determine my final judgment and my eternal destiny. Maybe I feel I have not tried hard enough to come closer to Him. Perhaps I avoided Him for fear of incurring more obligations than I might want. Then again, I may have failed to come closer because I did not really know Him or His message. Whatever the reason, it is not too late to begin again.

It takes time to know a person well enough to form a true and lasting friendship. I see this in everyday life. Though I have many acquaintances, I do not have many friends in the true sense of that word. A friend is one who understands and accepts me as I am. In his advice or disapproval, he is concerned about my welfare.

That Jesus understands me, I do not doubt, but that He accepts me as I am, this I often doubt, at least in my feelings. Whatever reasons I may give for feeling this way, my real reason is that I unconsciously think that Jesus sees me as a failure. I must try to appreciate what He really thinks of me. Until I do, I shall always have unsettling fears and doubts as to where I stand with Him. These emotions can gradually weaken my supernatural hope and confidence in God.

RESPOND O Jesus, divine Teacher, I desire to know You better, so that I may see You as the true friend You are, instead of the mere acquaintance I have made of You. Let me take time each day for a brief consideration of Your words, actions, and example. I hope eventually to know You so well that I may never doubt Your divine goodness, understanding, acceptance, and concern for me. Then, like those who marveled at Your Person and message, I too shall be amazed at the infinite depths of love that I find in You. Seeing myself through Your eyes, I shall respect myself, and love myself with that holy charity that brings peace to the mind and contentment to the heart. Amen.

26. HOLDING ON TO JESUS

READ   And rising up long before daybreak, he went out and departed into a desert place, and there he prayed. And Simon, and those who were with him, followed him. And they found him and said to him, "They are all seeking thee." (Mark 1:35–37)

REFLECT   The more the people listened to Jesus and the more they understood Him, the more they desired to stay with Him. Among these people there was every type of person I can imagine. He was sought by saints and sinners, old and young, strong and weak. In His person and words they found wisdom to solve their daily problems, strength to face life's daily obligations, and an interior peace that diminished their fears and dissolved their doubts.

REVIEW   Some people seek Christ's presence only as an obligation. They cannot be with Him too long. They become sad, too serious, anxious, or strangely devoid of thoughts or feeling. Do I experience this in any degree? Perhaps I am oppressed by the feeling that I am "not good enough" or just plainly "unworthy" of Christ's friendship. This attitude can do me as much spiritual harm as any attack of Satan.

I must strive to know myself ever better, so as to overcome such unhealthy attitudes. Be I ever so lacking in virtue, I must hold on to Jesus because without Him I cannot save my soul.

Jesus wants me to be impressed by my utter need of Him. He even warned His audience on one occasion that without Him they could do nothing worthy of heaven. Because of this, He stands by me throughout my daily life. Though He assists me in many hidden ways, His help is limited by my lack of sensitivity to His presence. If I could develop an easy sense of friendship with Him, His graces would bring me greater clarity of mind, strength of will, and peace of soul. I can grow into this state of friendship with Christ only if I work at it. Without strain or extraordinary measures, I must learn to come closer to Him through some reading, reflection, and prayer each day. I shall slowly learn to live in greater harmony with His words and example.

RESPOND   My Jesus, You have proven Yourself my friend in many ways. Not only in Your words, but also by Your example; You have shown that You understand the disturbed mind, the weak will, and even the sinner who desires to come to You in his last hour. Therefore, my Lord and Savior, I desire to change my mistaken notions of You, so that I may gradually find the peace and joy that You desire to bestow upon me. Amen.

27. JESUS FORGIVES SINS

READ   And behold, some men were carrying upon a pallet a man who was paralyzed, and they were trying to bring him in and to lay him before him. And as they found no way of bringing him in, because of the crowd, they went up on to the roof and lowered him through the tiles, with his pallet, into the midst before Jesus. And seeing their faith, he said, "Man, thy sins are forgiven thee." (Luke 5:18–20)

REFLECT   As Jesus pronounced the man's sins forgiven, the Scribes and Pharisees in the crowd became upset. Only God could forgive sin. Was this man claiming divine power? For the moment they were not sure what Jesus claimed, so they waited to hear more. Instead of explaining His power, Jesus proceeded to prove it by an evident miracle.

REVIEW   Jesus worked this miracle not only for those people, but also for me. By word and action, He tells me that He is an understanding Savior and a forgiving God. He does not expect me to appreciate His divine message fully in an instant. Like those who were with Him that day, I too shall have to think over His words and actions repeatedly. Slowly, with time, my understanding and appreciation will deepen. A number of people permit themselves to be blinded by their personal defects. They fail to look at their daily life in its totality. As a result, they underestimate the good deeds they perform and the sincerity with which they try to avoid sin. The mere presence of an imperfection or the commission of a venial sin convinces them that they are worthy only of total condemnation. Jesus is trying to show me that this is not His way of thinking. While He disapproves of my sins, He is pleased with my sincere efforts to live a good life. When I express sorrow for my sins, He is ready to forgive me, and offers me grace to continue my daily efforts.

Much as I may try to please God in all things, I must understand that I am a limited human being, with my personal measure of ignorance and weaknesses. As long as my failures are unintended and unwanted, I must accept them without undue shame or self-blame. If I sin, I ought to show enough trust in His divine mercy, to come to Him for pardon. Perhaps the greatest obstacle to my spiritual progress is an unconscious demand that I should be beyond the need for forgiveness. If this demand is conscious, I am either dominated by an overwhelming emotional pride or guilty of the sin of pride. In either case, my following of Christ will be greatly limited by my immaturity and lack of humility.

RESPOND   Jesus, my divine Redeemer, may I never believe that my sins outweigh the infinite reparation which You made for them by Your earthly life, labors, sufferings and death. Too often my small-minded outlook sees my sins as beyond Your patience and pardon. It is not You, but I who lack patience and forgiveness. I desire to avoid all sins in the future, but I shall never be surprised or discouraged when I do sin. With the healthy humility of a mature adult and the help of Your grace, I shall come to You for pardon. Amen.

28. JESUS, FRIEND OF SINNERS

READ   And it came to pass as he was at table in Levi's house, that many publicans and sinners were at table with Jesus and his disciples, for there were many and they also followed him. And the Scribes and the Pharisees, seeing that he ate with sinners and publicans, said to his disciples, "Why does your master eat and drink with publicans and sinners?" And Jesus heard this, and said to them, "It is not the healthy who need a physician, but they who are sick. For I have not come to call the just, but sinners." (Mark 2:15–17)

REFLECT   In this scene we see Jesus drawing sinners to Himself. The Pharisees and Scribes felt that He should turn His back on them. Jesus, however, declared that these were the people for whom He had come, since they needed Him more than the just. The just would readily cooperate with His grace, but sinners needed to see, hear, and understand how they might turn from their sins and develop their virtues.

REVIEW   What do I think of myself? Do I see my life as a mess and a failure? Do I feel guilty of not having lived up to my ideals? If so, I ought to consider whether my ideals are reasonable. Perhaps they are beyond my reach. If I am reasonably certain that I have really neglected the graces and opportunities God has granted me, I need only turn to this understanding and merciful Christ. According to His own statement, it is for the likes of me that He has come. Never shall I find a more accepting, more patient, more true friend than He.

However, I cannot undo the habits of years in a short time. I have many habits, both conscious and unconscious. These habits are constantly influencing my feelings, inclinations, thoughts, and decisions. In my effort to improve, I must be patient. As long as I remain emotionally disgusted with myself, I shall be unable to make an intelligent effort toward self-understanding and self-improvement. Either I shall consider myself unworthy of the effort; or I shall demand that I make one "perfect" resolution, and never again repeat any of my old defects or faults. This is the height of immaturity. It is neurotic pride, the kind of emotional pride that is seen in children, who do not understand their human nature. Jesus accepts me as I am, accepts my sincere resolutions, accepts my human efforts, and understands my unintended failures. When I see Jesus in this light, I shall enjoy the sunshine of His presence, the peace of His friendship, and the strength of His grace.

RESPOND   My Jesus, true Friend of sinners, grant me the grace to cast aside my emotional disgust with self and my insecurity with You. I will not make Your task more difficult by doubting Your infinite mercy and genuine concern for me. I hope to prove my friendship for You by striving each day to understand the emotions that draw me away from You and develop those virtues which I need most. Help me make this endeavor intelligently. It is the endeavor of a lifetime, and I shall need all my life to make the progress which You desire of me. Amen.

29. AN UNREQUESTED FAVOR

READ Now a certain man was there who had been thirty-eight years under his infirmity. When Jesus saw him lying there, and knew that he had been in this state a long time, he said to him, "Dost thou want to get well?" The sick man answered him, "Sir, I have no one to put me into the pool when the water is stirred; for while I am coming, another steps down before me." Jesus said to him, "Rise, take up thy pallet and walk." And at once the man was cured . . . Afterwards, Jesus found him in the temple and said to him, "Behold, thou art cured. Sin no more, lest something worse befall thee." (John 5:5–8, 14)

REFLECT From those last words of Jesus to the man, there would seem to be some connection between his former ailment and his sins. We can only conjecture what this connection may have been. It is quite probable that he had allowed himself to become rebellious against his physical deficiencies and embittered toward life. Perhaps it took him the greater part of his thirty-eight years to reach some measure of real resignation to his condition. Only then would he be ready for the unrequested favor which Jesus granted him.

REVIEW As fire purifies gold of its imperfections, so does my daily life offer me an opportunity to be purified of my defects. As I go about from day to day, I exercise a number of virtues in various degrees. However, among my good intentions, dispositions, and actions there are some defects which I can eliminate either fully, partially, or not at all. No matter how much I may desire to make my life more pleasing to God, I cannot do so without an intelligent appreciation of Who God is, what I am, why I exist, and how I am to obtain the peace and happiness I crave. Without this appreciation, I shall be doomed to frustration and death.

It is to my advantage to know my true self. Only the truth can make me the kind of person that God desires me to be, the kind of person I shall want to be when I see all things in the light of God's wisdom and judgment. Unconscious tendencies toward self-deception lie deep within every human being. Sometimes God sends me some hardship in order to bring me face to face with myself. As I see my immaturity, I come to know how incomplete my good desires have been. I face the choice of increasing my virtues or rejecting God's grace. Like the invalid in this meditation, I can make my problem a source of sin or a pathway to holiness.

RESPOND My God, help me to live my life as You made it. Let me not reach beyond my grasp, nor rebel at the limitations which You have placed upon my person and life. Teach me to make the most of the good things at my disposal, accept the privations which I must endure, and see that my true perfection lies in following Your divine will rather than my immature demands and expectations. I hope to practice humility by accepting my limitations with the same gratitude that I feel for Your gifts. Amen.

30. JESUS MY JUDGE

READ For neither does the Father judge any man, but all judgment he has given to the Son, that all men may honor the Son as they honor the Father. . . . "Amen, amen, I say to you, he who hears my word, and believes him who sent me, has life everlasting, and does not come to judgment, but has passed from death to life. . . . For as the Father has life in himself, even so he has given to the Son also to have life in himself; and he has granted him power to render judgment, because he is the Son of Man. Do not wonder at this, for the hour is coming in which all who are in the tombs shall hear the voice of the Son of God. And they who have done good shall come forth unto the resurrection of life; but they who have done evil unto resurrection of judgment." (John 5:22, 23, 24, 26-29)

REFLECT   Jesus, the God-man, Redeemer of the world, is to sit in judgment over all men. His judgment will be true, since it will be based upon the law of God. Those who have fulfilled God's holy Will have nothing to fear. Those who knowingly and freely opposed God's will, shall receive their just punishment.

REVIEW   It is a fact revealed by God through His divine Son, that I must one day render an account of my life. My judge will be Jesus Himself, Who came down to save me by a life of labor, prayer, and suffering. This thought ought to give me encouragement, since He has shown me in His gospels how understanding and forgiving He is. And yet, there is within me a feeling of uneasiness, a sense of uncertainty that He may reject me and condemn me for my sins. This feeling may be based on the fact that I have committed real sins, or again it may be a general, indefinite sense of guilt. If I have committed real sins, I have time now to express sorrow for having offended so generous a Father and so merciful a Savior. My acts of reparation, joined with the reparation and sacraments of Christ, will bring God's pardon and reward.

If, however, I find no peace in declaring my trust in Christ's pardon and mercy, I may be the victim of emotional guilt. This is not a virtuous fear of punishment for real sins committed and unrepented. It is merely an extension of the natural uneasiness I often feel when I am not sure of myself in some human situation. An emotional sense of inadequacy usually develops in early life. It can enter later on into my religious practices. I may now consciously feel that the only way to obtain God's approval is by being perfect. Since I cannot be perfect, I feel uneasy with God. If I have thought in this childish manner over a period of time, it will take time to eradicate it from my system. In the meantime, I must believe that as long as I am trying to know and fulfill God's holy Will, I shall never be condemned.

RESPOND Jesus, my Savior, how can I fear Your judgment when You have done so much to prove Your personal concern for me? I am truly sorry for my sins, both remembered and forgotten. Help me to prove this sorrow by my future efforts to fulfill Your holy Will. I shall fight my emotional fears and doubts by frequently affirming my confidence and trust in You. Amen.

31. READING THE SCRIPTURES

READ You search the Scriptures, because in them you think that you have life everlasting. And it is they that bear witness to me, yet you are not willing to come to me that you may have life. (John 5:39–40)

REFLECT The Jewish leaders had their own fixed ideas about God's plan of redemption. Though they daily read the Scriptures, they failed to recognize the Redeemer of Whom the Prophets spoke. So rigid was their thinking that they remained unimpressed by the wisdom, miracles, and personal holiness of Jesus.

REVIEW Before I was able to think for myself, I had already absorbed many of the thoughts, attitudes, emotional tendencies of my parents and other adults who influenced my early life. As I was growing into the age of reason, I was also developing a definite emotional slant on the truths which I now accept on the word of God.

Though that slant has been modified with age, education, and experience, some of its influence still sways me in my feelings, thinking, and behavior. This influence is felt not only in my self-regard and interpersonal relations, but also in my religious attitudes and conduct. It can make me misunderstand and misapply the teachings of Christ and the practices of His Holy Church.

Emotional thinking creates a blind spot in the mind and a one-sided view of God and religion. I may be impressed only with thoughts concerning "sinlessness," "self-punishment," "self-sacrifice," "work," etc. When I reflect on the words "virtue," "sin," "Christian perfection," etc., I may think only of my defects, faults, and sins. Or again, I may have an unwarranted fear of hypocrisy or self-deception. Actually, balanced religious living brings peace and contentment into the soul. It does not dwell morbidly on a sinful past, or strain for a perfection that tires the nerves and depresses the mind. Neither does it make one uneasy at the thought of death and judgment.

Christ preached the understanding, mercy, and love of God. If I feel that I should be working harder, praying more, and sacrificing myself more, I may be right. If, however, I feel uneasy simply because my life brings me satisfaction or reasonable pleasure, I might well suspect a morbid notion of virtue, holiness, and religion. Mistaken ideas can be as dangerous to my soul as really sinful habits. Such ideas can eventually draw me away from Christ. They make religion seem too difficult and God too demanding.

RESPOND My Jesus, King of divine truth, help me to understand myself well enough to detect any mistaken notions in my religious thinking. Let me know myself and let me know You. May I neither exaggerate nor minimize what You said and did. With truth in my mind and generosity in my heart, I wish to live my daily life as a sincere act of friendship with You. Amen.

READ   And it came to pass again as he was going through the standing grain on the Sabbath, that his disciples began, as they went along, to pluck the ears of grain. But the Pharisees said to him, "Behold, why are they doing what is not lawful on the Sabbath?" And he said to them, "Have you never read what David did when he and those who were with him were in need, and hungry? how he entered the house of God, when Abiathar was high priest, and ate the loaves of proposition, which he could not lawfully eat, but only the priests? and how he gave them to those who were with him?" And he said to them, "The Sabbath was made for man, and not man for the Sabbath. Therefore the Son of Man is Lord even of the Sabbath." (Mark 2:23–28)

REFLECT   Here again we find Jesus attempting to open the minds of the Pharisees to the real spirit of God's law . . . the spirit of wisdom and love. Unfortunately, the Pharisees were so rigid in their interpretation of the law that they insisted on the literal meaning, no matter how impossible or intolerable it might be at times.

REVIEW   Unless I learn to serve God with intelligence I too shall be rigid and narrow-minded in my religious thinking and practices. I must see God as a reasonable, understanding, and sympathetic Father. Only then can I live in the spirit of Christ's teaching. Am I able to exercise an intelligent good will toward myself or am I compelled to live the letter of every religious rule? Can I excuse myself in circumstances when God Himself might readily excuse me? Can I make the same allowances for myself as I can for those who are unable to fulfill some religious duty, or do I live in fear of self-deception or of God's "unbending" justice? Do I depend so rigidly on external performances that I cannot even accept the more lenient interpretations of competent counselors?

As long as I am dominated by an unreasoning fear of God, I shall never act as an adult in my religious activities. I must learn to think and act in the spirit of Christ. When I say that I do not want to sin, I must believe in my own sincerity. Unless I trust in my own intention, I shall never find peace of mind, no matter what Christ's Church tells me. There are times when I cannot wait for due permission or needed advice. At such times I am expected to form my own conscience and make my own decision. If the act is not wrong in itself, and my intention is good, and the circumstances require action, I must believe in myself, and act. I may inquire later to confirm or correct my decision. God does not mean to enslave me by His commandments. He desires only to show me the way to eternal life.

RESPOND Lord, unless I understand these principles and live by them, I shall hurt both myself and those who depend on me for guidance. I shall feel or act as though You were an unreasonable and cruel tyrant with no consideration for the natural weaknesses and normal needs of human nature. Such a notion will make religion repulsive to me and to those whom I influence. In our various activities, we will deal with You as little as possible. May I never forget this incident, in which You showed Yourself as a truly understanding and considerate Savior. Amen.

33. JESUS AT PRAYER

READ Now it came to pass in those days that he went out to the mountain to pray, and continued all night in prayer to God. And when day broke, he summoned his disciples; and from these he chose twelve. (Luke 6:12–13)

REFLECT It was the eve of a great day. Tomorrow Jesus would choose the twelve who were to occupy first place in establishing His earthly kingdom, the Church. Jesus had no real need to pray over the matter, since He was always in contact with His heavenly Father. However, He had come to teach us the Christian life. By His example, He showed us externally what was always going on within His soul. He thereby stressed the importance of prayer in everyday life.

REVIEW What does prayer mean to me? Is it merely the recital of a few formulas memorized in my early life, or is it more than that? Actually, prayer is a communication with God, whether with words or merely in my thoughts and desires. Any welcome awareness of God's presence is a prayer.

In prayer I can offer to God my adoration, thanksgiving, petitions, and reparation. When I adore, I give my highest respect and praise to Him, the Infinite Creator. I confess my utter and absolute dependence on Him for all that I am and have on earth, and for my eternal self-fulfillment in heaven. My thanks are offered for the gifts He has bestowed upon me, gifts so generous that I am usually unaware of their number and importance to me. My petitions are presented to Him for my own needs of body and soul, the needs of my dear ones, and the needs of people throughout the world. My reparation is offered for my sins and for the sins of others, whereby we have offended His goodness, opposed His wisdom, and abused His gifts.

The more I learn to share with God my thoughts, desires, intentions, and efforts, the more fully shall I imitate the example of Jesus, my divine Model. Prayer will change me because it will make me ever more conscious of God's nearness. My union with Him will influence my thinking and behavior even without my awareness. Those around me will somehow be affected by my interior union with God. However, I must not expect to become a man of prayer in a day. Like everyone else, I shall need God's grace, and my own persevering practice. The habit of prayer will grow with time.

RESPOND   My Jesus, I desire to imitate You in Your prayerfulness. Teach me to pray as You did, with an intimacy that will make me feel at home with the Father. Grant me a sense of my God-given importance, to help me respect myself and my prayer. Give me an appreciation of Your nearness and concern for me, to convince me that You are listening. My love for You will then urge me to live my daily life in prayerful union with You. Amen.

34. THE SERMON ON THE MOUNT

READ   And coming down with them, he took his stand on a level stretch, with a crowd of his disciples, and a great multitude of people . . . who came to listen to him . . . And he lifted up his eyes to his disciples . . . And opening his mouth he taught them . . . (Luke 6:17, 18, 20; Matt. 5:2)

REFLECT   Having chosen His special followers, Jesus now proceeds to teach them the basic principles of the New Law. On them He will later confer special graces to understand and interpret His doctrine as He Himself intends it. However, before receiving the graces of Pentecost, they will have to undergo several years of training. They will hear these doctrines explained again and again. On this foundation, the Holy Spirit will build the extraordinary spiritual life of the apostles.

REVIEW   To follow Christ intelligently, it is not enough

to know His words. I also need to know His meaning, His attitude and His intentions, before I can correctly apply His words to my daily life. This kind of knowledge is not gained by mere reading or memorizing. It is to be absorbed slowly through prayer, meditation, self-examination, and daily practice. Spiritual growth is achieved by faith in the supernatural dignity which Christ bestowed upon me in baptism; by humility to accept my limits, both temporary and permanent; by continued practice, in spite of my frequent partial failures and occasional total ones. Over and over I shall make the same mistakes. Again and again I may be corrected by my superiors or by my own conscience. My greatness lies in refusing to be discouraged by failures, limitations, or slow visible progress. Like the apostles, I too shall one day be ready for graces far beyond my present expectations.

This is a lesson that comes slowly to many people. They have too little patience with their nature's pace. They are too easily discouraged by their partial successes or repeated failures. In their immaturity, they are not willing to continue their efforts with such slow visible progress. They grow tired of reading the same matter, thinking the same thoughts, striving for the same virtues, and facing the same defects. They do not realize that as long as they are in this life, temptations will continue to face them. Labors will still require their attention and energy. Sufferings of body, mind or soul will always be present in some degree. Only when they have arrived before the judgment seat of God may they hope to hear the words: "Well done, thou good and faithful servant." Only then will their task of striving for Christian perfection be over.

RESPOND   My Jesus, let me not be so immature as to think that I know enough about Your teachings, and that I have no further need to strive for self-improvement. Since the ways of God are so mysterious, the temptations of Satan are so clever, and the weaknesses of my human nature are so complex, let me never tire of increasing my knowledge, progressing in prayer, frequenting the sacraments, and applying Your principles to my daily life. Amen.

35. LIVING WITHIN THE LAW

READ "Do not think that I have come to destroy the Law or the Prophets. I have not come to destroy, but to fulfill . . . Therefore whoever does away with one of these least commandments, and so teaches men, shall be called least in the kingdom of heaven; but whoever carries them out and teaches them, he shall be called great in the kingdom of heaven." (Matt. 5:17, 19)

REFLECT In order to settle the fears and doubts of some of His hearers, Jesus makes it quite clear that He is not attempting to destroy God's laws. For the benefit of those who might be listening to Him with the hope of breaking away from their religious training, He emphasizes His point: As He intends to fulfill God's law, so too must they respect and practice the commandments of God and the religious prescriptions of legitimate authority.

REVIEW Some people see religion as a burden, a frustration and hindrance to their spontaneous self-expression. They feel hemmed in and tied down by the requirements and laws of the Church. Due to their natural tendencies, emotional needs, and force of habit, they seek freedom from all restraint. In their quest for freedom, they talk themselves into some very convenient convictions. They specialize in some congenial virtues to satisfy their need for self-respect, and neglect those virtues which are not to their liking. This process of convenient selection is not always conscious or deliberate. God may see reasons to excuse these people to some extent. Nevertheless, their spiritual condition is not a healthy one. They are an easy prey to many temptations, and they can do a good deal of harm, even in the name of religion.

How do I feel about the commandments and laws governing my state in life? Is my desire for freedom so strong that I remain content with the minimum requirements? Do I habitually avoid extra good works or religious practices? Perhaps the pressure of my present obligations leaves me little time or energy for anything more. If so, I might consider whether this pressure is due to my faulty emotional habits, my immature attitude toward my obligations, or my childish uneasiness with God or others. Religion may be a burden to me because of my unreasonable demand for perfection in my religious performance. Or again, I may feel religion is a reminder of what I am not. Instead of seeing God as the loyal Father He is, I may feel the weight of my shame, self-blame and fear of punishment whenever I turn my mind to religious thinking.

RESPOND My Jesus, divine King of my life, I hope to imitate Your respect and fulfillment of Your Father's commandments and law. Only at the appointed time did You leave the Old Law for the New. Grant me a deep sense of loyalty to You as I follow Your principles in my daily activities. Teach me to be at ease with God and at peace with myself, so that I may never feel an unreasonable need to lose myself in worldly distractions. Amen.

36. CHASTITY OF MIND AND BODY

READ "You have heard that it was said to the ancients, 'Thou shalt not commit adultery.' But I say to you that anyone who so much as looks with lust at a woman has already committed adultery with her in his heart." (Matt. 5:27–28)

74

REFLECT Jesus is talking here of actual sin, and not of those spontaneous, unpremeditated, unintended, and unwanted tendencies of mind and body which arise within every normal person at one time or another. He stresses the point that sin is not merely a deliberate external action, but can also be a conscious and fully accepted desire.

REVIEW The sexual nature of man is the work of God. There is nothing ugly, repulsive, or evil in it. For good reasons, God made the sexual appetite the second strongest drive in human nature. Therefore, I must not be surprised, ashamed, or afraid when sexual tendencies appear spontaneously through my imagination, feelings, desires, or momentary actions. With God's help, I must be intelligent and mature enough to tolerate these uninvited tendencies, not confusing them with my freely chosen intention. In spite of my knowledge and good intentions, I shall often be unable to make a clear decision as to my degree of free consent, because of the complicated nature of my sexual tendencies.

I should know enough about sex to satisfy all normal curiosity about it. The more I fear sex, the more I shall be disturbed by it. My very fear will make me more aware of sex. Since sin is in the intention, and an intention is something I can always make, I must refuse to be disturbed by the indeliberate attraction of my eyes or imagination to sex.

Unfortunately fear of sex is sometimes taught to children in a morbid manner. As a result they become afraid to look at or touch their own body even when necessity requires it. They are convinced that any attention to their sexual parts is a serious sin, regardless of circumstances. This fear makes them unduly uneasy even in their adult social life. Their nervous self-restraint is far from the intelligent, virtuous self-control of the informed adult. Fear can create obsessions in the mind, so that one cannot help thinking of sex more frequently than is normal. It can so weaken the will that one is no longer able to control his actions in this matter. At such times, one can only declare his good intentions, and then believe in his own sincerity and in God's infinite reasonableness.

RESPOND O Jesus, I know that I am a complicated being, composed of body and soul. Teach me to accept both parts of my nature without contempt for its natural tendencies. I rely upon Your guidance and grace for the proper attitude and necessary strength to control the unreasoning tendencies of my sexual appetite. May I never be carelessly presumptuous or morbidly immature in my daily internal and external sexual attractions. While I intend to avoid all unnecessary occasions of sin, I hope also to be mature enough to face the necessary temptations of everyday human living. Amen.

37. THE SPIRIT OF CHRISTIAN FORGIVENESS

READ "You have heard that it was said, 'Thou shalt love thy neighbor, and shalt hate thy enemy.' But I say to you, love your enemies, do good to those who hate you, and pray for those who persecute and calumniate you, so that you may be children of your Father in heaven, who makes his sun to rise on the good and the evil, and sends rain on the just and the unjust." (Matt. 5:43–45)

REFLECT Jesus invites us to aim high in our interpersonal relations. He advises us to be Godlike, not with a false sense of superiority, nor with a subtle contempt for the ignorance and weaknesses of others, nor with a self-righteousness that is quick to correct or punish those who offend us. Our Godlikeness must consist in understanding the human limitations of our neighbor and in attributing their offenses to human weakness rather than to malice. He exhorts us to imitate the divine patience and mercy of the heavenly Father, Who gave every man a lifetime to see his errors and to repent of his sins.

REVIEW   At first glance, this counsel of Jesus can be quite discouraging. My habits of self-defense, my need for approval, and my fear of being rejected by others are well fixed by now. I tend to dislike those who dislike me, hate those who seem to reject me, fear those who are more gifted or stronger than I, envy those who seem content with themselves, and suspect those who appear to be taking advantage of me. I feel that others would go too far if I did not "put them in their place."

And yet, Jesus asks me to show good will to all, in spite of their small-mindedness, impatience, rash judgments, unkind dispositions and self-centered attitudes. He tells me to fix my eyes on the heavenly Father's way of dealing with such people. Many people are very immature. They are as self-centered in their adult years as when they were children. They may not even be aware of their immaturity. They may be victims of their inner emotional pressures. Their early life may have been difficult for them. In spite of their present good will and sincere efforts, they may be unable to overcome the unconscious anxieties and fears that now impel them to a neurotic self-defense. They may be suffering more than I from their mean disposition. When I treat them in like manner, I am being as immature as they are. If there be malice in them, I would do well to leave them to God. Of course, this does not mean that I am forbidden to defend my rights when the matter is important enough to warrant it. It simply means that I must strive to imitate the understanding, goodness, and patience of God by not magnifying every little incident.

RESPOND   My heavenly Father, where would I be today if You acted toward me with the same small mind that often incites me to strike back at others? Make me big enough to overcome my emotional smallness, and mature enough to look beyond the narrow vision of others. Let me see You at the side of those who provoke me to anger, so that I may never defend my rights with a spirit of revenge. Amen.

38. LESSER MOTIVES

READ Take heed not to do your good before men, in order to be seen by them; otherwise you shall have no reward with your Father in heaven. "Therefore when thou givest alms, do not sound a trumpet before thee, as the hypocrites do in the synagogues and streets, in order that they may be honored by men . . . Again when you pray, you shall not be like the hypocrites, who love to pray standing in the synagogues and at the street corners, in order that they may be seen by men . . . And when you fast, do not look gloomy like the hypocrites, who disfigure their faces in order to appear to men as fasting. Amen, I say to you, they have received their reward." (Matt. 6:1–2, 5, 16)

REFLECT Jesus urges us to get the most out of the good we perform. Why seek the recognition of men when we can have the recognition of God? Human admiration and esteem are usually unpredictable, often unreliable, frequently superficial, sometimes insincere, and mostly short-lived. God, on the other hand, sees our desire, knows our intentions, appreciates our endeavors, and rewards our efforts far beyond our fondest hope.

REVIEW A hypocrite is a person who is deliberately insincere in his good works. He pretends to be what he neither intends nor tries to be in reality. However, not every pretense is hypocrisy. Everybody "puts on a front" when dealing with those whose respect or admiration he desires. Such "putting on" may be a sincere effort to improve oneself.

There is a third type of pretense. This form of pretending is aroused by emotional immaturity. Childhood is a time of helplessness and dependency. During these early years everyone feels a need to obtain the acceptance and approval of those on whom he depends. Some traces of this emotional need persist in later life. These remnants of childhood insecurity sometimes constitute an obstacle to one's spiritual progress. Without being aware of it, I may use God, religion, or virtue as a means of obtaining the acceptance or esteem of people. I may sincerely believe that I am performing my good works for the glory of God or for other good intentions. And yet, in reality, I may be performing them principally for the lesser rewards they bring. True, I may not be able to eradicate these lesser motives entirely, but I can make frequent renewals of my highest intention, namely, to please God above all else.

I must not unduly accuse myself of being a hypocrite simply because I am aware of people when I perform my good works. If I choose to perform them for the glory of God, He will accept that as my foremost intention, no matter how much I may suspect my own sincerity.

RESPOND   My Jesus, though I must never willfully offend the people around me, let me never be more impressed by them than by You. Even when I am conscious of lesser motives in my prayers or good works, let me desire to please Your heavenly Father in these activities. May my motto always be: "All for the glory of God." Amen.

39.   THE PROBLEM OF ANXIETY

READ   "No man can serve two masters; for either he will hate the one and love the other, or else he will stand by the one and despise the other. You cannot serve God and mammon. Therefore, I say to you, do not be anxious for your life, what you shall eat; nor yet for your body, what you shall put on . . . For your Father knows that you need all these things. But seek first the kingdom of God and his justice, and all these things shall be given you besides. Therefore do not be anxious about tomorrow; for tomorrow will have anxieties of its own. Sufficient for the day is its own trouble." (Matt. 6:24–25, 32–34)

REFLECT Jesus now deals with one of the deepest and most subtle human problems, the problem of anxiety. Men do strange things when anxiety moves them. In varying degrees they lose their power to think clearly and their ability to make intelligent decisions. Many a sinful deed is committed under the influence of anxiety. Jesus gives us the best and highest solution to anxiety, namely, trust in God's wisdom, power, and fatherly concern for each individual.

REVIEW The first law of my nature is the law of self-preservation. From my earliest years, I became anxious whenever I felt insecure. In my anxiety I felt impelled to cry for help, or to help myself as best I could. Many of my present personal habits and attitudes are defenses against anxiety. My defenses become more complex with the changing circumstances of my life. My mind developed those defenses which were more available or satisfying to me. Consequently, I now have my predominant emotional needs and personal habits. I may be most at ease when I can cater to the wishes of others; or be contrary in my thoughts, words, or actions; or finally, remain aloof through silence, solitude, or other forms of isolation.

One of the means of overcoming anxiety is the possession of earthly goods. Men feel safe when they do not have to worry about their bodily needs. The possession of earthly goods is not evil, in itself. It is good as long as it is guided by God's Law and directed by His grace. It becomes dangerous only when it seizes control of my thinking and behavior. Only then is it capable of leading me into sin. Jesus tells me to keep anxiety under control by placing my security in the fatherly providence of God. He assures me that God will not fail me in my essential needs.

RESPOND Heavenly Father, my emotional tendencies often influence me without my awareness. My fears and anxieties have become so ingrained in my nervous system and mental habits, that I shall often have to tolerate them in spite of my supernatural trust in You. Only with grace, practice, and time shall I be able to diminish the undesirable pressure of natural anxiety. Teach me to be patient with myself when my feelings fail to follow my faith. Though I may feel emotionally anxious, I desire to oppose the feeling with a deep and firm trust in Your divine wisdom, infinite power, and fatherly care. Amen.

40. INTERIOR BLINDNESS

READ "Can a blind man guide the blind? . . . But why dost thou see the speck in thy brother's eye, and yet dost not consider the beam in thy own eye? And how canst thou say to thy brother, 'Brother, let me cast out the speck from thy eye,' while yet thou thyself dost not see the beam in thy own eye? Thou hypocrite, first cast out the beam from thy own eye, and then thou wilt see clearly to cast out the speck from thy brother's eye." (Luke 6:39, 41–42)

REFLECT Before I can help others amend their lives, I must first amend my own. I need to see myself as I really am, and correct what requires correction. Unless I know my real self, I shall be looking at others with a defective or distorted vision. I shall not have a full view of them because of the blind spot which I have toward myself.

REVIEW   If my past life was exposed to more criticism or correction than I was able to bear, I may well be hypersensitive to any reminder of my shortcomings. Any awareness of my limitations or defects may arouse in me an unbearable anxiety, sadness, or self-disgust. In my fear of these unsettling emotions I may have developed defenses against them. One way of blinding myself to my intolerable self-awareness is to center my attention on the defects and faults of others. By adopting a critical and disapproving attitude toward them, I acquire a self-respect that distracts me from my anxiety, self-disgust, or fear of punishment. If this emotional process is conscious and voluntary, I am guilty of sinning in some degree. I may also be guilty of hypocrisy, since I pretend to hate what I refuse to correct in myself.

However, this process can also develop in me without sin. If so, I still need to correct it as far as I can, since it constitutes an obstacle to the good which I might accomplish in my life. Those whom I attempt to correct or advise are not blind to my defects or faults. They will wonder how I can undertake to guide or correct them when I have the same or worse shortcomings. Instead of taking my words to heart, they will resent me, and refuse to follow my admonitions.

Jesus therefore advises me to see myself with the help of His grace, and to acknowledge my shortcomings without undue shame or blame. He will help me correct or diminish them in due time. With this healthy self-knowledge, I shall be a better counselor. Instead of feeling like a superior being, I shall feel like one of my fellow men, with my own quota of human frailties. I shall be less likely to project my personal problems into the words, actions, and attitudes of others. My humility and sincerity will impress on others the lesson which I intend to teach. If they are mature enough to avoid their own blind spots, I shall improve their lives with some of my personal richness.

RESPOND My Jesus, grant me the grace to meditate often upon my blind spots. Teach me to understand that any unwillingness to know myself as I am, is a sign of either immaturity or bad will. I wish to be neither a child nor a sinner. Therefore, I hope to follow the principles of this meditation. I do not expect to improve quickly nor perfectly, but I shall try each day to grow in this wise and holy attitude. Amen.

41. BUILDING ON ROCK

READ "Everyone therefore who hears these my words and acts upon them, shall be likened to a wise man who built his house on rock. And the rain fell, and the floods came, and the winds blew and beat against that house, but it did not fall, because it was founded on rock. And everyone who hears these my words and does not act upon them, shall be likened to a foolish man who built his house on sand. And the rain fell, and the floods came, and the winds blew and beat against that house, and it fell, and was utterly ruined." (Matt. 7:24–27)

REFLECT Jesus astounds His audience with both His manner and His message. He speaks with an authority that inspires confidence in some and fear in others. He claims to know the sure path to eternal life. Some would gladly follow Him, but others would turn away or even turn against Him.

REVIEW In these words Jesus offers me the security of His guidance and the strength of His assistance. And yet, much as I desire this security and strength, part of me is constantly moving away from Him. My mind finds it easier to dwell upon the visible attractions of this earthly life than upon the less tangible truths which Jesus presents. These external interests distract me from my "defects" and from my vague sense of God's disapproval. In spite of my explicit trust in God's understanding, acceptance, and mercy, my mistaken feelings accuse me of not doing enough, not trying enough, or not improving enough. I feel that I may be too selfish, lazy, or worldly.

Through His Church, Jesus tells me that I have more reason to rejoice than to fear. In baptism my natural life was joined to God by sanctifying grace. This state of grace makes every moment of my earthly life pleasing to God. Whatever I think, say, or do is pleasing to God even when it is not explicitly religious. Though I do not feel this connection of nature and grace within me, it is a fact. I displease God only by sin, and I cannot sin unless I knowingly and freely choose to do so. Therefore, though I am unaware of God throughout most of the day, I am actually in union with Him every moment by His grace. Though it would help me immensely to be more aware of God through prayer, reflection, or reading, be they ever so brief, I am mistaken to think that I have displeased Him because I was totally absorbed in my activities. If I have tried to live this day with a desire to please God, good will toward others, a positive hatred of all sin, and a reasonable contentment with myself, I may rest assured that I have advanced in wisdom and grace.

RESPOND   O Jesus, my Teacher and Master, grant me grace to understand my daily life in the light of what I have just read. With this outlook, I shall find peace instead of confusion, joy instead of fear and sadness, and an increasing sense of union with God instead of the feeling that I am a failure and disappointment to Him. I believe that You are with me even though I may not feel it. Help me to build my spiritual home on the rock of Your truth instead of the weak sands of my ignorance and mis-understandings. Amen.

42. AN URGENT REQUEST

READ Now a servant of a certain centurion, to whom he was dear, was sick to the point of death. And the centurion, hearing of Jesus, sent to him elders of the Jews, beseeching him to come and save his servant. And when they came to Jesus, they entreated him earnestly, saying to him, "He is worthy that thou shouldst do this for him, for he loves our nation, and himself has built us our synagogue." So Jesus went with them. And when he was now not far from the house, the centurion sent friends to say to him, "Lord, do not trouble thyself, for I am not worthy that thou shouldst come under my roof . . . But say the word, and my servant shall be healed . . ." Now when Jesus heard this, he marvelled, and turning to the crowd that followed him, said, "Amen, I say to you, not even in Israel have I found such great faith." (Luke 7:2–9)

REFLECT We see here two types of people. Some people feel the need to convince God that He should grant their requests. Others will ask God's help with a simple trust in His power, wisdom, and good will toward them.

REVIEW Both the elders and the centurion showed fear in their approach to Christ. The fear of the elders appeared as an uneasiness that He might refuse their request. The fear of the centurion took the form of an intelligent reverence for the power, wisdom, and holiness of Jesus. Instead of trying to convince Jesus that He should grant this petition for help the centurion declared himself unworthy of Christ's personal attention. He simply placed his request before Jesus and left the matter in His hands.

How do I approach Christ? Is my religious practice impelled by a fear of His rejection, or am I inspired by a healthy reverence for His infinite power, wisdom, and goodness? Does my sense of unworthiness make me uncomfortable in God's presence, or does it urge me to approach Him with a reverent appreciation of His infinite perfections. Actually, there are two kinds of unworthiness. There is the unworthiness of the malicious sinner, who has neither the desire nor the intention of amending his life. I can never be guilty of this unworthiness unless I choose to be. On the other hand, there is the natural unworthiness that belongs to every created being by its very nature. Neither angels nor men can realize what God is without at the same time realizing their own smallness and utter dependence upon Him. This sense of unworthiness should impel me to approach God with gratitude for His goodness, an intelligent fear of His justice, and a desire to give Him whatever honor my weak human nature can offer in my daily life.

RESPOND   My Jesus, though the centurion was well aware of his unworthiness before You, he still asked for Your help with confidence in Your understanding and goodness. Help me to imitate him by placing my petitions in Your hands, and trusting in Your personal concern for my needs. Whatever You decide about my requests, I hope that I may never try to convince You that I know better than You about my desires and needs. Amen.

43.   THE BAPTIST'S DISCIPLES

READ   But when John had heard in prison of the works of Christ, he sent two of his disciples to say to him, "Art thou he who is to come, or shall we look for another?" (Matt. 11:2–3)

REFLECT John was seeking a way to draw these men to Jesus. They felt such a debt of gratitude to the Baptist for his spiritual help, that they were reluctant to leave him. On this occasion, when they were reporting to John the raising of the dead man at Naim, John saw his opportunity to draw them toward Christ.

REVIEW John presents a wonderful example of supernatural tact. He knew that his work was nearing its end. He was eager to have these disciples join the followers of Jesus. At the same time, he did not want to hurt their feelings, since their refusal to follow Jesus was made in good faith. They knew John to be a true man of God. In their gratitude and loyalty to him, they remained with him. Seeing their sincerity, John could not be inconsiderate of their feelings. He did not want them to feel that he was eager to be rid of them. At the same time he knew that their welfare required that they approach their Savior.

He therefore sent them to Jesus with his question. Jesus understood. He kept them waiting while He performed a number of miracles. Then He listened to their question, and gave them a truly striking answer. His response came in the words of a prophecy, describing the powers which He had just manifested before their very eyes. Being men of good will, they would not reject this special grace. Their conversion was begun. John would complete it before dying in Herod's prison.

How considerate am I of other people's feelings? Even when I am right and they are wrong, I am still obliged to spare their feelings, as long as I can do it without causing scandal. Some people believe that they are not bound by the law of charity when dealing with those who are in error. This is not so. Jesus even urged us to love our enemies and do good to those who hate us. How much more true would this apply to those who are in error through no fault of their own! I can show them the truth by my good example at all times, and by my words when the opportunity arises naturally. But I shall do more harm than good if I try to force my convictions upon those who are unable or unwilling to accept them.

RESPOND O Jesus, may I never despise those who disagree with me. I shall not be right all the time, nor are others always wrong. I want to love the truth enough to admit my own errors when others are right. I also desire to love my neighbor enough to be tactful when I think he is wrong. May I never needlessly hurt the feelings of others when they are unable or unwilling to learn the truth. In my eagerness to help them, let me not push them farther from Your truth by my repugnant attitude or behavior toward them. Without compromising Your truth, I hope to show good will to every man. Amen.

44. AN OBSTACLE TO GRACE

READ "To what then shall I liken the men of this generation? And what are they like? They are like children sitting in the market place, calling to one another and saying, 'We have piped to you, and you have not danced; we have sung dirges and you have not wept.' For John the Baptist came neither eating bread nor drinking wine, and you say, 'He has a devil.' The Son of Man came eating and drinking and you say, 'Behold a man who is a glutton, and a wine-drinker, a friend of publicans and sinners!'" (Luke 7:31–34)

REFLECT These words of Christ came at the end of a discourse expressing exalted praises of John the Baptist. Jesus ends His discourse by declaring that those who had refused to accept the admonitions of John and His own personal message were immature. They were behaving like peevish children who rejected the pleas of their companions to play different roles in a game.

REVIEW Immaturity is a great obstacle to spiritual progress. The immature person is controlled by his emotions. He often becomes confused in his reasoning, uncertain in his judgments, and hesitant in his decisions. Then again, he may be unable to control his thoughts or his actions. As a result, his religious practices are superficial, unbalanced, rigid, or unrelated to his practical daily living. They have little or no influence upon his inner self-possession and his external behavior. Immature people usually shun any form of self-knowledge or self-control. They are creatures of feelings, slaves of their own emotions. For this reason Jesus compared them to children.

Immaturity does not necessarily excuse one from guilt. In some degree, he may be guilty of his immaturity or of the sins into which it leads him. He may be willfully careless about obtaining the knowledge necessary to alleviate his present condition, or about acquiring better habits of self-control. Or again, he may be culpably unwilling to do what little he can to curb his present habits of sin.

In many cases, however, one's present immaturity developed so imperceptibly through the years that it is largely without blame. Nevertheless, it does a great deal of spiritual harm, in the form of inferiority feelings, guilt feelings, self-hate, and fear of punishment. One who is at odds with himself will sooner or later transfer his feelings to God. He will feel that God is displeased or disgusted with him, or simply too busy with more important matters. He will then either strain for God's approval by a perfect performance in daily life, or he will eventually give up all religious endeavor because of fatigue, depression, and discouragement.

RESPOND My God, while I desire always to be a child of Yours, I pray that I may be a mature adult in my religious outlook and daily practices. I hope, with Your help, to learn Your truth without misunderstanding, and apply it to my daily life without misinterpretation. I shall always have a normal amount of involuntary immaturity, but I sincerely hope that it may never occur through my own fault. Amen.

45. THE CONDEMNING PHARISEE

READ   Now one of the Pharisees asked him to dine with him . . . And behold, a woman in the town who was a sinner . . . brought an alabaster jar of ointment; and standing behind him at his feet, she began to bathe his feet with her tears, and wiped them with the hair of her head, and kissed his feet, and anointed them with ointment. Now when the Pharisee, who had invited him, saw it, he said to himself, "This man, were he a prophet, would surely know who and what manner of woman this is who is touching him, for she is a sinner." (Luke 7:36–39)

REFLECT   In this scene I behold the penitent woman, the condemning Pharisee, and the understanding and forgiving Savior. How differently from the self-complacent Pharisee Jesus looked upon this sinner!

REVIEW   Too often I am inclined to fear that Jesus might judge me as the Pharisee judged this woman. My lack of confidence in my own sincerity makes me anticipate the condemnation of Jesus. And yet, He strove so hard to convince me that He is glad to forgive. The woman said nothing. She bathed His feet with her tears, anointed them with ointment, and dried them with her hair. She showed her sorrow in the unmistakable language of action. Jesus understood her message, and spoke the consoling words, "Thy sins are forgiven thee."

Jesus also reads my heart. He knows what I feel in the

depths of my soul. He knows the unexpressed desire, the unspoken word, the unexplained action, by which I say, "Lord, I am sorry for having offended You! My doubts and fears might make sense if I did not know Jesus. But in this scene He introduces Himself to me as the kind of Redeemer I need. He reads my heart and stands by me when others misunderstand, misjudge, or condemn me. May I never be so immature that I find it intolerable to acknowledge my sins, express my sorrow for them, and then leave the matter in Christ's hands. How can I fear to be judged when the Judge is this wonderful, accepting, forgiving Savior?

Unfortunately, this true image of the real Christ is sometimes distorted by people who are sincere, but mistaken in their view of Him. In spite of their good intentions, they repaint Him as sterner, more threatening, less understanding, and less forgiving than He really is. I must see Jesus as He shows Himself in His Holy Gospel and in the teachings of His Holy Church.

RESPOND   My divine Savior, if You cannot convince me by this touching incident, how can anyone else ever persuade me to expect understanding, pardon, and eternal life from You? If I had a choice of entrusting my judgment to anyone other than You, I would refuse to do so. I believe in You! I trust You! I love You, my Jesus! Help me prove my words by my daily efforts. Amen.

46. THE DIVIDED KINGDOM

READ   And . . . Jesus said to them, "Every kingdom divided against itself is brought to desolation, and every city or house divided against itself will not stand." (Matt. 12:25)

REFLECT Jesus had just cast a devil from a man. His enemies had witnessed the miracle. Since they could not admit that He worked by the power of God, they had to accuse Him of being in league with Satan. Jesus answers that: He could hardly be working for Satan and against him at the same time.

REVIEW My spiritual life is healthy in proportion as I am an integrated personality. Have I learned to subordinate all of my tendencies, energies, and desires under one principal intention and purpose? Or am I so divided within myself that I work for one goal at one time, and for the opposite at other times? As Jesus put it, "No man can serve two masters." I must make up my mind as to what I want from my life. Having done this, I ought to follow some sort of plan to achieve my chosen goal. I can seek to obtain whatever satisfaction this earthly life can give me, or I can live with an eye to obtaining eternal happiness. I do not have to neglect either of these goals, but only to subordinate one to the other. Otherwise I shall be a house divided against itself, and I shall fall either into the emotional confusion of immature fears, doubts, and indecisions, or into the moral corruption of sin.

The integration that I must seek is that of Christian perfection. I must strive to understand God's plan for my salvation. He has enabled me to serve Him in whatever walk of life is available to me. Having understood God's plan as best I can, I must try to make the most of my talents, graces, and opportunities. I must live each day as it comes, without straining beyond my strength, and without a voluntary neglect of the good within my reach.

I can exercise my virtues and earn my heavenly merits through the same things which might have drawn me away from God. Oftentimes the saint and the sinner differ not so much in what they do as in the attitude, intention, and purpose of their actions. The saint is integrated toward eternal life; the sinner, toward earthly satisfactions without God. In between these, there are many who are not sure what they want, or where they are going. Where do I belong? What can I do about it?

RESPOND My Jesus, help me attain a holy integration, so that I may have one main intention in my daily activities. Let me always see beyond the immediate earthly purpose of what I do, and let my principal desire be to please You every waking moment of my day. Make me mature enough to do this without foolish straining, and without a childish fear of the normal effort involved in every worthwhile purpose. Amen.

47. THE FRUITS OF A TREE

READ "Either make the tree good and its fruit good, or make the tree bad and its fruit bad; for by the fruit the tree is known . . . The good man from his good treasure brings forth good things; and the evil man from his evil treasure brings forth evil things." (Matt. 12:33–35)

REFLECT Just as we judge the value of a tree by its fruit, so does Jesus judge the worth of a man by the way he chooses to think, speak, and act in his daily life. The fruits and the actions are symptomatic of what is inside. They reveal the quality of the source from which they come.

REVIEW Jesus is speaking here of moral goodness. He is not referring to those spontaneous thoughts, feelings, emotions, and actions which arise without my forethought, and which may remain in my mind or impel my will without my free consent. In themselves, these spontaneous tendencies are neither morally good nor bad. Jesus has in mind those interior and exterior tendencies and activities over which I have some measure of control. No matter how I may feel about things or people, it is what I choose to think or do about them that makes me either virtuous or sinful.

Many people misjudge themselves, due to their ignorance of human nature. They believe that they should be able to keep perfect control over themselves, so that they may think only what they choose to think, feel only as they decide to feel, and do only what they freely intend to do. When their self-control is less than perfect in their emotions, imagination, thoughts, or actions, they accuse themselves of malice and sin. They do not realize that these deeper tendencies and spontaneous activities are an integral part of their human nature. This part is often beyond their control. It is governed by the instincts of self-preservation, self-expression, and self-defense, and modified by habits arising from past experiences. God's grace was not intended to destroy these tendencies, since they are necessary to normal human living. Grace can only help me attain some measure of control over them. This type of division within me does not destroy my moral integration and spiritual maturity. As long as I have a clear intention to follow Christ's principles, and make an intelligent effort to do so, I am morally integrated and a spiritual adult.

RESPOND My Jesus, it is such a relief to see that You are so much more reasonable with me than I am with myself. There is within me a cruel tyrant, an unforgiving, unreasonable master that would destroy me. I cannot live up to my own immature demands, but I can live up to the divine commands and counsels which You present to me. I am glad that You accept all of me, even that part of my nature over which I have little control. May I never again misjudge myself by my spontaneous likes and dislikes, but by my deliberate intentions and moral efforts. Amen.

48. THE GOOD SEED

READ "Behold, the sower went out to sow. And as he sowed, some seed fell by the wayside, and the birds came and ate it up. And other seed fell upon rocky ground, where it had not much earth; and it sprang up at once, because it had no depth of earth; but when the sun rose it was scorched, and because it had no root it withered away. And other seed fell among thorns; and the thorns grew up and choked it, and it yielded no fruit. And other seed fell upon good ground, and yielded fruit that grew up, made increase and produced, one thirty, another sixty, and another a hundredfold." (Mark 4:3-8)

REFLECT After showing the various obstacles to the growth of the seed, Jesus states that the seed which fell upon good ground was fruitful in varying degrees. Though all of this ground was good, still the produce was not equal in all places.

REVIEW If I can absorb this lesson by repeated meditation, and apply it in my daily life, I shall find great peace both within myself and in my dealings with others. I sometimes think like a child. I think categorically, without making necessary observations and distinctions. I think that good men are equally good and that the saints were all equal in their sanctity. It does not dawn on me that there are degrees of goodness. I fail to realize that each man's perfection differs from that of every other man because of talents, graces, limitations, experiences, and opportunities.

Though the above consideration seems obvious to me, the fact is that when I lament my shortcomings, I fail to apply this consideration to myself. I compare myself with others as though there were ground for a valid comparison. I judge my achievements in the light of other people's accomplishments or expectations. I am pleased or displeased with myself in proportion as I equal, surpass, or fall short of the qualities and successes of others.

Jesus Himself tells me how the good seed produced differently in different sections of the good ground. He does not compare me with others. Neither does He expect me to accomplish as much, or as well, as others. I am the individual I am because of many factors that have contributed to the formation of my present personality. I can only go about my daily activities with the graces, talents, and good will that are in me at the moment. The results will be my personal fruits for this day. God desires no more than this from me.

RESPOND My Jesus, please impress this message deeply upon my mind. I have been so ignorant, so immature in my attitude toward You, myself, and others. This lesson which You have taught me today can be the key to great peace of soul and greater personal accomplishment. I hope to diminish gradually the emotional strains and childish expectations which have unbalanced my religious endeavors in the past. I can now say, "All for Jesus," without feeling that I must push myself beyond all reasonable bounds. For this grace, I thank You from the bottom of my soul. Amen.

49. COOPERATING WITH GOD'S GRACE

READ "If anyone has ears to hear, let him hear . . . Take heed, therefore, how you hear; for to him who has shall be given; and from him who does not have, even what he thinks he has, shall be taken away." (Mark 4:23; Luke 8:18)

REFLECT In His own mysterious ways, Christ offers to

every man the graces needed to gain eternal life. Those who try to follow His words and inspirations, gradually come closer to God in their interior attitudes and exterior behavior. Those who neglect His teachings and graces, gradually become more vague in their religious outlook, more indifferent about God's commandments, and more helpless against life's daily temptations.

REVIEW The more I understand the mind of Christ, the more shall I appreciate the supernatural grandeur He has bestowed upon my daily life. Through His holy sacraments and His Church, I have the reassurance of His divine knowledge, the guidance of His infinite wisdom, and the support of His supernatural grace. He has promised me His personal friendship on earth and His visible companionship in Heaven. In His words I shall find an endless source of inspiration, good will, and peace throughout my earthly life.

And yet, in spite of this supernatural life, Jesus reminds me time and again, that I shall still be subject to the normal feelings and experiences of everyday human living. I shall still have my moments of spontaneous annoyance or anger, unintentional impatience or unkindness, unexpected doubts or fears, unmanageable desires or dislikes, intense concern for myself or inconsiderateness of others, bitter disgust with myself or hostility toward others, and an occasional sense of failure or hopelessness.

If I am mature enough to believe in God's infinite understanding and my own good will, these human emotions will not disturb me for any length of time. I shall look on them as normal experiences, which do not necessarily make me bad. I shall refuse to doubt my good intentions, but prove them by continuing to follow Christ's principles as best I can. If, on the contrary, I am immature, I shall be upset by these emotions and tendencies. My self-doubts will compel me to search endlessly for a clear and sure answer to every question arising from my fears: "Did I have a right intention? Did I consent to this evil thought? Did I offer sufficient resistance to that wrong desire? Did I cause others to sin by my words or behavior?" In my ignorance, I may believe that I have sinned by not maintaining perfect control over my feelings. In sheer discouragement, I may consider myself a hopeless case. I may even feel resentful against God in my mistaken notion that He has demanded the impossible of me. The truth of the matter is that Jesus knows my limitations and sees my good will. He is utterly reasonable in His expectations and infinitely sympathetic with me in my unintended failures.

RESPOND   My Jesus, make me content to be myself in my daily life. Help me believe that You do not expect more of me than I am, or demand more than I can accomplish. Without this conviction, I shall be unable to get along with people or be at ease with You. Grant me a reasonable self-love, so that I may feel that my friendship is worth offering to God and men. Amen.

50.   THE MYSTERY OF GROWTH

READ   "Thus is the kingdom of God, as though a man should cast seed into the earth, then sleep and rise, night and day, and the seed should sprout and grow without his knowing it. For of itself the earth bears the crop, first the blade, then the ear, then the full grain in the ear." (Mark 4:26–28)

REFLECT   Jesus compares His earthly kingdom to a seeded field. Once planted the crop grows by its own natural power. The farmer can help make conditions more favorable, but the actual growing is accomplished by nature itself. Day and night the mystery of life works its miracle, until the entire crop is ready for the harvest.

REVIEW   God implanted a supernatural life in my soul at baptism. Like all life, it grows unobserved. As I grew into the age of reason, I found my mind inclined to believe God's truth because He revealed it. I felt confident in His desire to help me obtain eternal life. I had a desire to love Him for what He is, namely, my greatest Good. These and other virtues began to grow by His grace. I fostered this growth by my conscious attempts to develop these virtues more fully in my daily life. Sometimes I fail to appreciate the fact that my spiritual growth occurs not merely when I am consciously performing some particular good work, but at every moment that I live in sanctifying grace. As long as my general attitude is one of good will toward the people and activities in my daily life, my spiritual life is growing, and my heavenly merits are increasing.

Some people fall into the error of judging their spiritual growth by their sentiments. They think if they feel the nearness of God or their own sincerity, they are advancing spiritually. This is not necessarily so. Feelings may proceed from wishful thinking. I must believe that God is near as much when He seems far from me as when I am aware of His presence. I must trust in His love and rely on His assistance as much when I feel undeserving or abandoned as when my emotions and enthusiasm overflow. I must be as loyal to His holy Will when I am repelled by those around me or by my daily duties as when I am inclined to be kind and diligent. I may take advantage of my feelings when they favor God's truth, but I must live above them when they are contrary to His holy word.

Another error that may lead me astray in my spiritual endeavors, is that of believing that my spiritual growth is to be measured by my direct control over myself in every situation. I am still advancing when I become emotionally upset or mentally disturbed in my relations with God or my neighbor. I am accountable only for that which lies within my present control. My lack of control always proves that I am a human being. It does not necessarily prove that I have rejected a grace. As long as I have good will, I must believe that my spiritual growth is proceeding according to God's plan.

RESPOND My Jesus, I believe what You have taught, I rely upon Your grace for the wisdom and strength to attain the eternal happiness of heaven, I desire to love You not only in Yourself but also in the people and duties that make up my daily life. Help me to live each day with the intention of pleasing You, and to leave my spiritual growth in Your hands. Amen.

51. THE TREASURE AND THE PEARL

READ "The kingdom of heaven is like a treasure hidden in a field; he who finds it hides it, and in his joy goes and sells all that he has and buys that field. Again, the kingdom of heaven is like a merchant in search of fine pearls. When he finds a single pearl of great worth, he goes and sells all that he has and buys it." (Matt. 13:44–46)

REFLECT Jesus compares His kingdom on earth to a treasure so precious that it surpasses the value of all else in this earthly life. He shows how those who appreciate its real worth are ready to purchase it in preference to their other earthly possessions.

REVIEW This discourse of Christ might come as a surprise to some people. They feel that they must lose all self-interest in their service of God. They sincerely believe that since God deserves to be loved and served for Himself alone, they ought to rise at once to utter selflessness in their daily relations with God and their neighbor. They demand of themselves that they be empty of all tendencies toward self-interest. Any desire for recognition or gratitude is looked upon as a sinful imperfection. They easily accuse themselves of "selfishness" whether they have committed a sin or performed a good work.

Jesus contradicts them by this present discourse. In these words He is clearly appealing to human nature's inborn tendency toward its own well-being. He does not consider me sinfully selfish if I serve Him with the intention of gaining the treasure which He offers me in this discourse. By the very nature He gave me, I am moved to seek what is good for me. Therefore my self-seeking is bad only if I knowingly and freely reach out for things which I cannot have without sinning. When I seek what He Himself permits or desires me to enjoy, I am not displeasing to Him.

Thus a pure intention does not mean that I must seek God without any consideration for myself, but that I must seek Him because I see in Him my highest good and greatest advantage. As I come to know Him better through the years, I shall find myself wanting to give Him more of myself. My prayers and good works will gradually change, so that I shall increasingly find my satisfaction in the mere fact of pleasing so wonderful a Father and so generous a Savior. Thus, the selflessness of true religion is a progressive growth in wisdom and prudence. I who now want Him for my own sake alone, shall later prefer Him to many other satisfactions because He is so precious in Himself. It will take years of daily fidelity to Christ's commandments and ideals before I can achieve this supernatural transformation of intention and purpose. In the meantime, however, I must not condemn myself for not yet having achieved the pure ideal. Without a special grace, I never shall. All I can hope for, is to come ever closer to it with the passing years.

RESPOND   My Jesus, I hope to absorb this lesson slowly and steadily. My desire to avoid hell or attain heaven's joys is inspired by Your grace. However, I do hope for further graces, so that I may appreciate the goodness of God more and more. Then I shall find more joy in pleasing the Father than in obtaining my own safety and satisfaction. Amen.

52. THE STORM AT SEA

READ   And he said to them on that day, when evening had come, "Let us cross over to the other side." And sending away the crowd, they took him just as he was, in the boat; and there were other boats with him. And there arose a great squall, and the waves were beating into the boat, so that the boat was now filling. And he himself was in the stern of the boat, on the cushion, asleep. And they woke him and said to him, "Master, does it not concern thee that we are perishing?" Then rising up, he rebuked the wind, and said to the sea, "Peace, be still!" And the wind fell and there came a great calm. And he said to them, "Why are you fearful? Are you still without faith?" (Mark 4:35-40)

REFLECT   In this incident we behold Jesus in His human weakness and His divine strength. Weighed down by exhaustion, He readily surrendered to this much-needed sleep. So soundly did He sleep that the violence of the storm failed to awaken Him. The confidence of the disciples gradually weakened as the violence of the storm increased. When fear finally took control of them, they cried for their Master's help. He awoke, rebuked them for their lack of faith in Him, then showed them a glimpse of His divinity. With a command He dissolved the violence of wind and waves.

REVIEW   In my daily life there are a number of human situations that arise like the sudden storm on the lake. I too am prone to fear. It may vary anywhere from slight uneasiness to extreme panic. My natural urge will always be to defend myself. There is no harm in doing do, as long as my self-defense is reasonable and orderly. However, there are situations when I am unable to help myself, or even to obtain the assistance of others. In such situations, Jesus demands that I place my faith in His personal concern, and trust in His divine assistance.

If insecurity and anxiety have played a prominent part in my early life, I shall often be uneasy, anxious, or afraid by force of habit. Moreover, the habits of my nervous system may add to, or emphasize the fears and doubts arising in my mind. My drive to self-preservation will impel me to defend myself in any available manner. Though my faith may tell me that Jesus is near, my emotions and feelings at the moment will make me uncertain of His assistance. I shall be torn between supernatural confidence and natural distrust. Eventually I shall either seek a solution without regard for morality, or I shall let God's commandments direct me in some degree.

RESPOND   My Jesus, I believe that You are truly divine. I gladly place my life in Your hands. Teach me to help myself with prudence and charity when the occasion demands it. Let me humbly ask the assistance of others when I need it. But most of all, grant that I may firmly trust in Your divine wisdom, power, and love when my drive to self-preservation threatens to make me unreasonable in my self-defense. Amen.

53. THE MYSTERY OF VOCATION

READ   And as Jesus was getting into the boat, the man who had been afflicted by the devil began to entreat him that he might remain with him. And he did not allow him, but said to him, "Go home to thy relatives, and tell them all that the Lord has done for thee, and how he has had mercy on thee." And he departed and began to publish in the Decapolis all that Jesus had done for him. And all marvelled. (Mark 5:18–20)

REFLECT   So grateful was this man for the restoration of his spiritual and mental health, that he desired to join the disciples. Jesus saw in him a valuable messenger of the gospel among his own people. However, to fulfill this role successfully, he would have to do so as a layman. His people would listen to him without the prejudice which they had already shown to Jesus. In this manner they would be better disposed to believe the disciples later on. This is the vocation which Jesus granted to this grateful soul.

REVIEW   Some people waste a good deal of time lamenting what they would do if only they could relive their life. Consciously or unconsciously, they have a constant dissatisfaction and disgust toward themselves. They may even feel guilty of having neglected their talents and opportunities. To relieve their inner emotional pressure, they will transfer their discontent to external situations and circumstances or to the people involved in their lives. They waste so much time in useless complaints or bitter attitudes, that they fail to make the most of their present circumstances.

I must learn to see the hand of God in all the circumstances of my life. He permits many situations to develop for reasons which He alone knows. Instead of useless wishing for a return to my earlier life, vain complaints about obstacles to my ambitions and efforts, or surrender to discouragement and self-pity, I would be wise to see my present situation as a vocation from God. He places many opportunities before me, by which I can make the world around me a little better.

There is a great deal of good which I alone can do because I alone am in a position to do it. The people I meet may be helped by my readiness to accept them, encourage them, and help them. My smile may melt their frown; and my greeting can bring a ray of sunshine to those who are shrouded in fears and doubts. I can make the presence of God felt through my Christlike attitude and generosity. As Jesus spent most of His earthly life in the little carpenter shop and town of Nazareth for my sake, so may I be His representative in my personal walk of life.

RESPOND   O Jesus, this is my vocation: To make the most of what I am without undue disgust; use my present talents and opportunities with dignity and prudence; strive to improve myself without undue strain; and help enrich the lives of others without feeling imposed on by God or compelled by men. With this sense of vocation I shall see the glory of heaven as the goal of my earthly life, and I shall find that deeper contentment I often desire. Amen.

54. A HIDDEN CURE IN A CROWD

READ   And there was a woman who for twelve years had had a hemorrhage, and had suffered much at the hands of many physicians, and had spent all that she had, and found no benefit, but rather grew worse. Hearing about Jesus, she came up behind him in the crowd and touched his cloak. For she said, "If I touch but his cloak, I shall be saved." And at once the flow of blood was dried up, and she felt in her body that she was healed of her affliction. (Mark 5:25–29)

REFLECT   There is something unique about this woman. She had endured twelve years of suffering, of repeated hopes and disappointment, successive occasions of discouragement as each doctor admitted that he had done all he could. And yet, after all this she was still willing to continue her quest for her lost health. Even in her method she was unusual. She spoke no word and made no effort to arouse Christ's pity. She simply touched His garment and left the cure to His power and good will.

REVIEW Illness can be one of man's greatest hardships on earth. It can weaken his better self, rendering the mind unable to think and the will devoid of all control. Self-concern is usually so prominent in the sick that they temporarily lose their normal interests. As their nature yearns for health, moments seem like hours and nights appear to be endless.

My religious strength and ideals can be utterly overwhelmed by the instincts and drives aroused by illness. As I restlessly crave the return of health, energy, and peace of mind, I may become extremely inconsiderate of those who are concerned for me and work for my comfort and recovery. I may even experience spontaneous surges of impatience with God. In protracted illness I may gradually develop a sense of helplessness, hopelessness, and aloneness. I may be surprised by momentary outbursts of anger against God and resentment at His Saints. Prayer and religious considerations may become utterly repulsive to me. Disgust with life may bring on a longing for death as a relief from the intolerable torment of being alive.

This is why the woman in this gospel is such a shining example of supernatural faith and fortitude. Before her illness she must have been a prayerful woman with a healthy understanding and balanced appreciation of God. Though illness may strengthen one's virtues, it rarely establishes virtues one never bothered to develop. Though I may never have to bear the cross of illness, my best preparation for such a cross is my present daily life. As I intensify my awareness of God's personal love for me, and strengthen my determination to embrace His holy Will in all things, I shall receive greater graces to carry me through whatever difficulties lie ahead.

RESPOND Lord, I offer to You my entire life. Help me embrace each day's problems and burdens as coming from

Your hand. Let me never fear the future, but leave it in Your loving hands. With this disposition, I shall be better prepared to bear the cross of illness if You so desire. Amen.

55. THE DAUGHTER OF JAIRUS

READ And behold, there came a man named Jairus, and he was a ruler of the synagogue; and falling at the feet of Jesus, he entreated him to come to his house, for he had an only daughter about twelve years of age, and she was dying . . . While he was yet speaking, there came one from the house of the ruler of the synagogue, saying to him, "Thy daughter is dead; do not trouble him." But Jesus on hearing this word answered the father of the girl, "Do not be afraid; only have faith and she shall be saved."

And when he came to the house, he allowed no one to enter with him, except Peter and James and John, and the girl's father and mother. And all were weeping and mourning for her. But he said, "Do not weep; she is asleep, not dead." And they laughed him to scorn, knowing that she was dead. But he, taking her by the hand, cried out, saying, "Girl, arise!" And her spirit returned, and she rose up immediately. (Luke 8:41–42, 49–55)

REFLECT Jairus had hardly presented his plea, when his servant told him that it was too late. As Jesus looked upon the sorrowful father, He told him not to lose hope. Jairus' tottering hope was bolstered by the grace of Christ, and was rewarded with a miracle.

REVIEW At one time or another every man must face situations which are beyond his control. How he reacts to these depends on his emotional maturity, moral strength, and trust in God. Some people simply disintegrate when faced with any problem, difficulty, or sorrow beyond the most ordinary routine. In their dependency on others, they react to these situations more like helpless children than like adults. Others respond to life's hardships with hostility. They become resentful and envious of those who seem to have less troubles than they. They may even accuse God of discrimination, injustice, or cruelty.

Being human, I too can respond to my hardships and sufferings with some of these immature emotions and attitudes. I must endeavor to help myself when possible, seek the aid of others when necessary, and never cease to doubt God's personal interest in me. I must try to develop this emotional maturity and spiritual strength by practicing it in the ordinary occurrences of daily life. I must frequently express my faith and trust in Christ. Jesus wants to share my daily activities, joys, sorrows, and burdens. He asks me to see His hand in everything that occurs throughout the day. As I become more aware of His nearness and concern for me, I shall be less likely to offend Him by rebelling against the inevitable or surrendering to my doubts about His goodness, wisdom, and love.

RESPOND   O Jesus, Master of my life, in all my needs and problems, I hope to help myself as best I can, with the help of Your grace. At the same time, however, I beg for such faith in Your divine power, trust in Your all-wise providence, and love of Your holy Will, that I may accept gratefully whatever burdens, problems, or sorrows You may choose to send into my life. Amen.

56.   A RETURN TO NAZARETH

READ   And he came to Nazareth, where he had been brought up; and according to his custom, he entered the synagogue on the Sabbath and stood up to read . . . *The Spirit of the Lord is upon me; because he has anointed*

*me; to bring good news to the poor he has sent me, to pro-
claim to the captives release, and sight to the blind; to set
at liberty the oppressed, to proclaim the acceptable year
of the Lord, and the day of recompense.* And closing the
volume . . . he began to say to them, "Today this Scripture
has been fulfilled in your hearing." And all bore him witness, and marvelled at the words of grace that came from
his mouth. And they said, "Is not this Joseph's son?"
(Luke 4:16, 18–22)

REFLECT After the many reports of Christ's public teachings and miracles, the Nazarenes were curious to hear Him
and to see His powers at work. His present claim to this
Messianic role, shocked them. They could not forget that
He was their former carpenter. They were unable to open
their minds for a fair hearing of His message.

REVIEW As long as I remain in this earthly life, I shall
always have to contend with the inner emotions of the
people around me. Just as I am often swayed by emotional
tendencies of which I am totally or partially unaware, so
are they. Like me, they resent others for a number of reasons. Their resentment may be aroused by their own unconscious feelings of inferiority or guilt, or by a natural
aversion for what they see as pretense, artificiality, or unwarranted haughtiness.

Fear of human resentment, criticism, or rejection has
prevented many a person from going beyond the bounds
of mediocrity in his service of God. As Jesus stood before
His townsmen, He knew that they would reject Him for
proclaiming Himself their Messias. He also knew that His
Father wanted Him to prefer the truth to their acceptance.
I too have a choice before me. I can make my first choice
the approval of men or the esteem of God.

However, in my effort to become more loyal to the principles of Christ, I must beware of the human tendency
to antagonize others by undue defiance or unnecessary ex-
hibitionism. The resentment of those around me may not

be altogether unwarranted. I cannot expect them to accept my external change as a permanent part of me, until I have made it such. To accomplish this, I need to change from within. As my faith and love of God urge me on to a more Christlike behavior, I shall become more spontaneous in my attitudes, responses, and behavior. It will require some time before others become convinced that my new behavior is a sincere effort for God. Slowly my well-intentioned neighbors will accept my changing personality as genuine.

RESPOND   O Jesus, my divine Model, in my efforts to imitate You more fully in my daily life, let me always be considerate of the reasonable feelings of others. Help me follow my higher intentions and practice my virtues without belittling others or exalting myself. Amen.

57. WORKING FOR CHRIST

READ   And he summoned the Twelve and began to send them forth two by two; and he gave them power over the unclean spirits . . . And he said to them, "Wherever you enter into a house, stay there until you leave the place. And whoever does not receive you, or listen to you—go forth from there, and shake off the dust from your feet for a witness against them." (Mark 6:7, 10–11)

REFLECT   Jesus now gives His disciples their first taste of the active ministry. He tells them to impart their message and offer assistance to all men of good will. As for the others, the disciples are not to become involved with emotional attitudes or useless efforts to convert them against their will.

REVIEW   In its own way, my daily life is a ministry for

Christ. As my knowledge of His truth and my personal acquaintance with Him improve, I shall become more aware of little ways to help others see themselves in the light of God's truth. However, I can be my own greatest hindrance in this work for Christ. In spite of my sincere desire to draw others closer to Christ, I may actually cause them to resent my efforts, and resist the grace at their disposal.

Deep within me there are emotional tendencies which can make me inconsiderate of the mental dispositions, emotional leanings, and human weaknesses of those whom I attempt to help. Their previous training and fixed opinions are not to be despised. I must not think that because I have the truth, I have a right to disregard their sincere convictions. Though I may hate error, I must always respect the sincerity of those in it. To act otherwise is a sign of my immaturity and unfitness to help these people in the name of Christ.

A true follower of Christ is too charitable to hurt the feelings of those who try to serve God with the partial truth at their disposal. If they are not ready for Christ's full message, I must leave them to Him. In His own good time and in His own way, He will help them gain eternal life. As for malicious people, I shall not help them by open signs of contempt or condemnation. Only Christ and His Church can safely deal with them. I must leave them alone without arousing greater obstinacy and malice in them.

RESPOND   My Jesus, though I am to serve You by my daily example to others, let me always remember that I am not God, but just a human being, open to many blunders in whatever I do. This awareness will make me humble, prudent, and charitable in my efforts to help others know Your message and love You. I must always be aware of my human tendency to feel superior at the expense of others. With loyalty to You and consideration for the emotional needs and weaknesses of others, I shall never hold others back from You. Amen.

58. WISDOM AND SIMPLICITY

READ "Behold, I am sending you forth like sheep in the midst of wolves. Be therefore wise as serpents, and guileless as doves. But beware of men; for they will deliver you up to councils, and scourge you in their synagogues, and you will be brought before governors and kings for my sake . . . No disciple is above his teacher, nor is the servant above his master. It is enough for the disciple to be like his teacher, and for the servant to be like his master. If they have called the master of the house Beelzebub, how much more those of his household!" (Matt. 10: 16–18, 24–25)

REFLECT Jesus here teaches His disciples an important principle. They are to be sincere and singleminded in their dealings with others. At the same time, they must be aware of the emotional undercurrents that influence the people with whom they deal. Whether through ignorance, misunderstanding, or malice, a number of people would give them a hostile reception. In Christ's personal example and grace the disciples are to find inspiration and strength.

REVIEW   If I make a consistent effort to follow the principles of Christ in my daily life, I shall make enemies. A number of people will be antagonized for various reasons. Some will be reminded of their shortcomings and weaknesses. Others will feel an implicit rebuke in my behavior. Feelings of inferiority, inadequacy, self-disgust, or guilt will incline them against me.

This opposition will often be hidden. Some will act as though I did not exist. Others will be painfully formal with me. Others will find fault with those qualities of other people which they resent in me. Others will contradict, distinguish, doubt, or slight whatever I say. Others will

112

exaggerate my defects and mistakes, and minimize my virtues and accomplishments.

At times I may feel inclined to respond to this opposition on the same immature level of these people. Christ asks me to remember that He underwent the same experience for my sake. He invites me to imitate His example and offers me grace to rise above these passing human hurts. I can choose to grow toward the glorious stature of Jesus or remain immature like these "small" people. My simplicity will consist in exercising the good will of Christ toward them. My wisdom will shine in my understanding of the childish emotions that govern their minds and dominate their behavior.

RESPOND My Jesus, make me humble enough to admit when others are right and I am wrong. Make me strong enough to be independent of the praises, blame, or contempt of those who shun Your principles. With justice in my mind and charity in my heart, let me please You without desiring to displease them. When this is impossible, I hope to imitate Your loyalty to the Father's will. Amen.

59. THE PROBLEM OF HUMAN RELATIONS

READ "Do not be afraid of those who kill the body but cannot kill the soul. But rather be afraid of him who is able to destroy both soul and body in hell . . . Therefore, everyone who acknowledges me before men, I will acknowledge him before my Father in heaven. But whoever disowns me before men, I, in turn, will disown him before my Father in heaven . . . He who loves father or mother more than me is not worthy of me; and he who loves son or daughter more than me is not worthy of me . . . He who finds his life will lose it, and he who loses his life for my sake, will find it." (Matt. 10:28, 32–33, 37–39)

REFLECT These words are not so much a threat as a statement of fact. If I am afraid of the disapproval, rejection, or harm which human beings can inflict on me, how much more should I fear the disapproval, rejection, and punishment of the Divine Justice? If I crave peace, contentment, and love, will I sacrifice the all-satisfying life of heaven for the sake of the passing, short-lived satisfactions of this world? To sin because of my earthly fears or loves, is folly and suicide.

REVIEW I am afraid of many people in one way or another. This fear began in the early years of my life. In my childhood helplessness, I was defenseless against the moods, expectations, and demands of the adults who governed me. As I advanced in my interpersonal experiences, I learned ways of defending myself against my fears. I learned to avoid or hide what might annoy, displease, or anger those whose good will I desired. I discovered how to win their approval, acceptance, and help. I felt secure and content with the friendship and love of those on whom I depended. In gratitude for their approval and help, I was disposed to give them whatever pleasure or service I could render. This was the beginning of love in me. In proportion as I felt loved by others, I was inclined to return love.

These two emotions of fear and love have swayed my thoughts and actions all through my life. Even after the age of reason they have exerted their influence upon my conscious judgments and willful actions. Many a deliberate decision of mine is made only after it has undergone the inspection and approval of my fears and loves, likes and dislikes. I am often so completely unaware of this mental process, that I sincerely believe I am making my decision solely through unbiased reasoning or purely by the grace of God.

However, conscious or not, these two emotions can incline me toward deliberate sin. For this reason Jesus reaches deep down within me to arouse my instinctive drive to self-preservation. He advises me to fear no man as much as God, and to prefer no person to God. God's justice can punish me more than any human opposition, and His goodness can satisfy me far beyond any human friendship or love.

RESPOND My Jesus, by my very nature, I am constantly reaching out for my advantage, benefit, and contentment. Since God alone is my highest, most enduring, and most complete Good, help me prefer Him when any person or thing threatens to separate me from Him. Amen.

60. THE BEHEADING OF THE BAPTIST

READ And a favorable day came when Herod on his birthday gave a banquet for the officials, tribunes, and the chief men of Galilee. And Herodias' own daughter having come in and danced, she pleased Herod and his guests. And the king said to the girl, "Ask of me what thou willest, and I will give it to thee." And he swore to her, "Whatever thou dost ask, I will give thee, even though it be half of my kingdom." Then she went out . . . and she came in at once . . . and asked saying, "I want thee right away to give me on a dish the head of John the Baptist." And grieved as he was, the king, because of his oath and his guests, was unwilling to displease her. (Mark 6:21–26)

REFLECT Herodias had urged the death of John before this. Herod resisted her wish because he feared John's holiness, and respected his wisdom. On this occasion, however, John was doomed by the fierce hatred of Herodias and Herod's overwhelming fear of appearing weak before his friends.

REVIEW The interests of these two people were centered entirely on this earthly life. Herodias left her husband for

Herod in order to attain greater worldly prestige. The Baptist's denunciation of her action had been a public humiliation. For this she could never forgive him. Herod, on the other hand, found his satisfaction in exhibiting his pomp and power before his friends. He was compelled to keep his boastful promise, by his fear of the crowd's contempt and his own inner disgust with any sign of personal weakness.

It is normal to have some regard for the opinions and judgments of others. I have always needed the acceptance, approval, and good will of others. In childhood, I learned to evaluate my personal worth by the judgments of the adults who governed my life. Their displeasure upset me, while their approval brought me a sense of satisfaction. When their demands or expectations were beyond my power, I tried to tell myself that I did not care for their approval, but I suffered some pain nevertheless. The need for human approval has gradually become so much a part of me that I often act under its influence without being aware of it.

However, this need for acceptance and approval becomes a major problem when it disturbs my peace of mind or stops me from being myself. If I am unable to express my thoughts or follow my judgments, I ought to consider how to free myself from this unreasonable slavery. Otherwise I may, like Herod and Herodias, seek false solutions to my problem.

RESPOND My Jesus, other people's opinions of me are often influenced more by their inner emotional needs, preferences, and habits, than by my personal qualities or behavior. Help me to be enough of an adult to maintain a reasonable self-respect, a charitable consideration for the personal weaknesses of others, and an utter fearlessness of their unreasonable expectations or demands on me. Amen.

61. A SPIRITUAL RETREAT

READ And the apostles came together to meet Jesus and reported to him all that they had done and taught. And he said to them, "Come apart into a desert place and rest a while." For there were many coming and going, and they had no leisure even to eat. And they got into the boat and went off to a desert place apart. (Mark 6:30–32)

REFLECT The apostles were thrilled and overjoyed at the powers Jesus had granted them. They had brought His message to many, healed the sick, and cast out devils. On their return, they were eager to tell Him what they had said and done. Even as they spoke, people continued to come for help. Seeing how tired the apostles were, Jesus took them away from the crowd to a lonely spot where they might rest.

REVIEW Day to day living demands a good deal of my attention and energy. During most of the day, I am the servant of my duties and obligations. As I proceed through the day, my mind tends to become weary and my spirit loses its freshness. With advancing fatigue my nature begins to resist the requirements and demands of others. I incline more easily toward impatience and unkindness.

An occasional bit of restful solitude, prayerful reading, and peaceful reflection will help renew my bodily energies, mental alertness, emotional balance and moral strength. I can review my day, reconsider some of my judgments, re-evaluate some of my decisions, and weigh my behavior in the light of Christ's principles and example. Many a future attitude, judgment, and decision will be the better for my having contemplated it in prayerful solitude.

As I learn to enjoy being alone with Christ, I shall also grow in the understanding, acceptance, and possession of myself. Free from immature shame and self-blame, I shall be better able to look at my spontaneous tendencies, emotions, feelings, habits, desires, judgments, intentions, and efforts. I shall better appreciate the difference between the uncontrollable part of myself and the thinking, reasoning, moral level of my personality. With this knowledge I shall gradually be more disposed to assume an intelligent responsibility for my decisions and efforts. I shall grow out of my undue fear of making mistakes and my immature dread of criticism from others. In solitude I can more easily perceive the facts, possibilities, and limitations of my life, and more serenely accept the realities to which I am bound. With this clearer perspective of my life, I can reasonably consider how to make the most of my circumstances, without childish expectations and infantile anxieties.

RESPOND My Jesus, teach me to find myself and You in prayerful solitude. Help me overcome the immature shame, blame, disgust, and discouragement that often prevent me from seeing my real self. Let me view myself with the same justice and charity that You show me, so that I may gradually achieve a reasonable contentment with myself and a satisfying companionship with You. Amen.

62. IN THE COMPANY OF CHRIST

READ And when he landed, Jesus saw a large crowd, and had compassion on them, because they were like sheep without a shepherd. And he began to teach them many things. (Mark 6:34)

REFLECT These people came to Jesus with a hunger for His grace. His words gave them a deeper understanding of their difficulties, and a greater courage to face their problems. He cured not only their bodily infirmities, but also their more disturbing ills, those of the mind and spirit.

REVIEW As God looked upon Adam, He said that it is not good for man to be alone. However, necessary as human companionship is, there is another companionship which is also indispensable to my earthly existence, namely the companionship of God. When the second Person of the Holy Trinity chose to work out my redemption in human form, He offered me a visible companionship with God. In the company of Christ I can obtain knowledge that is essential to my earthly and eternal welfare, and strength to overcome the moral weaknesses of my nature.

Christ offers me a friendship that is closer, more reliable, and more enduring than all other friendships. He offers me His understanding in my fears and self-doubts, His acceptance in my self-disgust, His pardon in my sinfulness, His unflagging interest in my personal longings and efforts, His constant concern for my needs, His ready assistance in my problems, His sure guidance in my mental confusion and doubt, and His supernatural strength against my temptations. His offer of friendship is wholehearted. The only limit to it is my lack of knowledge. My only obstacle to it is sin.

A well-developed friendship with Jesus is the closest thing to heaven on earth. Unfortunately, many people are acquaintances rather than friends of Christ. They know Him, as it were, in passing, but not with the understanding and ease that comes from frequent association. Instead of seeing Him as He showed Himself in the gospels, they know Him only as He was presented by others and imagined by themselves. The image of Christ often suffers when transmitted through the limited knowledge of others or one's own emotional leanings. Through a daily prayerful reading of His life, I can modify my mistaken notions about Jesus, and slowly draw closer to Him in true friendship.

RESPOND   My Jesus, as the woman in the gospel searched for a mere farthing, so do You eagerly seek my friendship. I desire to accept You as my proven friend. Help me grow in my acquaintance with You, so that I may become ever more aware of Your guidance and assistance, and firmly convinced of Your understanding, acceptance, forgiveness, and concern for me. Help me believe that I can satisfy You with my good will and daily efforts, in spite of repeated mistakes and sins. Amen.

63.   TESTING CHRIST

READ   And immediately afterwards he made his disciples get into the boat and cross the sea ahead of him . . . And when it was late, he was there alone, but the boat was in the midst of the sea, buffeted by the waves, for the wind was against them. But in the fourth watch of the night he came to them, walking upon the sea. And they, seeing him walking upon the sea, were greatly alarmed, and exclaimed, "It is a ghost!" And they cried out for fear. Then Jesus immediately spoke to them, saying, "Take courage; it is I, do not be afraid."

But Peter answered him and said, "Lord, if it is thou, bid me come to thee over the water." And he said, "Come." Then Peter got out of the boat and walked on the water to come to Jesus. But seeing the wind was strong, he was afraid; and as he began to sink he cried out, saying, "Lord, save me!" And Jesus at once stretched forth his hand and took hold of him, saying to him, "O thou of little faith, why didst thou doubt?" (Matt. 14:22–32)

REFLECT   Jesus showed His personal concern for His disciples by coming to them through the storm. Since they were not yet full grown in their faith and understanding of Him, they were frightened by this unusual appearance.

Peter was no better off than the rest. He too had his fears and doubts. But he decided to put this apparition to the test by requesting a miracle. At Christ's word, he descended upon the water. However, after a few steps away from the boat, his fear and doubt overcame him, his faith weakened, and the miracle ceased.

REVIEW What Peter did happens every day to many people in different ways. When troubles arise, they become anxious and confused. God offers them His help in His own way but they do not recognize His hand. They are blinded by their fears and doubts. They put Christ to the test. They ask for some explicit sign to convince them beyond all doubt that He is interested in them.

If I desire to follow Christ in my daily life, I must do so not on my terms, but on His. I must not expect more than my personal share of talents and graces, nor demand the removal of obstacles or situations which God may expect me to bear with intelligence and grace. If miracles were the immediate reward for performing one's daily duties, there would be many more virtuous people in the world. Faith in Christ is proven when the wind blows strong and the waves run high. Trust in Him is shown by continuing to row, whether I make little or no progress. I may see Him coming to me through the tempest, or again I may see nothing except the threatening storm. Nevertheless He expects me to believe on His word that He stands by to protect me.

RESPOND My Jesus, whatever my troubles, whatever my problems, I do not face them alone. I shall never hesitate to ask Your help when I consider it necessary. However, I shall always believe that I row my boat with You at the helm. I cannot sink or be lost on the sea of life, because You are my Captain. Amen.

64. HIGHER MOTIVES

READ When therefore the crowd perceived that Jesus was not there nor his disciples, they themselves got into the boats and came to Capharnaum, seeking Jesus. And when they had found him, they said to him, "Rabbi, when didst thou come here?" Jesus answered them and said, "Amen, amen, I say to you, you seek me, not because you have seen signs, but because you have eaten of the loaves and have been filled. Do not labor for the food that perishes, but for that which endures unto life everlasting, which the Son of Man will give you. (John 6:24–27)

REFLECT These people were so impressed by the miracle of the loaves and fishes, that they wished to make Jesus their king. Then they would be free of anxiety for their material wants. Jesus urged them to develop a fuller vision of life. They were created for eternity. They should therefore subordinate their temporal needs to the eternal goal of this earthly existence.

REVIEW There are many motives that induce men to fulfill their religious obligations and follow the moral law in their daily life. These motives may range from the sheerest desire to avoid God's punishment to the purest wish to show more generosity to the all-lovable Creator. Besides these supernatural motives, there is a wide variety of natural motives which also incline people to reverence and service of God. They look to Him for nourishment, health, peace, success in their undertakings and social standing, and innumerable other earthly advantages.

These lesser motives are not to be despised as long as they are regarded in their proper place. The self-concern that moves men toward these benefits was created by God. It inclines men to reach for things which are necessary or helpful to their daily lives, and impels them to reject what may harm them in any way. This concern is evil only when it induces me to disagree with God's truth and reach for what is forbidden by His infinite wisdom.

On this occasion, Jesus exhorts his hearers to show wisdom and prudence in their self-concern, by placing their eternal welfare before their temporal well-being. My spiritual combat consists in trying to purify my God-given self-concern, so that it may constantly reach for God's will in all things. The more I diminish unnecessary natural wants, the more grace and energy shall I have to devote myself to His holy Will. In this way I shall be directing my earthly life toward the all-satisfying life of heaven.

RESPOND   O Jesus, King of wisdom and holiness, enlarge my vision of life, so that I may see beyond the immediate advantages and satisfactions which I encounter today. Let me choose these good things in so far as they make me more pleasing to You, and turn away from them whenever they are unnecessary occasions of sin. Amen.

65. FAITH IN CHRIST

READ   "For I have come down from heaven, not to do my own will but the will of him who sent me. Now this is the will of him who sent me, the Father, that I should lose nothing of what he has given me, but that I should raise it up on the last day. For this is the will of my Father who sent me, that whoever beholds the Son, and believes in him, shall have everlasting life, and I will raise him up on the last day." (John 6:38–40)

REFLECT   With these words Jesus proclaims Himself the Savior of all men. The heavenly Father will admit into eternal life all those who believe in His divine Son. Jesus willingly accepts the will of His Father, and takes upon Himself the responsibility of our salvation.

REVIEW Too often I forget the plan which God has devised for my salvation. I feel that the burden of reparation for my sins rests fully upon my weak human shoulders. This thought makes me insecure, uneasy, and afraid. I am not so sure that I can measure up to the requirements of Divine Justice. The memory of my past sins, and the awareness of my present weaknesses and faults, make me reluctant to think of God, death, and judgment. My fear is a great obstacle to my coming closer to Jesus in my daily life.

In this present message, Jesus reveals to me the marvelous plan which His heavenly Father has devised for my redemption. The divine Son will obey His heavenly Father, and by His obedience will make ample reparation for my disobedience. By my faith in Christ, I shall be so joined to Him, and He to me, that the greater part of my burden will be carried by Him. The scanty reparation of which I am capable will bear the dignity of the Son of God. In Him and through Him I shall find a marvelous union of Divine Justice and Infinite Mercy.

Contrary to what I sometimes feel, God does not want to condemn or punish me. Like the true Father He is, He wants to forgive, assist and reward me with a glory I cannot even imagine. When my fears blot out this truth, I must fight them with my faith in Jesus. If He could deceive me, I might have reason to follow my emotions, but if He is the Word of God, I must hate the falsehood that my fears express. A frequent, prayerful consideration of the encouraging message of Jesus will help me grow strong in my faith and trust. Slowly, with grace, practice, and time, I shall learn to assert my confidence in Christ so firmly that my doubts will diminish and my fears will weaken. Then I shall know the peace of His friendship and the joy of His daily companionship.

RESPOND Jesus my Savior, what a relief to realize that my salvation depends more upon You than upon myself. Without Your grace, I would be hopelessly confused and weak against every temptation, but with Your help I can always offer whatever resistance is within my power. My constant resistance to temptation and my daily efforts to follow Your principles, are all I need, to receive the benefits of Your earthly obedience to Your Father's will. I can never be condemned unless I knowingly and freely choose to turn my back on You by sin. Rather than do this, let me prefer any earthly pain, sorrow or burden. Amen.

66. THE BREAD OF LIFE

READ "I am the bread of life. . . . This is the bread that comes down from heaven, so that if anyone eat of it he will not die. I am the living bread that has come down from heaven. If anyone eat of this bread he shall live forever; and the bread that I will give is my flesh for the life of the world. . . . Amen, amen, I say to you, unless you eat the flesh of the Son of Man, and drink his blood, you shall not have life in you. (John 6:48–52, 54)

REFLECT Jesus continues His efforts to impress these people with the true nature of their redemption. As surely as food is destroyed to give life to its consumers, so will the Son of God offer Himself to men as Food and Drink for their souls. The supernatural life which flows from Him to them must be nourished by the flesh and blood of His suffering human nature. The Self-offering of Calvary will be repeated over and over in the Holy Eucharist until the end of time.

REVIEW Again Jesus tries to impress His hearers with the fact they must never again believe that they are working out their salvation unaided and alone. So much would He be part of that work that He would become their Food and Drink, to give them the supernatural life and strength to gain heaven. What a relief and consolation to me as I meditate upon this divine revelation. My littleness disappears into the bigness of Christ; my weakness is bolstered by His strength; my guilt is wiped out by His infinite redemption; my ignorance is enlightened by His shining truth; my efforts are guided by His example and encouraged by His companionship.

All of these facts, however, are not a matter of feeling. If I expect to feel the grandeur of His presence and the glory of His grace, I do not yet understand His message. He wants me to live by faith, not by the unreliable emotions of the moment. If Jesus said that He is in the Holy Eucharist, I must believe it on His word. My feelings may tell me that He is a million miles away from me, but He said that He is present under the appearance of Bread and Wine. I would rather believe His word than the sight of my eyes or the sound in my ears. Only in this way can I be a man of faith. As this faith is strengthened it will brighten every other truth which He has revealed. Many facts which I now believe in a theoretical manner, will gradually exert greater influence in my daily life. From Jesus in the Holy Eucharist will come my greatest spiritual growth and strength.

RESPOND My Eucharistic King, I believe, on Your word, that You are present upon the altar. When my mind hesitates to face You, because of my sense of unworthiness and guilt, let me remember that You have worked hard to make reparation for my defects and sins. Let me not minimize Your work and sacrifice, but help me believe that You understand, forgive, and encourage me to continue trying for Your sake. Amen.

67. DOUBTING CHRIST

READ "The words that I have spoken to you are spirit and life. But there are some among you who do not believe." For Jesus knew from the beginning who they were who did not believe, and who it was who should betray him. And he said, "This is why I have said to you, 'No one can come to me unless he is enabled to do so by my Father.'" From this time many of his disciples turned back and no longer went about with him. (John 6:64–67)

REFLECT In these words we behold people who had looked on the face of Christ, heard from His lips the message of salvation, and yet turned away from Him because they felt a repulsion for what He required of them. The thought of eating His flesh and drinking His blood made them recoil in disgust. Jesus then revealed that no man can accept His invitation without supernatural grace.

REVIEW From this narrative I can see how necessary it is for me to understand my emotions and direct them into healthy channels. These powerful forces can hinder my co-operation with God's grace. Even without my awareness, they can influence my thinking, sway my will, and dominate me in numberless ways. They incline me to like some things, fear some things, and hate some things. How I feel about Christ is often a result of the emotions that control my mind and blind my good will.

In my ignorance I tend to hold myself accountable for my feelings as though they were entirely under my control. Such, however, is not the case. They developed long before I could understand or control them. In my first years of life my emotions were spontaneous and uncomplicated. I wanted what pleased or satisfied me, feared what was painful or disagreeable, and hated what caused me annoyance or suffering. As I advanced in my interpersonal experience, these emotions became more complex. I could love and hate at the same time. Fear could so intermingle with my love that I became insecure with some of the things I desired. With experience I learned to control, disguise, or ignore my real emotions, so as to avoid possible punishment or retaliation.

My present behavior is the result of my defenses against the expectations and demands of others. These are my habitual solutions to the problems arising in my daily life. The more I understand this behavior the less likely am I to reject God's grace as these disciples did on this occasion.

RESPOND   My Jesus, I often misunderstand You because I think with my emotions and feelings, instead of thinking with my intelligence and faith. Help me see how blind I am to the real You. Help me to appreciate how understanding and wise You are in Your attitude toward me. May I never believe that You look at me with the narrow view and rash judgment that often hems me in and oppresses my spirit. Amen.

68. THINKING WITH GOD

READ   And the Pharisees and some of the Scribes who had come from Jerusalem gathered about him. And when they saw that some of his disciples were eating bread with defiled (that is, unwashed) hands, they found fault. . . . But answering he said to them, "Well did Isaias prophesy of you hypocrites, as it is written, *This people honors me with their lips, but their heart is far from me; and in vain do they worship me, teaching as doctrine the precepts of men.* For, letting go the commandment of God, you hold fast the tradition of men, the washing of pots and of cups, and many other things you do like these." (Mark 7:1, 6–8)

REFLECT   Jesus points out the error of these men. They were placing the customs and traditions established over a period of time, on the same level as God's commandments. In fact they even permitted men to neglect some of God's commandments in preference to these man-made regulations.

REVIEW   In one way or another, a number of people fall into this error. They usually begin with a sincere desire to give greater attention and praise to God. To satisfy this desire, they increase their daily prayers, begin some pious practice, e.g., a daily visit to church, or perform some other good work. In time they feel so obliged to perform these prayers or good works, that they are unable to diminish or omit them even for a reasonable cause. Be they ever so tired from their day's occupation, they feel that God expects or demands this self-imposed service from them. If circumstances make it impossible for them to do so, they feel as guilty as if they had violated one of God's commandments. Others are subject to this error in a different manner. They become so fixed in the local customs and traditions of their earlier life, that they are unable to adapt to the customs of new places. Even when the authority of the Church inaugurates a change of disciplinary regulations, they are hesitant or reluctant to make the change.

Many of these people eventually find their self-imposed burden repulsive. They feel guilty of this repulsion, and this guilt feeling adds to their already intolerable burden. They may distract themselves from this inner pressure by being demanding or critical of those who seem less strict and rigid in their religious practices. Inwardly, however, they envy these others for being free of the burden which weighs heavily upon them. They may teach their mistaken notions and practices to those under their authority. This immature distortion of religion may eventually draw them or others away from God.

RESPOND   My Jesus, impress upon my mind the reasona-

bleness and freedom which You preached on this occasion.
Show me how to follow Your will without adding imaginary obligations to those which reason and faith have already placed upon my shoulders. Amen.

69. TRUE SELF-PURIFICATION

READ "But the things that proceed out of the mouth come
from the heart, and it is they that defile a man. For out
of the heart come evil thoughts, murders, adulteries, immorality, thefts, false witness, blasphemies. These are the
things that defile a man; but to eat with unwashed hands
does not defile a man." (Matt. 15:18–20)

REFLECT Jesus does not mean to minimize the importance of duly authorized external observances or personal
preferences. He is simply pointing out that external observances can never be a substitute for internal service and
honor to God.

REVIEW A number of people estimate their religious
worth and progress by the mere performance of external
religious activities. Their fidelity to prayers, private devotions, and prescribed external observances, would seem to
indicate an unflagging readiness to offer praise, gratitude,
and reparation to God. And yet, their religious performance is unrelated to their interpersonal relations. In dealing with others, these seemingly religious people are often
unkind, inconsiderate, impatient, unduly critical, irritable,
unforgiving, prone to rash judgments, and rigidly opinionated.

Jesus condemns this segregation between our dealings
with God and our relations with our neighbor. He asserts
that true self-purification and service to God must begin
from within. I must adopt a supernatural intention to give

glory to God in all His works, especially the works He loves most in this world, namely my fellow men. Only such an intention can enrich my external religious performances with the most precious of all virtues, Christian charity.

I too can make the mistake of measuring my religious perfection by the number of my prayers, external observances, and private good works of my own choosing. I may feel quite content in the conviction that these prove my self-dedication to God. Jesus urges me to examine the attitude and intention with which I perform these religious activities. I may feel a sentimental good will toward people in general, and at the same time show little or no consideration for the particular individuals involved in my daily life. The self-offering to God which I profess in my prayers and religious observances, must prove itself in my daily self-giving to Him, where He needs me most, namely in the people with whom I deal. With eyes on Christ, I must extend to the people around me the sign of good will, the proofs of generosity, and the many little helps which will encourage, strengthen, and console them.

RESPOND My Jesus, grant me light to see how I may enrich the lives of people around me by my good will and sincere self-giving. Teach me to understand, accept, and assist them as best I can. May their daily burden be a little lighter, and their daily tasks a little easier because of my moral support and personal assistance. May my external religious observances be pleasing to You through this inner spirit of generosity and good will. Amen.

70. HUMILITY IN PRAYER

READ And behold, a Canaanite woman came out of that territory and cried out to him, saying, "Have pity on me,

O Lord, Son of David! My daughter is sorely beset by a devil." . . . But he answered and said, "I was not sent except to the lost sheep of the house of Israel." But she came and worshipped him, saying, "Lord, help me!" He said in answer, "It is not fair to take the children's bread and to cast it to the dogs." But she said, "Yes, Lord; for even the dogs eat of the crumbs that fall from their masters' table." Then Jesus answered and said to her, "O woman, great is thy faith! Let it be done to thee as thou wilt." And her daughter was healed from that moment. (Matt. 15:22–28)

REFLECT Even though the gentiles were to receive His message and gifts later on, Jesus could not resist this woman's petition. She won Him over through two great virtues, i.e., her unwavering faith in Him and her humble acknowledgment of her inferior position as an outsider.

REVIEW A number of people find it difficult to pray for God's help. Consciously or unconsciously, they fear that He may rigidly insist that they bear their burden with patience and resignation. Their fear usually causes them to doubt that God will help. Sometimes their mental confusion is intensified by guilt-feelings, because they look on their fears and doubts as a proof that they lack faith and trust in God. This accumulation of desire, fear, doubt, and guilt makes prayer burdensome and repulsive. Under this emotional strain, they become tired, depressed, and discouraged.

The truth of the matter is that the fears and doubts of these people are no proof that they lack faith and trust in God. The fact that they turn to Him at all, is proof of their faith. Their very petition shows that they have some measure of hope and trust in God's help. Their real problem lies buried deep within their mind. They have a low self-esteem and a mistaken evaluation of their personal worth. This unfavorable self-regard developed over the years. It is now so ingrained in them that they are largely unaware of it. They are so displeased with themselves, that any sign of neglect, disapproval, or rejection by others is a painful experience to them. Consequently, they fear either that they do not deserve God's help, or that He may look on their petitions with a rigid demand that they suffer for their defects and sins.

RESPOND My Jesus, help me know myself well enough to avoid or correct this unhealthy situation within myself. Teach me to have a proper self-love. My prayers are important to You. My smallness disappears in the light of Your love, and my sins are erased by Your divine reparation and pardon. Every activity of my daily life is stamped with Your dignity and bolstered by Your supernatural grace. May I always present my requests with trust in Your personal concern for me, and with a willingness to accept Your fatherly decision in the matter. Amen.

71. JESUS CURES THE SICK

READ And when Jesus had departed from there, he went along the sea of Galilee; and he went up the mountain and sat there. And great crowds came to see him, bringing with them the dumb, the blind, the lame, the maimed, and many others; and they sat them down at his feet, and he cured them; so that the crowds marvelled to see the dumb speak, the lame walk, the blind see. And they glorified the God of Israel. (Matt. 15:29–31)

REFLECT Jesus performed these wonders not only to help the needy, but also to impress the world. As the crowd beheld the power of God in Him, they were impelled to express admiration and praise of their Father in heaven.

REVIEW Most people are willing enough to offer thanks

and praise to God as long as all goes smoothly in their daily life. However, many react differently when faced with trouble and affliction. Some pray for God's help with a stubborn insistence that He grant their request unconditionally. Others blame God for their trouble, as though He were at fault in some way. Others doubt or deny the existence of God, since they cannot understand how a good God could ever permit such suffering. Thus, in one way or another, suffering and affliction arouse these people to rebel against God or to reject Him altogether.

Though these people may attribute their reactions to logical reasons, there is no logic in their thinking. Their attitude is inspired by emotions that sway them more than they realize. In their life history we will find that these emotions were developed as a self-defense against the conditions and circumstances of their earlier life. They are now habits employed against any unpleasant turn of events. Whether God or men be involved, these people will react with equal vigor against what they see as injustice. Unconsciously they are unwilling or unable to adapt to difficult circumstances. Rather, they insist that these circumstances be adapted to their way of thinking and living.

Where do I belong in this matter? Am I able to see God when my routine is disturbed by problems and sufferings? Can I live the advice that I give to others in their afflictions? Do I continue to praise God's goodness and wisdom when I am weighed down by anxiety, pain, or grief? In these circumstances it is not God Who changes, but I. Through greater knowledge, understanding, appreciation, and religious practice, I must endeavor to acquire the spiritual strength to see beyond the trials of the moment and rise above the natural desires of this earthly existence.

RESPOND My Jesus, as I consider the human experiences, burdens, and affliction which You bore for my sake, can I refuse to bear my share of these? Teach me to look upon my daily life as a true partnership with You. I shall become wiser by entering into Your earthly experiences, and stronger by bringing You into mine. Amen.

72. MISUNDERSTANDING CHRIST

READ And they had forgotten to bring bread, and they had but one loaf with them in the boat. And he began to charge them, saying, "Take heed; beware of the leaven of the Pharisees, and of the leaven of Herod!" And they began to argue among themselves, saying, "We have no bread." But Jesus knowing this, said to them, "Why do you argue because you have no bread? Do you not yet perceive, nor understand? Is your heart still blinded? Though you have eyes do you not see, and though you have ears do you not hear? And do you not remember? When I broke the five loaves among five thousand, how many baskets full of fragments did you take up?" They said to him, "Twelve." "And when I broke the seven loaves among four thousand, how many large baskets of fragments did you take up?" They said, "Seven." And he said to them, "How is it that you do not yet understand?" (Mark 8:14–21)

REFLECT Jesus was using a figure of speech to teach a lesson to His disciples. They were so disturbed at having forgotten the bread that they thought He was referring to this. Jesus reminded them of His power to produce bread when necessary, and then they understood His true meaning.

REVIEW What the disciples did on this occasion, happens every day with many people. They project their emotions and thoughts onto Christ. Instead of understanding His teachings and example as He intended, they interpret them in accordance with how they feel or think. They so color the Person and doctrine of Jesus that they change

Him rather than themselves. This projection is generally caused by unhealthy emotions. When one is disturbed by feelings of inferiority, guilt, unworthiness, and fear of disapproval and punishment, he tends to see others as having the same opinion of him as he has of himself. One who has a reasonable self-esteem is not disturbed by these emotional distortions. His mind is not tied down by fears and doubts. It is free to take people at face value and to profit by interpersonal experience.

This power which emotions have over the mind can affect me without my awareness. It may be the principal reason why my religious endeavors and practices are strained and burdensome. It is often the cause of tension and friction between others and me. Psychological projection may be at work in me, or in the person with whom I deal, or in both of us. I must endeavor to develop an awareness of it, so that I may counterbalance it in myself and tolerate it in others. Most of all, I need this self-awareness in order to improve my relations with Jesus and His heavenly Father.

RESPOND My Jesus, help me free myself from my fears, doubts, and self-disgust, so that I may never lose sight of what You really are. Do not let my emotions and imagination see You as anything other than what You have proven Yourself, that is, my Redeemer, my Lord, and my closest Friend through life. Amen.

73. THE GIFT OF FAITH

READ Now Jesus, having come into the district of Caesarea Philippi, began to ask his disciples, saying, "Who do men say the Son of Man is?" But they said, "Some say, John the Baptist; and others, Elias; and others, Jeremias, or one of the prophets." He said to them, "But who do you say that I am?" Simon Peter answered and said, "Thou art the Christ, the Son of the living God." Then Jesus answered and said, "Blessed art thou, Simon Bar-Jona, for flesh and blood has not revealed this to thee, but my Father in heaven. (Matt. 16: 13–17)

REFLECT Those who saw and heard Christ, had different notions concerning His true identity. Unfortunately, many of these notions were wrong. Peter gave the correct answer, and Jesus declared that he did so by the grace granted him by the heavenly Father.

REVIEW Though I do not hesitate to agree with Peter's profession of faith in the divinity of Christ, there are times when I have my share of mistaken notions about Him. In spite of all that He has said and done to convince me that He understands me, accepts me as I am, and desires to share my daily life, I have my moments of fear or doubt whether He is really concerned about me. Though I may read or hear of His proven love for me, my contrary feelings still sway my thinking and influence my behavior toward Him.

My misunderstanding of Christ is not always a simple matter of defective knowledge. It also has other roots. One of these roots is a faulty self-regard. Due to past experience, some people look upon their natural limitations with shame. Some blame themselves for any show of human weakness, be it ever so slight or blameless. Some are incapable of being at ease with others, even with Christ.

Without being aware of it, I too can be influenced by these emotional tendencies. Thus, the thought of Christ may remind me of my sins and judgment rather than my efforts and glory. I may feel a vague hesitancy rather than a peaceful anticipation as I approach Him in prayer. I may more easily feel that He is not satisfied with me rather than that He is glad to have me near Him. These and other misunderstandings can limit my friendship with Jesus. They can even incline me to follow Him at a distance.

RESPOND O Jesus, I believe that You are the Son of God, Second Person of the Holy Trinity. You are truly God and truly Man. As God-man You are my Savior, my divine Model, and my invisible Companion every step of my earthly path toward eternal life. Let me become ever more aware of this truth, and my spiritual progress will improve. Amen.

74. A REBUKE TO PETER

READ From that time Jesus began to show his disciples that he must go to Jerusalem and suffer many things from the elders and Scribes and chief priests, and be put to death, and on the third day rise again. And Peter taking him aside, began to chide him, saying, "Far be it from thee, O Lord; this will never happen to thee." He turned and said to Peter, "Get behind me, satan, thou art a scandal to me; for thou dost not mind the things of God, but those of men." (Matt. 16: 21–23)

REFLECT Jesus now begins to prepare His disciples for the shock which they would undergo in the near future. His brief announcement of His capture, suffering, and death stunned them. Under the influence of his impetuous emotions, Peter rebuked his Master for even thinking such things. Only strong language could quiet the turbulent emotions of Peter. Jesus called him a tempter, a worldly minded man.

REVIEW Peter had just been appointed head of Christ's Church. The graces of that sacred moment were still upon him. And yet, the emotional shock of Christ's announcement was too much for him. From the supernatural level of His conscious life, he made an instantaneous descent to the emotional level. Though he was still impressed by his glorious appointment, he was swayed more by natural feelings than by supernatural thinking. Jesus understood that Peter was momentarily upset by the announcement. Nevertheless, He scolded Peter for allowing his emotions to do his thinking and make his decisions. Worldly people might act in this manner, but not a chosen follower of Christ. He called Peter a tempter because he was influencing the others to adopt his own faulty attitude.

What happened to Peter also happens to me on a number of occasions. There are so many factors that make up my daily life. Some of them are pleasant and easy to manage. Others are neither pleasant nor easy. Between my interior habits of thought and behavior, and those of the people whose lives are intertwined with mine, I have my share of misunderstandings, doubts, slights, oppositions, contradictions, and tensions.

Amid this distracting and upsetting emotional atmosphere, my inner insecurity distracts my mind from the inspiring ideas and ideals presented by Christ. My drive to self-preservation arouses me to defend myself against painful experiences. I do so with emotional responses that tend to blot out the warnings of reason and the urgings of grace. Like Peter I have many an occasion to regret my spontaneous tendencies and behavior. But like him, I can eventually learn to think more like Christ and less like the immature self that developed within me through past experience. Slowly, with time, grace, practice, and more practice, I can change as truly as Peter did, if not as much.

RESPOND My Jesus, let me not be disgusted by my spontaneous emotions and tendencies. Peter is a good example of what may yet happen to me. Help me live in closer contact with You, so that I may daily learn a little more, practice a little better, and advance a little closer to the attitude and conduct that You desire of me. Amen.

75. THE TRANSFIGURATION

READ Now it came to pass . . . that he took Peter, James and John and went up the mountain to pray. And as he prayed, the appearance of his countenance was changed, and his raiment became a radiant white. And behold, two men were talking with him. And these were Moses and Elias, who, appearing in glory, spoke of his death, which he was about to fulfill in Jerusalem. (Luke 9:28–31)

REFLECT In order to strengthen His disciples during the turbulent crisis which lay ahead, Jesus granted this extraordinary privilege to these three leaders of the group. With the memory of His glory they would bolster the faltering faith of the rest during the dark days of His passion and death.

REVIEW The holy Scripture calls man's earthly life a warfare. The struggle to earn a living for oneself and his dependents, the weight of responsibilities, the insecurity engendered by possible difficulties and problems, the aggravation caused by interpersonal misunderstandings and friction, all of these bring anxiety to the mind, confusion to the intellect, and indecision to the judgment. Faced with these tangible threats and possible dangers, the individual is easily swayed by his drive to self-preservation and self-defense. He is so distracted by the needs and wants of the moment, that he is more disposed to calm his inner uneasiness than to consider the morality of his dispositions and behavior.

Like the apostles, I too need an inner vision powerful enough to counterbalance my unthinking emotional tendencies. I need to see an advantage, a benefit, a goal so desirable that no earthly crisis can turn me away from the principles of Christ. The vision of Christ in His glory can become so real to me that it will overcome the emotional insecurity and unreasoning anxiety which might lead me into sin. It is significant that in this glorious vision Jesus spoke with Moses and Elias about the sufferings and death which he was soon to endure. In this manner He reminds me that the way to everlasting glory is the way of the cross. My cross is my daily life, by which I may rise above my spontaneous instincts, unreasoning drives, and emotional habits with the help of God's grace, the guidance of Christ's teaching, and the inspiration of His personal example.

RESPOND   O Jesus, Master of truth, King of glory, and Guide to eternal life, lead me through the pressures, problems, and temptations of my daily life. Help me see beyond the inconveniences, anxieties, and tempting attractions of the moment. With eyes upon the all-satisfying glory of heaven, I shall find strength to reject those partial satisfactions and incomplete joys that involve sin. Amen.

76. NATURAL DOUBTS

READ   And on coming to his disciples, he saw a great crowd around them, and the Scribes arguing with them. . . . And he asked them, "What are you arguing about among yourselves?" And one of the crowd answering, said, "Master, I have brought to thee my son, who has a dumb spirit . . . And I told thy disciples to cast it out, but they could not."

And he answered and said to them, "O unbelieving generation, how long shall I be with you? How long shall I put up with you? Bring him to me." . . . But Jesus said to him, "If thou canst believe, all things are possible to him who believes." At once the father of the boy cried out, and said with tears, "I do believe; help my unbelief." (Mark 9:13-23)

REFLECT In this scene we find the disciples unable to work this cure. Jesus told them later that they had failed because of their faltering faith. And yet, the father of the boy admitted both his faith and his lack of it. Jesus granted the cure because of the sincere desire of this man to believe in spite of his doubts.

REVIEW To doubt is so natural to human nature, that even one who believes by the grace of God, may occasionally feel some surges of doubt within himself. I need not be troubled by these spontaneous involuntary tendencies toward fear and doubt. They arise from my natural sense of inadequacy in certain situations. I must understand that this sense of helplessness is not due to a lack of faith. As with the father of this boy, it can spur me on to a firmer desire to believe. Instead of doubting my sincerity because of unwanted emotional fears and doubts, I must believe in the genuineness of my desire. God will judge me more by this desire than by any contrary feelings within me.

However, my faith must be more than a belief that God can help me. It must also contain a conviction that He knows what is best for me, and desires whatever will do me the most good. Without this fullness of faith, I shall make the mistake of those who present God with demands rather than requests. Implicitly they tell Him what to do, regardless of His wisdom in the matter. They even try to strike a bargain with Him, with promises of returning one favor for another.

Such behavior is the height of immaturity. It is a symptom of emotional thinking and childish fear. Though I may loudly assert my faith in the power, wisdom, goodness, and love of God, I prove what I really think of Him in my moments of need. How I behave when some crisis enters into my life, is the real proof of my faith or lack of it. Though I may have little control over my emotions,

I must constantly affirm my desire to leave all things in
His hands.

RESPOND Lord Jesus, sometimes I too have reason to ex-
claim with the father in this gospel, "I believe; help my
unbelief!" However, I will not hesitate to affirm my faith
and trust in You, regardless of my feelings. Feelings of
anxiety and doubt will be no surprise to me, nor will they
make me ashamed of myself. They are old habits, and
will probably remain with me, in some measure, all through
life. I do believe, Lord! Help me prove it in action. Amen.

77. OPPOSITION TO FAITH

READ Now the Jewish feast of Tabernacles was at hand.
His brethren therefore said to him, "Leave here and go
into Judea that thy disciples also may see the works that
thou dost . . . If thou dost these things, manifest thyself to the world." For not even his brethren believed in
him. Jesus therefore said to them, "My time has not yet
come, but your time is always at hand. The world cannot
hate you, but it hates me because I bear witness concerning
it, that its works are evil." (John 7: 2–7)

REFLECT Christ's relatives had heard reports about His
amazing miracles. They had also heard the doubts and
comments of their townsmen. They were more inclined to
share the doubts of their friends than the faith of those
who had seen the power of Jesus. They therefore told Him
to prove Himself by working His miracles indiscriminately,
instead of confining them to particular persons and places.

REVIEW Though Jesus did not explicitly accuse these relatives of being members of the "world" that opposed Him,
it would seem that He might well have done so. After all,

they too disbelieved. Could it be that He saw excusing causes in their lack of faith? Since they had known Him all their lives, were they emotionally incapable at this time, of believing in His Messianic mission? Perhaps they needed more time to absorb the graces which He was offering them. Moreover, there was the emotional pressure exerted on them by the incredulity of their fellow Nazarenes. It was difficult for them to live in this atmosphere of doubt and opposition, without some measure of internal confusion and indecision. At any rate, Jesus treated them with understanding, patience, and kindness. He made no accusation of guilt or bad will.

In my own way, I too am hindered from coming closer to Jesus by my inner feelings and the external interpersonal influences on me. It is not easy for me to change at will the attitudes and deep feelings about Christ which have developed in me through the years. Though I know by faith that He is an understanding, accepting, merciful redeemer, I cannot dispel at once the feeling that perhaps He sees me as a sinner who deserves a heavy punishment for many neglected graces and lost opportunities. Moreover, I too am influenced more easily by the human attitudes and behavior of others than by the words and example of Christ. Much as I may desire to come closer to Him in my daily thoughts, intentions and practices, I may fear the reactions of others so much that I restrain these supernatural desires.

RESPOND My Jesus, help me to see clearly how far my emotions hold me back from You. Help me, Lord, to understand what holds me back. Let me see why I tend to become distracted, tired, and vaguely uncomfortable in my religious activities. With this knowledge I may be better able to reconstruct my mistaken notions, attitudes, and feelings concerning You. Amen.

78. THE POWER OF GOOD WILL

READ   And the Jews marvelled, saying, "How does this man come by learning, since he has not studied?" Jesus answered them and said, "My teaching is not my own, but his who sent me. If anyone desires to do his will, he will know of the teaching whether it is from God, or whether I speak on my own authority." (John 7:15–18)

REFLECT   So blinded were these men by their fixed ideas that they resisted every attempt of Christ to win them over. He therefore accused them of bad will.

REVIEW   The first requirement of all religious living is good will. Unless I am disposed to learn God's holy Will and to follow it as best I can, my religious activities are but an empty shell. Good will inclines one to make an effort at self-improvement even when he is convinced that he will probably fail. He is willing to make a start, with the hope that God will lead him toward a successful conclusion. Though he may be caught in an apparently hopeless situation, he is willing to try. He may feel weighed down by definite fears or vague anxieties, held back by uncertainties and doubts, repelled by the effort required or the responsibilities that might arise, but through it all he is willing to try. Such is the man of good will.

However, good will alone cannot make me a true follower of Christ. It must be guided by His truth and bolstered by His supernatural assistance. In spite of my good will, I can be blinded to Christ's message by fixed ideas and personal preferences. My good will may be misguided by my deep prejudices or fears. As a result of these mistaken interior emotions and dispositions, I may be able to offer Christ only a partial service, in which I consciously or unconsciously place a limit on my self-giving.

145

I too may need to know Jesus better, understand His message more fully, and be convinced that He is entirely devoted to my true and lasting welfare. Only with this knowledge and conviction will I be more disposed to change my old habits of thought and conduct. Spurred on by God's grace, I will try to walk more fully with Christ by practicing attitudes and virtues that will bring me closer to Him and to those involved in my daily life. I shall no longer look upon this effort as an impossible strain or an unreasonable restriction of my liberty. I may still feel the tug of old emotional habits that turned me away from God in the past. And yet, in the light and strength of His grace, I shall want to develop new habits for His glory and my own everlasting happiness.

RESPOND My Jesus, due to my developed fears and doubts, and my acquired preferences and prejudices, I shall continue to feel an occasional aversion to Your truth or a passing opposition to Your grace. Let me understand the normalcy of these contrary tendencies. Instead of condemning myself for them, let me calmly counterbalance them with a supernatural good will and a daily effort to cooperate with Your holy graces. Amen.

79. CONFLICTING OPINIONS

READ Some of the crowd, therefore, said . . . "This is truly the Prophet." Others said, "This is the Christ." Some, however, said, "Can the Christ come from Galilee? Does not the Scripture say that it is of the offspring of David, and from Bethlehem . . . that the Christ is to come?" So there arose a division among the crowd because of him. (John 7:40–43)

REFLECT In all this discussion and argumentation, there

were many emotional undercurrents. Some people were frankly puzzled, while others were trying to gain the upper hand in the discussion. The wise people in the crowd did more thinking than talking, more praying than arguing.

REVIEW   Living among my fellow men means being exposed to their emotional tendencies, needs, and demands. Every human being is, by his very nature, inclined in his own favor. Consciously or unconsciously, guiltlessly or maliciously, directly or indirectly, most people will, at one time or another, expect me to see things their way and behave in accordance with their emotional leanings. If I have achieved a reasonable self-esteem and a fair measure of moral strength, I can tolerate the pressure of these interpersonal relations. On the other hand, beneath my external front and intellectual camouflage, I may still be resorting to childish forms of self-defense. If I am unable to maintain my self-respect when others oppose, resent, or reject me, I am immature.

The mature man can hear his opinion contradicted without becoming unduly perturbed. In his love of truth, he can give an unbiased consideration to differences of opinion, and acknowledge his error if he perceives it. He respectfully defers to those who have greater knowledge in what they say, and to those who have authority to command what they require of him. When, however, he has reason to believe his own opinion or respect his own judgment, he can do so without fearing the disapproval of others. My authority for my religious convictions and moral principles, is the Church of Christ. Those who disagree with me in these matters, disagree not with me personally, but with Christ Himself. The best I can do for these people, is to presume their sincerity, stand by my convictions, live by my principles, and let God govern and judge the world.

RESPOND   My Jesus, help me attain true emotional adulthood in my interpersonal relations. Let me respect the rights of others and presume their sincerity, without compromising my own rights and principles. Teach me to exercise charity without weakness, and strength without severity. I hope to find my peace in Your truth, and my self-reliance in Your divine assistance. Amen.

80. REFUSAL TO CONDEMN

READ   Now the Scribes and Pharisees brought a woman caught in adultery, and setting her in the midst, said to him, "Master, this woman has just now been caught in adultery. And in the Law Moses commanded us to stone such persons. What, therefore, dost thou say?" . . . But Jesus, stooping down, began to write with his finger on the ground. But when they continued asking him, he raised himself and said to them, "Let him who is without sin among you be the first to cast a stone at her." . . . But hearing this, they went away, one by one . . . And Jesus raising himself, said to her, "Woman . . . has no one condemned thee?" She said, "No one, Lord." Then Jesus said, "Neither will I condemn thee. Go thy way, and from now on sin no more." (John 8:3–11)

REFLECT   After the crowd departed, Jesus spoke to the woman and to the world. Rather than condemn, He would have us go forth and sin no more.

REVIEW   One of the greatest obstacles to closer friendship with Jesus, is a morbid memory of past sins. A number of people are unable to forget their sins, even after confessing and doing penance for them. In spite of Christ's sacramental reassurance of His pardon, they continue to despise themselves, accuse themselves, or fear that there may still be some unforgiven remnant of sin in them. Even as they express their desire to love God, or sorrow for their sins, they feel uneasy or strained. In their natural lack of self-confidence and self-respect, they suspect themselves of selfishness, insincerity, or hypocrisy. Since their principal motive may be to avoid the punishment of hell, they consider themselves unworthy of pardon. They forget that the fear of hell is also a grace from God.

These people can read the above narrative, acknowledge the understanding and forgiveness of Christ, and still feel that none of it applies to them. Little as they realize it, their real problem is not religious but emotional. Due to past experience, they find it impossible to forgive themselves for their weaknesses and failures. They cannot feel at peace unless they do things perfectly. Only then can they feel safe from their unsettling self-disgust, the disapproval of others, and the justice of God.

These people never really grew up emotionally. They never learned to respect the natural limitations and normal weaknesses of their God-given human nature. They do not appreciate the difference between their feelings and their intentions, their spontaneous tendencies and their free decisions, their involuntary imperfections and their voluntary sins. In practice, they never cease accusing themselves of intentions they never made, and sins they never chose. Having lost faith in themselves, they find it hard to understand how anyone else, even God, can see any value in them. Being unable to forgive themselves, they cannot be sure that Christ understands their condition and pardons their sins.

RESPOND   Lord, there is a trace of this problem in many people. Help me recognize it if it exists in me. Grant me the grace and emotional strength to develop a healthier attitude toward myself and my failures. Let me look back only long enough to learn a valuable lesson from my faults. Then help me work toward self-improvement with confidence in myself, trust in Your pardon, and reliance on Your constant assistance. Amen.

81. TRUTH AND INTERIOR FREEDOM

READ   When he was speaking these things, many believed in him. Jesus therefore said to the Jews who had come to believe in him, "If you abide in my word, you shall be my disciples indeed, and you shall know the truth, and the truth shall make you free." (John 8:30–32)

REFLECT   Jesus makes a remarkable promise to these new converts. He claims that His truth will not cripple their natural desire for freedom, but will guide that desire along the life-giving path of true freedom, namely, freedom to build their lives on the firm foundation of His truth.

REVIEW   Self-expression is one of the basic drives of human nature. I feel impelled to satisfy a number of appetites and wants which developed in me through the actual circumstances and situations of my early life. They are now habits which demand expression in the particular manner and matter that brought me satisfaction in the past. Some of these forms of self-expression are undesirable. Though I have learned to cloak them in the language and behavior of an adult, deep within me they are still as unreasoning and unreasonable as they were in my childhood. In time of emotional stress they incline me to disregard the commandments of God and the example of Christ.

The truth of Christ is the path to real self-expression. It can guide me to my highest self-fulfillment. It can free my mind of the fears and doubts which arise from my natural limitations, insecurity, and anxiety. It can dispose me to live within the reality and facts that govern my life. It shows me what is truly good for me and what is harmful. Through Christ I can pierce the camouflage of appearances and feelings, and look beyond the pleasures and satisfactions of the moment.

With the truth and grace of Christ, I am free to find my true self, develop my real powers of body, mind, and soul, and attain the all-satisfying life of heaven's eternal glory. I shall no longer demand of myself what is beyond my strength, nor despise myself for being what I must necessarily be in my present circumstances. There will be peace in my present efforts, and satisfaction in the achievements of each day. In my limited way, I shall know the true God as He is, without distorting Him through my childish misunderstandings. Thus, the truth of Christ will set me free from my present slavery to emotional thinking and unreasoning wants.

RESPOND   O Christ, King of true freedom, I rely upon Your truth to show me the way to eternal life, and I trust in Your assistance for the strength to walk that path. There will be obstacles, threats, and dark days. But I shall not be walking alone. With the eyes of faith I shall see You walking with me. With the shining light of Your words and example, I hope to arrive in due time at my heavenly home. Amen.

82. THEORY AND PRACTICE

READ   "If you are the children of Abraham, do the works of Abraham. . . . Why do you not understand my speech? Because you cannot listen to my word. . . . If I speak the truth, why do you not believe me? He who is of God hears the words of God. The reason why you do not hear is that you are not of God." (John 8:39, 43, 46, 47)

REFLECT   Jesus again accuses His enemies of bad will. They had closed their minds to His message and shut their eyes to His holy example. While claiming fidelity to God through their ancestor, Abraham, they offend the Father by rejecting His Son.

REVIEW   There is a wide gap between man and God, a gap filled with ignorance, misunderstanding, and misleading emotions. Jesus came to build the bridge which would cross that gap and unite man to God. That bridge is none other than my daily life, raised up by the grace which Jesus merited for me through His work of redemption. His truth and grace have diminished the power which my ignorance and natural appetites had over me. Though I seem no different externally from any other man, I live a more-than-natural life. Every thought, word, desire, and voluntary act of my day is stamped with the mark of my baptism, the mark of Christ's salvation. What was once a merely natural life, has been raised up to the level of God.

However, Christ's work of redemption must be completed by my daily cooperation with His truth and my fidelity to His principles. This cooperation has its own distinctive problems. The emotions, attitudes, wants, and habits in me and in others are constantly obstructing my supernatural efforts and influencing my daily behavior. True, many of my infidelities to Christ are not fully conscious or wholly deliberate, and many are not serious infractions of His law. However, conscious or not, deliberate or not, they can eventually become more serious.

The enemies of Jesus permitted themselves to be dominated by their emotional preferences and prejudices. Jesus finally accused them of sinning in their opposition to Him. This can also happen to me. I am therefore obliged to take due precautions against such a development. Through an ever growing knowledge of Him, an ever deepening appreciation of His truth, and a mature, peaceful effort to be more aware of His nearness, I can gradually become so strongly attached to Him that I will prefer to please Him rather than satisfy my unreasonable natural tendencies. As long as I am still overcome by these tendencies, I shall continue to be partially deaf to His words and blind to His divine goodness. I shall find myself ill at ease, disinterested, or even repelled by religious activities and spiritual efforts.

RESPOND Lord Jesus, help me give calm and peaceful thought to my daily conduct, so that I may see where I can improve myself in accordance with my present strength of body, mind, and soul. Without nervous strain and with a sincere intention, let me follow the light You grant me in this meditation. Amen.

83. JESUS CLAIMS TO BE DIVINE

READ Jesus answered, ". . . Amen, amen, I say to you, if anyone keep my word, he will never see death." The Jews therefore said, "Now we know that thou hast a devil. Abraham is dead, and the prophets, and thou sayest, "If anyone keep my word he will never taste death. Art thou greater than our father Abraham, who is dead? And the prophets are dead. Whom dost thou make thyself?" Jesus answered, ". . . Abraham your father rejoiced that he was to see my day. He saw it and was glad." The Jews therefore said to him, "Thou art not yet fifty years old, and hast thou seen Abraham?" Jesus said to them, "Amen, amen, I say to you, before Abraham came to be, I am." (John 8:49, 51–54, 56–58)

REFLECT At this point in Our Lord's public life, we behold the sad condition of people hampered by bad will and hardened by continual resistance to grace. So many reports by eyewitnesses and their own observations, had succeeded only in making them hopelessly stubborn in their opposition. At first Jesus tolerated their mental block in an effort to win as many of them as possible. The time had now come for Him to declare His full identity. "I am" is the name by which God called Himself when Moses asked His name. Jesus used it so effectively on this occasion that they sought to stone Him for doing so.

REVIEW There must have been some defect in the religious performance of these men. They were leaders of the people, well versed in the laws and traditions of their race. Their external observance of the religious regulations and practices was exemplary. They fulfilled their daily prayers, gave alms, taught others, and were considered men of God. Yet, when they met Jesus they became upset at first, then hostile, and finally, utterly dedicated to His downfall by any available means.

Why this opposition from these leaders of the people? Jesus called them whitened sepulchres, all white outside, but inside filled with corpses. They had relied upon a hollow external union with God. They had used their religion to obtain an earthly superiority, prestige, and power over the people, not to make themselves generous, self-giving servants of God. In their own way, they had much in common with Pilate and Herod. They were seeking the same worldly self-fulfillment.

Since Christ did not fit their prescriptions, they rejected Him. I too can reject Jesus in some measure because of faulty notions and emotional attitudes in my religious practices. I must learn to hear His voice in the teachings and guidance of His Holy Church. My daily life must be judged not by the virtues I prefer, but by the virtues I need in my particular circumstances. In my spiritual endeavors I must satisfy not myself alone but Christ, who has proven Himself to be my Lord and my God.

RESPOND My Jesus, I accept You as my God, Redeemer, Teacher, and Model. Help me see how I may imitate You more faithfully in my daily attitudes, words, and behavior toward my fellow men. Make me willing to strive daily for a prayerful union with God and a sincere good will toward my neighbor. Amen.

84. THE NEED TO BLAME

READ   And as he was passing by, he saw a man blind from birth. And his disciples asked him, "Rabbi, who has sinned, this man or his parents, that he should be born blind?" Jesus answered, "Neither has this man sinned, nor his parents, but the works of God were to be made manifest in him." (John 9:1–4)

REFLECT   Having seen in the history of their race, how God punished the disobedience of His people with physical tribulations and sufferings, the disciples wondered what sin had brought about the blindness of this man. Jesus points out that God has many reasons for permitting men to suffer.

REVIEW   The tendency to see blame in oneself or others, is much more common than I may suspect. I often hold myself accountable for anything in me that is open to the least suspicion or question. Though I readily admit that I am subject to human limitations and shortcomings like everyone else, I find it difficult to forgive myself for revealing these human traits in my daily activities.

If I am to bring this tendency under control, I must understand it as fully as possible. The main root of this unhealthy tendency is fear—fear of being hurt by the disapproval, rejection, or punishment of God. Though this natural fear may be intermingled with the supernatural gift of "fear of the Lord," it deprives me of the interior peace and strength which the supernatural gift would ordinarily bring. Natural fear inclines me to judge my human defects and faults more harshly than they deserve. It makes me eager to win God's mercy by my merciless self-condemnation, and to avoid His punishment by my uncharitable self-disgust and self-punishment. Natural fear tends to interpret every pain, disappointment, and problem as a sign of God's displeasure. This fear makes me expect only the worst from the hands of God. In my need to relieve the inner pressure of this natural fear and self-rejection, I may turn my attention outwardly to the defects and faults of others. This transference may make me feel that I am proving my love of God by hating the sins of others.

RESPOND My Jesus, help me understand the lesson which You tried to teach Your disciples on this occasion. Let me see more clearly the emotions which hinder me from drawing closer to You. I wish to fight my childish fears and my immature behavior with the wisdom of a true adult. Grant me a fuller knowledge of Your teachings, prudence to apply Your truth to my daily living, wisdom to relish Your inspiring principles, and charity to keep me trying in spite of my human failures. Let me love myself as You love me, and help me hate the unreasoning anxieties and unreasonable fears that turn my mind and my heart away from You. Amen.

85. SPIRITUAL BLINDNESS

READ And Jesus said, "For judgment have I come into this world, that they who do not see may see, and they who see may become blind." And some of the Pharisees who were with him heard this, and they said to him, "Are we also blind?" Jesus said to them, "If you were blind, you would not have sin. But now that you say, 'We see,' your sin remains." (John 9:39–41)

REFLECT These teachers of Israel were better prepared than the common people to recognize the signs of the Messias in the person and life of Jesus. And yet, while less educated people advanced in their supernatural power to recognize the true identity of Christ, their instructors became willfully opposed to His divine message. Jesus now pronounces their opposition sinful, since it was born of prejudice and sustained by bad will.

REVIEW Consciously or unconsciously, I can imitate these enemies of Christ in my own way. I can become so set in my personal habits as to be foolishly content with my present degree of self-knowledge, religious practices, and moral conduct. I can be so fixed in my thinking as to resist further growth of mind and spirit.

Whether or not I am aware of it, my life is never at a standstill. On the surface it may seem to go along the same channels year after year. And yet, this is not so. Like the working of erosion on the shores of rivers and streams, the channels of my life are constantly changing. Changes occur in my reflections on the past, my outlook on the present, and my hopes for the future. In the tomorrows yet to come, these changes will make themselves felt. I shall need to see God's hand in the situations that develop, and Christ in the people involved in those situations. I shall have to practice patience, prudence, and charity toward myself and others. Unless I keep my mind alive with religious thinking and my spirit strong with a conscious daily practice of Christ's ideals, I may be more foolish in old age than I was in my youth.

This tragedy does occur in a number of people. They seem to have been more generous with God and men in their younger days. With advancing years, they seem to become less concerned with others, less sensitive to God's nearness, and less aware of Christ's sufferings and personal love. They become more critical of people and more resentful toward God. Instead of advancing in the strength of faith, the cheerfulness of hope, and the sweetness of charity, they become weak against their own feelings, sad with discouragement, and bitter toward others.

RESPOND My God, let me never tire of drawing closer to You throughout my daily life. Help me broaden my knowledge of Your divine Son and deepen my appreciation of Him through the years. Help me enrich each day with a bit of prayer, some brief consideration of His words and example, some small reflection on my daily behavior. Thus do I hope, with Your help, to avoid the spiritual deterioration that comes from stagnant thoughts and fixed attitudes. Thus do I hope to avoid blindness to Jesus, deafness to His voice, and resistance to His graces. Amen.

86. THE GOOD SHEPHERD

READ "I am the good shepherd, and I know mine and mine know me . . . and I lay down my life for my sheep. . . . For this reason the Father loves me, because I lay down my life that I may take it up again. No one takes it from me, but I lay it down of myself. I have the power to lay it down, and I have the power to take it up again. Such is the command I have received from my Father." (John 10:14, 17–18)

REFLECT Once again Jesus reaches out for the hearts of those who, for one reason or another, are slow to believe in Him. To counteract the possible fears and doubts aroused by His recent claim to divinity, He affirms that He has come to help, not harm, to give, not demand, to sacrifice Himself for them far more than they would have to sacrifice themselves for His sake. And all of this would be done in fulfillment of His Father's plan of redemption.

REVIEW Jesus knew how easy it is for men to hear His

words without appreciating His message. He knew that His truth would influence men's lives only in proportion as they tried to understand it more fully, appreciate it more deeply and apply it more faithfully in daily life. Over and over, He repeated His life-giving message, adding greater insight with each repetition. All this would require time for His hearers to recall the old, understand the new, and integrate both into new habits of thinking and living.

How impressed am I with this constant insistence of Christ that He loves me and is deeply concerned with everything that concerns me? He here calls Himself my good shepherd, who knows me to the very core of my being; knows every spontaneous tendency, every feeling and intention, every weakness and effort of mine. He declares that He is ready to lay down His life for me, and that He will do just that when the heavenly Father requires this as a reparation for my sins. I must be very precious to Him if He thinks me worth all this! However, I cannot fully appreciate the height, the depth, the breadth, and the intensity of His love by merely hearing about it, or reading about it. I must reflect on it again and again. Gradually I shall be so impressed by His personal concern for me that my daily attitudes, disposition, and behavior will be inspired by an active gratitude for so perfect a friend.

RESPOND   O Jesus, my good shepherd, may I never wander away from You because of self-disgust or discouragement at my personal limitations, defects and faults. I want to make this daily life of mine a sincere, mature effort to please You in all things. When I fail, may I approach You with confidence in Your understanding and trust in Your desire to help me begin again. Amen.

87. INTERPERSONAL COMPETITION

READ   And they came to Capharnaum. When he was at home, he asked them, "What were you arguing about on the way?" But they kept silence, for on the way they had discussed with one another which of them was the greatest. And sitting down, he called the Twelve and said to them, "If any man wishes to be first, he shall be last of all, and servant of all." (Mark 9:32–34)

REFLECT   Jesus teaches His disciples a lesson in Christian greatness. Instead of surrendering to the natural urge to raise themselves above others, they ought to help others feel their own importance. Thus, they will be imitating their divine Master, Who made Himself the servant of all.

REVIEW   One of the most common problems of everyday life, is that of interpersonal competition. In numberless ways people assert themselves at the expense of others. They contradict, distinguish, criticize, scold, advise, urge, judge, or condemn, with the belief that they are acting purely for the sake of truth or for the benefit of others. And yet, the inner force that drives them, lacks that moderation and consideration that would convince us of this pure intention. We cannot help sensing the presence of other motives which corrupt or control their good intention.

This battle for superiority is a natural development from the real inadequacies of infancy and childhood. In spite of the love and care of adults, every infant has his moments of insecurity and anxiety. Even though, with experience, the growing child gradually learns to help himself in many ways, he continues to depend on others for a long time. Since this dependence subjects him to the domination of others, it is a painful experience. He gradually yearns to feel the self-assurance and superiority which he believes every adult enjoys. This yearning moves him to compete with others in a number of ways.

My emotional need to feel superior accounts for a number of my uncharitable attitudes, unkind words, and inconsiderate actions. My tendency to "put others in second place" is the root of many a defect or sin in my interpersonal relations. In spite of my good will and God's graces, I need more than a mere resolution to be humble, kind, unselfish, helpful, etc. I need to look beyond my attitudes and external behavior, and recognize the root of my defects and faults. With God's help I must see the childishness of my attitudes and the immaturity in my conduct. Fortified with a natural understanding and a supernatural good will, I shall be better able to think as an adult and act as a mature follower of Christ. I shall be more disposed to take the time and practice required for the growth of new habits in my thinking and daily conduct toward others.

RESPOND My Jesus, You made Yourself the servant of all who needed You. Can I rise any higher in true greatness than by reflecting Your divine Self-giving? My greatest obstacle to this greatness is my lack of maturity. Unconsciously I often behave like a child in my attitudes and behavior toward others. Make me aware of the immature emotions that incline me to prove myself better, brighter, stronger, or greater than others. May I desire only to be myself in my relations with You and with others. Amen.

88. SUPERNATURAL CONSIDERATION FOR OTHERS

READ "See that you do not despise one of these little ones; for I tell you, their angels in heaven always behold the face of my Father in heaven. For the Son of Man came to save what was lost. What do you think? If a man have a hundred sheep, and one of them stray, will he not leave the ninety-nine in the mountains, and go in search of the one that has strayed? And if he happen to find it, amen I say to you, he rejoices over it more than over the ninety-nine that did not go astray. Even so, it is not the will of your Father in heaven that a single one of these little ones should perish. (Matt. 18:10–14)

REFLECT   Jesus continues His appeal for good will and reverence toward others. He states that even children are not too little for our consideration. As the good shepherd will go out in search of a single lost sheep, so must I develop a deep appreciation of every person who crosses my path. This appreciation will enable me to resist any unreasonable tendency to favor myself without due consideration for others.

REVIEW   Due to the inborn need to feel safe from upsetting experiences, I may tend to be childishly self-centered in my attitudes, feelings, judgments, and behavior toward others. This immature self-concern must be counterbalanced by supernatural charity. The more I consider the personal love which Jesus has shown me, the more I shall feel inclined to offer Him a return of love. He asks that I return my love through the people around me. Though the help be so little a thing as a simple greeting, He will take it as offered to Himself.

For His sake I must try to understand why I demand that others meet my specifications before I offer them my good will or friendship. As I acquire Christ's understanding and good will toward others, I shall be more disposed to accept people as they are, rather than reject them because of my immature inability to adapt myself to circumstances.

In His command that I show consideration and concern for others, Jesus is reasonable. He knows that I cannot outgrow my immaturity overnight. He does, however, expect me to make a sustained effort to develop this supernatural attitude. I must begin by seeing my own immaturity, acknowledge it without undue shame or blame, and oppose it with a more adult understanding of myself and others. Secondly, I must realize that I am offering good will to others not only because they are my fellow men, but also because they are reflections of God, and brethren of Christ. I must learn to see Jesus in them, so that I may be strong enough to do for His sake what I cannot do for their sake alone.

RESPOND My Jesus, make me so aware of You in my neighbor that I may overcome the pride and prejudices that turn me against others. Help me grow in Your attitude. Let Your understanding enlighten my mind and Your generosity fill my heart, so that I may make other people's lives easier and better by my good will and self-giving. Amen.

89. EXERCISING ONE'S RIGHTS

READ "But if thy brother sin against thee, go and show him his fault, between thee and him alone. If he listen to thee, thou hast won thy brother. But if he do not listen to thee, take with thee one or two more, so that on the word of two or three witnesses every word may be confirmed. And if he refuse to hear them, appeal to the Church, but if he refuse to hear even the Church, let him be to thee as the heathen and the publican." (Matt. 18:15–17)

REFLECT As Jesus spoke to the crowd, He read their hearts. He saw the inevitable question arising within them. How far were they to go in their concern for the welfare of others? What of their God-given urge and right to satisfy their own basic needs? Jesus tells them how to proceed when others are unreasonable and incorrigible in their hostility and aggression.

REVIEW The urge to strike back in self-defense is so necessary to daily human living that God incorporated it into my primary drive to self-preservation. I spontaneously rise to defend myself by holding back, turning away, or offering some positive resistance to those who threaten, offend, or hurt me. In spite of my sincerest efforts to show good will toward others, sooner or later I shall have to cope with some who oppose me in one way or another. I may be obliged to defend myself. Jesus shows me how to seek justice with charity in my heart.

To save their reputation and spare them any unnecessary embarrassment, I may present my case to them in private. If they are unable or unwilling to accept my views or claims, I can seek the assistance of some prudent persons. If this accomplishes nothing, I may seek the aid of legitimate authority. If my opponents refuse to obey authority, I may turn my back on them and leave them to God. I am never obliged to surrender my necessary rights and possessions for the sake of those who have lost all respect for my needs and obligations.

If I feel responsible or guilty when faced with these unpleasant situations, I am behaving immaturely. I must not demand of myself more than I can achieve. There are so many emotional and moral factors influencing the behavior of others, that I shall sometimes be unable to win their good will. I must try to develop enough maturity to accept my limitations in these situations. In spite of the continued bad feelings of these people, I shall be able to go about my business with peace of mind and good wishes for them.

RESPOND My Jesus, even You faced failure in Your effort to help some people find their true advantages and welfare. You did not hesitate to blame them publicly when they attempted to pervert the truth and hinder Your divine mission. Nevertheless, You remained ready to receive those who might yet be helped by a last effort. You called Judas "friend" a moment after he betrayed You. May this divine blend of truth, justice, and charity fill my soul in all my dealings with others. Amen.

90. UNCONSCIOUS MOTIVATION

READ Now it came to pass, when the days had come for him to be taken up, that he steadfastly set his face to go to Jerusalem, and sent messengers before him. And they went and entered a Samaritan town to make ready for him; and they did not receive him, because his face was set for Jerusalem. But when his disciples James and John saw this, they said, "Lord, wilt thou that we bid fire come down from heaven and consume them?" But he turned and rebuked them, saying, "You do not know of what manner of spirit you are; for the Son of Man did not come to destroy men's lives, but to save them." And they went to another village. (Luke 9:51–56)

REFLECT Jesus knew that these disciples were sincere in their zeal to defend His honor, but He pointed out that the predominant source of their anger was not supernatural. Though they were conscious only of the insult cast at their beloved Master, their inclination to exterminate the offenders stemmed from an unconscious natural resentment at being rejected.

REVIEW In spite of my sincere desire and earnest intention to live my daily life in accord with Christ's teaching and example, I am constantly influenced by the spontaneous drives and emotional preferences that lie deep within me. What I intend as a service to God, may be performed imprudently or fanatically. Instead of acting with charity in my heart, I may be dominated by unconscious hostility.

Due to the influences of my early life, some of my inborn drives and emotional tendencies developed less healthily than others. The healthier inclinations help me to cooperate with God's inspirations, whereas the less healthy ones make this cooperation more difficult and even repulsive. Though I am accountable to God only for what lies within my conscious control, I do have some obligation to diminish, as far as possible, the power of those inner tendencies which incline me toward sin. With God's help, I must daily endeavor to recognize these deep emotional forces, face them without undue shame, blame, or disgust, and strive patiently to build a more adult attitude toward myself, my life, God, and others.

RESPOND   My Jesus, at times I respond to the unpleasant situations of my daily life with the immature attitude and behavior of Your apostles. Instead of seeing the deeper, childish emotions that move me, I either try to defend my behavior with false reasoning or I crush my spirit with undue shame, blame, and discouragement. Help me understand the deep insecurity, anxiety, fears, and doubts that move me to anger and hate. Since I am no longer the helpless child I once was, I no longer have reason to see a major crisis in every misunderstanding and adversity that occurs. I must expect some human error and weakness within myself and others, and accept interpersonal misunderstandings, tensions, and friction as part of ordinary living. Only then shall I be able to live and let live. Amen.

91. LABORING FOR THE LORD

READ Now after this the Lord appointed seventy-two others, and sent them forth two by two before him into every town and place where he himself was about to come. And he said to them, "The harvest indeed is great, but the laborers are few. Pray therefore to the Lord of the harvest to send forth laborers into his harvest." (Luke 10:1–2)

REFLECT The twelve apostles had been given a special place in Christ's work of redemption, but they could not perform their assignment alone. They would need many helpers. This is Christ's first call for assistants to His apostles.

REVIEW Regardless of my station in life, I have a commission to labor in the Lord's harvest. I received this commission in my baptism. In that sacrament God joined me to Christ in a supernatural manner, and enjoined on me the privilege and obligation of fulfilling Christ's will through the duties and opportunities of my daily life. In confirmation I was appointed to live my life as a soldier of Christ. Jesus expects me to develop His thinking through His teachings, sacraments, and grace, and extend His earthly mission of redemption by my prayers, good example, and active good will toward others.

Too often I tend to think that there is nothing outstanding about my person or daily activities. I even consider my occupations purely self-centered, since I work mainly for my personal needs and interests. Christ wants me to believe differently of myself. He teaches through His Church that I am not alone against my problems, burdens, and difficulties. Christ faces them with me. My work is a continuation of His daily work in Nazareth. My ideals are to reflect His personal example and teaching. My daily purpose is to include His messianic purpose to draw all men to God.

Like natural life, this supernatural life of mine is mostly hidden within me. Few of its effects are visible to the eye. Only God sees how my daily routine, disposition, and intention help souls in need of supernatural grace. The more I know of Christ's truth, the more fully shall I appreciate my dignity as a Christian and my power as a member of His Church. In spite of my feelings, Christ walks, works, suffers, and lives in me. As God was glorified in the daily life of His Son, so is Christ glorified in my daily life. This is the divine plan of redemption. Though there is no other name by which men may be redeemed, He granted me the privilege of helping Him in His divine mission.

RESPOND My Jesus, grant me a growing knowledge, understanding, and appreciation of the glorious privilege You bestowed on me in my baptism and confirmation. By Your union with me, You have granted my limited human activities the power to inspire good desires in others and to obtain for them the supernatural strength to draw closer to God. May I be ever aware of this holy privilege and dignity as I go about my daily activities. Amen.

92. DAILY CONTACT WITH JESUS

READ "Come to me, all you who labor and are burdened, and I will give you rest. Take my yoke upon you, and learn from me, for I am meek and humble of heart; and you will find rest for your souls. For my yoke is easy, and my burden light." (Matt. 11:28–30)

REFLECT Jesus reveals the secret to success in my Christian vocation. Though His grace helps me live my daily life, I shall need rest and renewal of spirit from time to time. He tells me to seek this spiritual refreshment directly from Him. As I develop His virtues of meekness and humility I shall find His service becoming less difficult.

REVIEW Christ is the soul of my supernatural life. From His divine merits flow the graces that will enlighten my mind and incline my will to fulfill His intention in my personal life. He will make His presence felt in me through the supernatural graces He bestows on me. He will continue to live, labor, and pray within the narrow limits of my personal being and individual circumstances. In order to refresh and renew my supernatural energies, I shall need to make conscious contact with Him through reading, reflection, prayer, and sacraments.

Two great obstacles in my daily following of Christ are my natural fear and hate. These two emotions have numberless degrees, and each degree is called by a different name. Consequently, I am often unaware of their influence on my daily behavior. Anxiety and fear are aroused by a sense of impending danger or harm. These emotions either incline me to avoid the trouble or incite me to anger and resistance. Fears arising from ignorance or misunderstanding are overcome by the virtue of humility. The humble man sees things in their right perspective and estimates their real advantage or disadvantage. He perceives the folly of his unwarranted fears, and finds courage in the support and companionship of Christ. Thus he is able to relax from the tensions created by these fears, and obtains peace by bringing Jesus into his problems.

Humility will bring me a readiness to accept reality, and to adjust to the facts of daily life. It will help give me strength to embrace the yoke of Christ's leadership and bear the burden of His commandments. The virtue of meekness is a result of that strength. I shall no longer be aroused to unjustifiable anger, resentment, and hate, because I shall no longer be unduly afraid of the people or situations involved in my daily life.

RESPOND O Jesus, meek and humble of heart, many of my present fears are remnants of my childhood anxieties. A number of my present dislikes, resentments, and interpersonal frictions are due to my hidden fears. Help me grow in humility and meekness, so that I may cease to be a child in my emotional tendencies, and grow in those virtues which are now blocked by these unwarranted anxieties and fears. Amen.

93. THE LAW OF CHARITY

READ And behold, a certain lawyer got up to test him, saying, "Master, what must I do to gain eternal life?" But he said to him, "What is written in the Law?" He answered and said, *"Thou shalt love the Lord thy God with thy whole heart, and with thy whole soul, and with thy whole strength, and with thy whole mind; and thy neighbor as thyself."* And he said to him, "Thou hast answered rightly; do this and thou shalt live." (Luke 10:25–28)

REFLECT Since God is man's highest Good, man's first obligation is to love God above all else. Man's second obligation is that he love all reflections of God, according to their proper relationship to his daily life. Since human beings are God's fullest reflection on earth, each man is obliged to love himself and his fellow men in accordance with the laws of natural reason and supernatural charity. Jesus urges all men to develop the same kind of concern and consideration for others as they feel for themselves.

REVIEW Love in general is an impulse or tendency of the soul toward what is perceived as good. This is the most powerful drive in every man, and it is constantly influencing men, with or without their awareness. From his first moments of life, man tends toward whatever brings him satisfaction. The unreasoning child feels these things as good, and he soon learns to fear and hate whatever disturbs his contentment. In adult life, this infantile idea of good and bad is not entirely eliminated by man's adult ability to think on a higher level. Though he knows by reason and faith that God is his highest Good, he often finds himself attracted to lesser benefits, which may satisfy him here and now.

Why this inner conflict, which is the root of many a sin? The unfavorable influences and unfortunate experiences of the past have left their mark upon his mind, emotions, and nervous system. Through the years, he has developed preferences, prejudices, and habits which tend to influence his religious attitudes and moral behavior. In spite of his best intentions and efforts to cooperate with God's graces, he continues to feel the downward tug of his unreasoning drives, misguided tendencies, and fixed habits.

The more I understand and appreciate the above facts, the less will I shy away from this commandment to love God and my neighbor. As I consider my unintended failures and unwanted reluctance to practice charity, I shall accept my contrary tendencies as traces of original sin and past experience, rather than proofs of bad will. I do want to love God above all else, and I am sincere in my desire to love Him also in my neighbor. I must never forget that love is more than a mere feeling. It is an intelligent appreciation of God's goodness, not only in Himself, but also in His created images. As long as I try to fulfill His holy Will as best I can, I must believe, in spite of my repeated failures, that my love is acceptable and satisfactory to Him.

RESPOND My God, my highest Good, I desire to love You above every created thing. Help me prove the purity of my desire by a sincere effort to please You in my daily behavior toward others. When my feelings overcome me and my mind turns away from You, let me not despise myself without cause. May I never confuse my unmalicious weaknesses with my real sins. Grant that I may offer You a sincere love in this life, and enjoy the full return of Your love in the next. Amen.

94. THE BETTER PART

READ   Now it came to pass as they were on their journey, that he entered a certain village; and a woman named Martha welcomed him to her house. And she had a sister called Mary, who also seated herself at the Lord's feet, and listened to his word. But Martha was busy about much serving. And she came up and said, "Lord, is it no concern of thine that my sister has left me to serve alone? Tell her therefore to help me." But the Lord answered and said to her, "Martha, Martha, thou art anxious and troubled about many things; and yet only one thing is needful. Mary has chosen the best part, and it will not be taken away from her." (Luke 10:38–42)

REFLECT   In these few words Jesus gave a profound lesson to Martha and to the world. The depth of His wise counsel left her more puzzled than enlightened for the moment. Later, however, as she pondered over His words, she may have seen the solution to her anxious manner of facing life's daily duties.

REVIEW   There is many a Martha in this world. These people are sincere, honest, and self-sacrificing in the performance of their daily duties. And yet, they lack that calm self-possession that characterizes the soul at peace with God. They seem to contradict Christ's statement that His yoke is easy and His burden light. There is a great deal of misunderstanding and uneasiness in these good people. They see themselves and God through the distorted vision of their own emotional fears and doubts.

They labor under the strain of trying to alleviate their self-disgust, win the approval of others, and avoid God's rejection and punishment.

They need to develop some of Mary's sense of values. She saw in Jesus the love, the wisdom, and the strength she needed, to face life's responsibilities and problems. As a result of her contact with Him, she was able to place a wiser emphasis upon the various duties and good things of this world. At the feet of Christ she found freedom from undue fears and liberation from useless anxiety. She could now live her life at peace with herself because she knew that Christ understood her and accepted her as she was. Confident of His love, she felt no need to win His approval. She could perform her daily tasks at her normal human pace, instead of nervously laboring with the anxiety and nervousness of her sister.

In my own way, I too am subject to some measure of insecurity and anxiety with God. I would do well to become more aware of the mistaken notions and unreasonable attitudes that prevent me from enjoying a greater closeness with Jesus and a calmer service of God. The better I come to know Jesus and appreciate His divine understanding and acceptance, the more shall I lose the anxiety of Martha and acquire the spiritual contentment of Mary.

RESPOND My Lord, teach me to look upon the people and activities involved in my daily life without undue anxiety and tension. Make me reasonably content with my life and glad to offer it to You. I desire to fulfill my duties without immature demands of a flawless performance. Let me find my contentment in the conviction that You gladly accept my intentions and efforts as proof of my sincerity. Amen.

95. RESISTANCE TO GRACE

READ And Jesus was walking in the temple, in Solomon's portico. The Jews therefore gathered round him, and said to him, "How long dost thou keep us in suspense? If thou art the Christ, tell us openly." Jesus answered them, "I tell you and you do not believe. The works that I do in the name of my Father, these bear witness concerning me. But you do not believe because you are not of my sheep. My sheep hear my voice, and I know them and they follow me. And I give them everlasting life; and they shall never perish . . ." (John 10:23–28)

REFLECT On the surface these men seem to be making a sincere request that Christ reveal His true identity. And yet, so firmly were they set against Him that they had become deaf to His words and blind to His miraculous powers. They saw only what they wanted to see and listened only for what might be used against Him. Jesus describes this behavior as a resistance to God's grace.

REVIEW The problem of resistance to God's grace is a complex one. Even though every man tends toward his own good, he usually seeks it in those forms to which he has become accustomed through past experience. Since novelty and change require some inconvenience and effort, men are usually reluctant to leave old habits and familiar things. Moreover, every man feels an unwillingness to face unpleasant reality and disagreeable facts about himself. Human nature spontaneously resists what is new or unpleasant because it fears the upsetting sense of insecurity and anxiety aroused by such things. When God's grace inclines a man toward self-improvement, it is met by nature's resistance. This resistance does not always appear in the form of conscious reluctance. Nature often fights grace, through feelings of fatigue or drowsiness, through distractions, or even through an intense preoccupation with other interests and activities.

In my own way, I too have my measure of deafness and blindness to Christ. Some of His teachings never really become a part of my daily thinking and behavior. Some of my most glaring defects are seen by everyone but me. My good will is limited by my immature attitudes and childish responses to the circumstances, situations, and people associated with my daily life. Through my personal mannerisms I protect myself from possible human hurts, shut out unpleasant facts and disagreeable reality, and often limit as far as possible my religious duties and moral responsibilities.

RESPOND My Jesus, help me to see You as You really are, and not as I fear You may be. You are so reasonable in Your demands, so understanding toward my human weaknesses, so forgiving when I sin. When You do not conform to my expectations, it is because my expectations are mistaken or malicious. Only reality, facts, and truth can guide me safely toward eternal life. Grant me the knowledge, willingness, and strength to adjust to the facts and truth which govern my daily life. Amen.

96. THE TRUE SOURCE OF BLESSEDNESS

READ Now it came to pass as he was saying these things, that a certain woman from the crowd lifted up her voice and said to him, "Blessed is the womb that bore thee and the breasts that nursed thee." But he said, "Rather, blessed are they who hear the word of God and keep it." (Luke 11:27–28)

REFLECT Jesus seized this opportunity to lay stress and

emphasis on the very soul of His message. Man's greatest happiness will come from his fulfillment of God's holy Will.

REVIEW The state of blessedness is such a fulfillment of man's highest powers and yearnings, that he will forever enjoy a contentment far beyond his fondest hopes. Jesus never tried to describe the blessedness of heaven because there is nothing on earth that might serve as a basis for comparison. So full, so rich, so all-satisfying is the heavenly blessedness that man's imagination is inadequate to picture it, and words are useless to describe it. Long or monotonous as eternity may seem to men on earth, it will never exhaust the happiness or dim the joy of the blessed in heaven.

In my own limited way, I reach for an all-satisfying contentment, happiness, and joy even in this earthly life. Every drive, urge, desire, preference, and effort is but a feeble expression of my yearning for self-fulfillment. I constantly seek the satisfaction of my appetites and fulfillment of my desires in what I think, say, and do throughout the day. Jesus tells me that this earthly contentment is but a shadow of the perfect contentment that God has prepared for me in heaven. He advises me to lift my vision and yearnings higher by faith, reach for eternal self-fulfillment and contentment through hope, and live for the all-satisfying friendship and love of God in heaven through charity.

Jesus tells me that my way to the heavenly blessedness is God's holy Will. By word and example He tries to show me not only the goodness and lovableness of God, but also the goodness which He has bestowed upon me through His work of redemption. The more I understand God through the Person and example of Jesus, the more easily shall I overcome my unreasoning fears, and the doubts about God's approval and acceptance of me, control my unreasonable hatred of my normal human imperfections, grow out of my childish expectations of more than I can achieve, and destroy my immature disgust and discouragement at my unintended failures.

RESPOND   My Jesus, Image of the Father, with the inspiration of Your example and the assistance of Your grace, I embrace the Father's will. Help me see it not through my emotions and imagination, but through the eyes of informed faith. Through the teachings of Your Holy Church and the strength of Your life-giving sacraments I hope to see each action and situation of this day as a part of my path to heaven. Amen.

97. SPECIALIZING IN RELIGION

READ   Now after he had spoken, a Pharisee asked him to dine with him. And he went in and reclined at table. But the Pharisee began to ponder and ask himself why he had not washed before dinner. But the Lord said to him, "Now you Pharisees clean the outside of the cup and dish, but within you are full of robbery and wickedness. Foolish ones! did not he who made the outside make the inside too? Nevertheless, give that which remains as alms; and behold, all things are clean to you. But woe to you Pharisees! because you pay tithes on mint and rue and every herb, and disregard justice and the love of God. But these things you ought to have done, while not leaving the others undone." (Luke 11:37-42)

REFLECT   These men had learned to specialize in certain virtues and religious practices, while neglecting others. Jesus accuses them of selecting a convenient religious pattern for themselves, and then considering this pattern as God's will for everyone. Jesus denounces their virtues and practices as a sham, since they were empty of justice, charity, and consideration for their fellow men.

REVIEW The tendency to specialize in certain virtues and religious practices is not to be condemned so long as one does not willfully neglect or minimize other virtues. Some people lean more easily toward prayer, others toward external works, others toward sympathy and service to their neighbor, and others toward solitude. As there is a variety of religious apostolates within Christ's Church, so is each man permitted to develop his supernatural life upon the natural foundation of his character and personality.

The danger comes when one measures the moral worth of others by the norm of his personal preferences and emotional prejudices. He may be critical of those who seem too carefree, too relaxed, or too ready to make excuses for the apparent defects and faults of others. He does not consider that God Himself made each person different from others. He may even be unable to accept the teachings of those qualified to interpret the mind of Christ's Church, when their teaching does not conform to his personal pattern of religious behavior. If he is in a position of authority, he may so confuse his subjects as to make them feel hopelessly incapable of pleasing God.

I share the common lot of every man. I too have my personal religious preferences and prejudices. Part of my daily self-purification must consist in correcting the undesirable attitudes which these emotional leanings create in me. I am not God, but a human being, woefully limited by my ignorance, my distorted views, and my errors in judgment and behavior. I can only follow my lights in accordance with the teachings and authority of Christ's Church, but I must leave all undue criticism and judgment of others in the hands of God.

RESPOND My Jesus, may I never hold others back or turn them away from You by my mistaken ideas or distorted view of You. Help me understand You so well and love You so ardently that I may reflect Your wisdom, understanding, and acceptance in my daily relations with others.

Thus I shall draw them closer to You more by what I am than by what I say. Amen.

98. FEAR OF PEOPLE

READ "But I say to you, my friends; Do not be afraid of those who kill the body, and after that have nothing more that they can do. But I will show you whom you shall be afraid of; be afraid of him who, after he has killed, has power to cast into hell. . . . Are not five sparrows sold for two farthings? And yet not one of them is forgotten before God. Yes, the very hairs of your head are all numbered. Therefore do not be afraid, you are of more value than many sparrows." (Luke 12:4–7)

REFLECT A number of people in the crowd desired to declare themselves openly in favor of Christ. However, their fear of reprisal from the men in power prevented them from doing so. Jesus admonishes them to face facts. They ought to overcome their fear of men's injustice by an intelligent fear of God's justice.

REVIEW From earliest childhood every man has a natural need to feel understood and accepted for what he is; approved and defended in his legitimate spontaneous self-expression; and needed and wanted by those involved in his daily life. When these emotional needs become so overwhelming that one's peace of mind and power of self-determination are disturbed, then these needs are no longer healthy. They arouse such a deep sense of insecurity and anxiety, that one feels compelled to be and act as others expect or demand. He will be unable to be himself, and may even lose all feeling for himself. His ideas, feelings, desires, and decisions will be dominated by his fear of emotional hurt or physical harm.

What spiritual writers call "human respect" is nothing else but a surrender to this interpersonal insecurity and anxiety. Many a person has been deterred from following the standards and ideals of Christ, because of his fear of the open displeasure or indirect disapproval of others. They are afraid of ridicule, criticism, physical harm, or rejection in any form. I too have my fear of human disapproval and rejection. Jesus wants me to be myself within the bounds of reason and charity. When human offenses or injuries are directed toward me because of my religious principles, Jesus wants me to stand by His teachings and follow His example. Better to suffer this unjust punishment of men than the just punishment of God.

RESPOND My Jesus, make me so aware of Your presence in my life that I may never be overwhelmed by the human threats and hurts which occur in my daily life. As long as I try to please You, I must necessarily offend those who do not want to be reminded of You. I shall try to avoid all unnecessary offenses to others, but I will not do so by compromising Your principles. I hope to prefer God's will to the demands and expectations of the worldly minded. Amen.

99. USELESS ANXIETY

READ "Therefore I say to you, do not be anxious for your life, what you shall eat; nor yet for your body, what you shall put on. . . . Consider the ravens: they neither sow nor reap, they have neither storeroom nor barn; yet God feeds them. Of how much more value are you than they! But which of you by being anxious about it can add to his stature a single cubit? Therefore if you are not able to do even a very little thing, why are you anxious concerning the rest?" (Luke 12:22–26)

REFLECT   Jesus is not speaking of intelligent self-concern, which arouses people to plan and work toward the solution of their problems. He is simply warning us against useless anxiety, which aggravates our problems by tiring the mind and wearing down our nervous energy. He urges us to see not only our limited human resources, but also the wisdom, power, and fatherly concern of God.

REVIEW   No man can solve all his problems all the time. At one time or another, everyone has reason to be unsure of himself or uneasy about some situation. When this happens to me, I can react as a child by letting my feelings overwhelm my thinking and judgment, or respond as an adult by trying to adjust my emotions to reality. The mature man looks at all the facts. He sees not only the natural solutions at his disposal, but also the place which God holds in his daily life. If I am immature, I shall be incapable of accepting inevitable disappointments or privations without shame, self-blame, or unreasoning hostility toward others. Even when matters are going smoothly, I shall be vaguely uneasy about possible problems or disappointments. Though I may be unaware of my anxiety, I shall feel tense, nervous, hypersensitive, or over-cautious.

Jesus urges me to face the full truth about my daily life. Besides my personal abilities, my present opportunities, and the sincere concern of my relatives and friends, I also have the fatherly love and assistance of God. Relying on all these remedies to my daily problems, I have more reasons for interior peace than for surrendering to my natural anxiety. Moreover, since anxiety does me no good, but only adds to my problems, I ought to strive for enough common sense and supernatural trust in God to leave matters in His hands. As I become less childish and more mature, I shall also become intelligently angry at my useless fears and destructive anxieties. This healthy anger will urge me to do my human best to solve my problems, and my supernatural best to let God arrange the final outcome.

RESPOND My Jesus, help me be deeply impressed by the harmfulness of useless anxiety. Let me rise in anger against this unreasoning, misguided self-concern which breeds so much needless suffering, wastes so much of my energy, destroys my peace of mind, and saps my spiritual strength. May I be mature enough to direct this anger not against myself, or people, or God, but only against this destructive enemy, my own useless anxiety. Amen.

100. SECURITY AND CONTENTMENT

READ "Do not be afraid, little flock, for it has pleased your Father to give you the kingdom. . . . Make for yourselves purses that do not grow old, a treasure unfailing in heaven, where neither thief draws near nor moth destroys. For where your treasure is, there also will your heart be." (Luke 12:32–34)

REFLECT Jesus urges us to seek first things first in our earthly quest for security and contentment. Without neglecting our natural needs, we are to use earthly goods and advantages in such a way as to merit the eternal security and all-satisfying contentment of heaven. Under the guidance of His Church, we are to grow in the knowledge, appreciation, and acquisition of spiritual riches, and thereby overcome our blind unreasoning tendency to seek security and contentment exclusively in the perishable satisfactions of this world.

REVIEW The good things of this world were created by God to help man satisfy his needs and develop his earthly life in accordance with reason and faith. Man's dependence on these things is natural, and it can be elevated by God's grace to a supernatural plane. My only real problem is how to become master of my earthly needs, instead of being their slave. My inborn drive to self-preservation inclines me toward whatever may seem to satisfy my sense of security and contentment. As long as I can think clearly, I may be able to control any unreasonable inclinations. When, however, my need for security is unbalanced by uncontrollable anxiety, my emotions will dominate my thinking and overpower my will.

In this state of mind, I may reach out for help like a drowning man grasping at a straw. I may seek my security in earthly advantages, without regard for justice or charity. My misguided need to feel safe and content, can even make me forget God's wisdom and commandments. In so far as these tendencies are conscious and within control, I am accountable for them. However, even when I am not guilty of them, they constitute obstacles to my lasting peace of mind and spiritual progress. Being the slave of my earthly needs, I cannot see my eternal advantages too clearly nor reach too firmly for my spiritual welfare.

RESPOND   My Jesus, King of wisdom, teach me to look upon my earthly needs with Your full view. Help me see them as the imperfect, temporary satisfactions they are. Let me dispose of things I do not need and use with due moderation those I do need. Make me so keenly sensitive to the desirability of heaven that I may be strong against the unreasonable urgings of useless anxiety. In my efforts for contentment and peace, let me not reach for earthly straws but for the firm life line of Your truth. Only in heaven shall I possess the all-satisfying security which my nature craves. Amen.

101.   DISSENSION FOR CHRIST

READ   "Do you think that I came to give peace upon the earth? No, I tell you, but division. For henceforth in one house five shall be divided, three against two, and two against three. They will be divided, father against son and son against his father; mother against daughter and daughter against the mother . . ." (Luke 12:51–53)

REFLECT   Jesus has promised interior peace to those who embrace His truth and follow His example. However, He also warns us that our loyalty to Him will bring us the resentment and hostility of those who find His teachings repugnant. We must therefore keep our peace of mind when this interpersonal friction occurs. We cannot always live at peace with both Christ and His enemies.

REVIEW   A number of people see religion and moral goodness as a disapproval, a restraint, or condemnation of their personal life. This may be so because of emotional developments over which they have no control. Or again, it may be due to some measure of moral weakness or bad will. Whatever the reason, I shall feel the disagreeable consequences when my religious effort becomes a source of annoyance to them. No matter how secretly I may try to follow Christ's principles and ideals, I shall be noticed sooner or later. These people will resent me for the uneasiness they feel at the sight or mention of me. They will blame me for it, when actually it is caused by their own conscience or emotional sense of guilt. They will seek to regain their self-possession by finding fault with me, or making me suffer in some way.

Jesus warns me against this inevitable interpersonal friction. It is part of my following of Christ. As he was opposed by the worldly minded, so too must I.

If I am too immature to live without the acceptance, approval, or companionship of these people, I shall offer a lesser service to Christ for their sake. On the other hand, I may go to the other extreme and give unnecessary provocation by my defiant attitude or behavior. Such conduct would prove either my immaturity or a sinful pride. I am not to maintain my self-esteem by criticism or judgment of others. The mature spiritual man has no need to defend himself from the harmless smallness of others, nor is he inclined to pass judgment on their guilt. He leaves all judgment to God and seeks his own contentment in the friendship of Christ.

RESPOND Jesus, my King, teach me to expect dissension and adversity as a normal part of human living. Then I will not be prone to childish retaliation when I suffer from the immaturity or malice of others. As a true disciple of Yours, I wish to exercise only good will toward others for Your sake. Even when I can see no reason for excusing their conduct, I must remember that You may see a thousand excusing causes where I see none. Grant me the wisdom to let You be God, and the strength to keep my place as an imperfect human being. Amen.

102. HEALTH AND HOLINESS

READ And behold there was a woman who for eighteen years had had a sickness caused by a spirit; and she was bent over and utterly unable to look upwards. When Jesus saw her, he called her to him and said to her: "Woman, thou art delivered from thy infirmity." And he laid his hands upon her, and instantly she was made straight, and glorified God. (Luke 13:10–13)

REFLECT The gospel narrative does not say that this woman was possessed by this evil spirit, but only that it was the cause of her bodily infirmity. At the word and touch of Christ, her body felt a return of health and energy. As she straightened up, her soul poured out gratitude and praise to God.

REVIEW Having contended with human nature since the creation of Adam, Satan is well versed in the art of temptation. He has found that the easiest way to a man's soul is through his body. Bodily appetites, needs, and habits strongly incline me toward comfort, satisfaction and contentment. My drive to self-preservation is aroused by discomfort and indisposition of the body. This drive moves me to reach for whatever may restore my sense of well-being and contentment. Moreover, since my brain and nervous system play an active part in the movements of my emotions and imagination, the devil can more easily tempt me when my body is indisposed or low in energy. I am then more inclined to be irritable, anxious, impatient, suspicious, unkind, and even unjust.

When Satan is unable to tempt me by a direct attack on my imagination or emotions, he may do so indirectly by arousing the bodily feelings that usually accompany my sinful attitudes toward others. Thus, in spite of my sincere desire to pay no attention to an occasion of sin, I may experience physical feelings of fear, anger, or hate. I must learn to tolerate these feelings with the conviction that I am not accountable for what I feel, but only for what I intend.

With this knowledge I may more easily relax in spite of my feelings. Instead of straining tensely and nervously against my unwanted physical feelings, uninvited phantasies, and unintended emotions, I must assert my spiritual convictions, believe in my good intentions, and conserve my bodily energies. I shall thereby lessen the danger of fatigue, depression, sadness, and discouragement.

RESPOND Lord, since it is easier to serve You in health than in sickness, help me to beware of Satan's attempts to overcome my soul by weakening my body. Teach me to have a proper respect for the reasonable warnings of my body. Let me take necessary nourishment, relaxation, and rest with an intelligent respect for my body's legitimate needs. A sound mind can help me more fully in a sound body than in a tense or sick one. As the woman in this gospel glorified God when she was freed of her ailment, so let me improve my spiritual efforts by safeguarding the health of my body. Amen.

103. THE SEED AND THE LEAVEN

READ He said therefore, "What is the kingdom of God like, and to what shall I liken it? It is like a grain of mustard seed, which a man took and cast into his own garden; and it grew and became a large tree, and the birds of the air dwelt in its branches."

And again he said, "To what shall I liken the kingdom of God? It is like leaven, which a woman took and buried in three measures of flour, until all of it was leavened." (Luke 13:18–21)

REFLECT Many times during His public life Jesus repeated this basic truth in an effort to impress it indelibly upon His followers. The kingdom of God, both the visible Church and the interior life of each member, was to achieve the amazing proportions of the mustard plant through a process as hidden and marvelous as the leavening of dough.

REVIEW During a mission, retreat, special religious function or moment of grace, many a man obtains an inspiring insight into the supernatural glory and joy possible to him. With sincere intentions many resolve to change their future behavior. And yet, with the passage of time, these sincere intentions and earnest resolutions cool and settle down to a mediocre level.

This happens so often because people do not let their theoretical knowledge enter into their practical thinking. They see how the young spend the first quarter of their lives, if not more, preparing for the responsibilities and accomplishments of their adult life. The most ordinary human life requires a good deal of preparation, training, repeated efforts, overcoming of obstacles, learning wisdom from mistakes and prudence from failures. Yet, in the matter of religious development or renewal of spirit, many people seem to forget the ordinary procedure of mental and moral growth. In effect, they demand a miracle . . . a sudden achievement of knowledge without the necessary learning; an instant acquisition of a new attitude, outlook and judgment, without the aid of time and experience; the immediate elimination of undesirable old habits, without the patient development of new ones.

RESPOND My Jesus, grant that this lesson may not be lost on me. I must understand that You respect the laws of growth and progress. In arousing my good will, You are merely inviting me to take the first of many steps along a surer path to eternal life. Each day will require many more steps, as I try to see my earthly life through Your eyes and live it under Your divine leadership. As the tiny mustard seed needs to be cultivated, protected from weeds, insects, and animals, and nourished by sunshine and water, so must I develop Your graces with a growing knowledge, a persistent practice, a humble acceptance of setbacks, and a stubborn refusal to compromise my principles or abandon my daily effort. Amen.

104. JERUSALEM, JERUSALEM

READ "Jerusalem, Jerusalem, thou who killest the prophets, and stonest those who are sent to thee! how often would I have gathered thy children together, as a hen gathers her young under her wings, but thou wouldst not!" (Luke 13:34)

REFLECT This was one of those rare appeals of the heart

of Christ to those who would not let Him help them. Here He speaks not as a judge, but as a parent whose only thought is to protect the children. He refuses to force their will, but endeavors to draw them by appealing to their need of Him, and His desire to assist them.

REVIEW How often I too am blind to the real Christ! In spite of the books I have read, the sermons I have heard, and the lessons I have received concerning His infinite goodness, understanding, power, and personal concern for me, I continue to keep aloof from Him. It is not so much malice as my emotional habits that hold me back.

I am so used to thinking of what I am not, ought to be, have not done, should have done, or may yet do in some distant tomorrow! I simply do not appreciate the fact that Jesus loves me as I am right now. Though He does not approve of my sins and urges me to oppose whatever may lead me toward evil, at the same time, He is not as discontent with my natural, inculpable, unintended defects and shortcomings as I am.

Due to past experience, I have learned to see everything in black and white. My thoughts, words, and behavior are considered either bad or good. This is wrong thinking, since each thought, word or action has its percentage of goodness, of possible improvement, and of natural limitation or faultiness. I usually become so distracted by the imperfection or fault in my behavior that I overlook the goodness in it. I am like the pupil who hates himself for having achieved only an eighty-five or ninety on a test. I must learn to strive for one hundred percent without straining beyond my strength or forgetting to thank God for the percentage I achieve.

The truth of the matter is that I do not intend to turn my back on Jesus. Even when I offend Him by sin, I frequently do so through ignorance, inadvertence, or momentary weakness. If I have ever offended Him in a serious way, He asks only that I repent, and prove my sincerity by a constant effort against sin in the future. As long as I am a man of good will, I must regard the above words of Christ as a personal request for my friendship and loyalty.

RESPOND My Jesus, may I take these words of Yours to heart, and come to You? Grant me a mature acceptance of my personal limitations, an unconquerable trust in Your sincere desire to bring me to my highest welfare, a firm confidence in Your understanding of my weaknesses, an immovable faith in Your pardon of my sins, and a deep gratitude for Your goodness and love. Amen.

105. FOOLISH PRIDE

READ But he also spoke a parable to those invited, observing how they were choosing the first places at table, and he said to them, "When thou art invited to a wedding feast, do not recline in the first place, lest perhaps one more distinguished than thou have been invited by him, and he who invited thee and him come and say to thee, 'Make room for this man'; and then thou begin with shame to take the last place. But when thou art invited, go and recline in the last place; that when he who invited thee comes in, he may say to thee, 'Friend, go up higher!' . . . For everyone who exalts himself shall be humbled, and he who humbles himself shall be exalted." (Luke 14:7–11)

REFLECT Jesus tries to make His hearers aware of their tendency to appear superior to others. He warns them that they may be forced by circumstances to recognize the superiority of someone else. If, however, they make no pretentions, they can never be humiliated.

REVIEW Since my childhood I have felt a natural uneasiness about my ability to take care of myself in some situations, and a natural dislike for my real or imagined inferiority to others. In my need to live free of self-disgust and other people's power to make me uneasy, I tried to believe myself independent of others, self-sufficient in my ordinary needs, and superior to others in most things. Consciously or unconsciously, I acquired the habit of competing with others in a thousand ways. This interior struggle for a sense of peace with myself and security with others, is so much a part of me now, that I am often unaware of it. It is frequently present in my attitudes, moods, desires, thoughts, words, and actions. Thus, I may be reluctant to confess my sins because of my inner sense of self-disgust, of hopelessness against my repeated fall into the same sins, or my fear of what the priest may think of me.

Jesus tells me to recognize my talents, virtues, limitations, and faults realistically. The mature man is more interested in facts than in imagination or feelings. With gratitude to God for my gifts, with mature acceptance of my inevitable limitations, and with consideration for the emotional needs of others, I ought to avoid any tendency to prove myself better than others. Even with God's grace, this is not easy to achieve unless I first attain an intelligent emotional contentment with myself. Only then can I gradually become at ease in my interpersonal relations. I shall no longer tend to envy the success or good fortune of others, or to assert myself against them in my attitudes or behavior.

RESPOND My Jesus, You made Yourself the servant of all for my sake. Through this self-abasement, You made reparation for my sins of vanity and pride, and You showed me the way to a lasting interior peace. Help me absorb Your words and example so thoroughly, that I may gradually overcome my immature tendency to appear superior to others. May I eventually be convinced that I need not be afraid or ashamed to be myself. Even in my efforts to improve myself, let me do so intelligently and peacefully. Amen.

106. A HOLY HATRED

READ "If anyone comes to me and does not hate his father and mother, and wife and children, and brothers and sisters, yes, and even his own life, he cannot be my disciple. And he who does not carry his cross and follow me, cannot be my disciple." (Luke 14:26–27)

REFLECT In this shocking remark, Jesus states once again the first rule of all reasonable and virtuous living. Since God is man's first need, man must place Him first in his set of values. Since God is man's highest fulfillment, satisfaction, and joy, man must never permit any created being to separate him from God by sin.

REVIEW To people who think more through their emotions and imagination, this declaration of Jesus seems cruel and harsh. And yet, if we consider the natural life of man, we find that his love for his parents, brothers, and sisters, undergoes a change as he proceeds from childhood to adulthood. During the years of his greatest dependency, he feels an exclusive attachment to his immediate family. As he grows into manhood, his love extends to others. Eventually he develops such a love for his wife and children, that if parents, or brothers, or sisters interfere with his marital love, he will drift from the family of which he was once a part.

If this is so in one's natural inclination to his self-fulfillment on earth, how much more should it be true in seeking one's eternal self-fulfillment? The more I grow in my acquaintance with God, the more will I refuse to let anyone on earth come between Him and me. As I would oppose anyone who interferes with my earthly contentment, so must I be ready to oppose anyone who endangers my eternal happiness. The security, love, and happiness I find in my earthly family is but a faint spark of the security, love, and happiness I shall one day possess in God's heavenly family.

RESPOND Lord, may I never be ungrateful to my dear ones and friends for the love they have shown me and the help they have given me. However, let me not remain a child in my attachment to them. If they are ever inconsiderate enough to interfere with my loyalty to You and endanger my eternal welfare, make me wise enough and strong enough to leave them rather than You. Amen.

107. THE LOST SHEEP

READ "What man of you having a hundred sheep, and losing one of them, does not leave the ninety-nine in the desert, and go after that which is lost, until he finds it? And when he has found it, he lays it upon his shoulders rejoicing. And on coming home he calls together his friends and neighbors, saying to them, 'Rejoice with me, because I have found my sheep that was lost.' I say to you that, even so, there will be joy in heaven over one sinner who repents, more than over ninety-nine just who have no need of repentance." (Luke 15:4–7)

REFLECT Many men tend to feel lost in the mass of humanity . . . To Jesus there is no crowd, but only individuals. In this parable He tries to impress this truth upon His hearers.

REVIEW At times I am so distracted by the crowd around me that I forget that God deals with me as a person, the individual person He created, sustains each moment of the day, and assists in every action. I must meditate often on Christ's discourse concerning God's care of the grass of the fields and the birds of the air. And He bids me consider how much more precious I am than the grass and the birds.

The awareness of my personal defects, the memory of my sins, and my concern about other people's opinions about me blot this precious truth from my mind. I tend to think that I am hopelessly little and unimportant to God, or that I am utterly displeasing to Him. When will I understand that God loves me because I am a human being for whom His divine Son died upon the cross. My fears, doubts, and discouragement might be justified if I had to achieve my salvation by my own merits alone. But I am not alone in my supernatural effort to gain God's favor and heaven's eternal joys. Jesus became my Shepherd and shed His blood for me. He came to me when I sinned, in order to lead me back by His truth and His grace. He begs me to look more at Him than at myself. With frequent reflections on His message and constant endeavors to feel it in my daily life, I shall find peace of mind and strength of soul, regardless of other people's opinions about me and in spite of my own emotional self-doubt and self-disgust.

RESPOND My divine Shepherd, You come looking for me much more eagerly than I come looking for You. When shall I be deeply impressed by Your infinite consideration and personal love for me? You are personally interested in all that concerns me. I shall remind myself of this over and over again. My gratitude will be shown in a sincere endeavor to be more pleasing to You through the remaining years of my life. Amen.

108. THE PRODIGAL SON

READ "A certain man had two sons. And the younger of them said to his father, 'Father, give me the share of the property that falls to me.' . . . And not many days later the younger son gathered up all his wealth, and took his journey into a far country; and there he squandered his fortune in loose living. . . . and he began himself to suffer want . . . And he longed to fill himself with the pods that the swine were eating, but no one offered to give them to him. But when he came to himself, he said, 'How many hired men in my father's house have bread in abundance while I am perishing here with hunger. I will get up and go to my father!' . . . And he arose and went to his father. But while he was yet a long way off, his father saw him and was moved with compassion, and ran and fell upon his neck and kissed him. And the son said to him, 'Father I have sinned against heaven and before thee. I am no longer worthy to be called thy son.' But the father said . . . 'Let us eat and make merry; because this my son was dead, and has come to life again; he was lost, and is found.'" (Luke 15:11–24)

REFLECT Jesus continues His endeavor to present a correct picture of His heavenly Father in the limited language of men. He attempts to break through the barrier of ignorance, misunderstanding, vague fears, unreasonable doubts, and unreasoning guilt-feelings. To those who, either explicitly or implicitly, feel like the prodigal son, Jesus says that God is an understanding Father, desirous to love rather than hate, eager to forgive rather than punish, more willing to help rather than to hurt.

REVIEW There are times when I too feel somewhat like the prodigal son. As I become aware of my hunger for peace, my aloneness in so many uncertainties, fears, doubts, and guilt-feelings, I feel a longing to come closer to God. I become conscious of my sins, and experience some vague fear whether they are all forgiven. I feel a yearning for understanding, acceptance, and assistance in my needs and doubts. I think of drawing closer to God with humble acknowledgment of my errors, sincere contrition for my sins, and a heartfelt petition that He receive me even as the last of His household. At His feet I hope to receive the security of His support, the peace of His forgiveness, and the joy of His heavenly fatherly acceptance. Jesus tells me that the heavenly Father is watching and waiting for me, comes part of the way to meet me, and in his joy over my return, will not even let me express shame or blame. He wants me to feel not as a servant, but as a son who has come home. Until I have absorbed this picture of God into the depths of my soul, I shall never find the peace, comfort, and strength which Christ's truth was intended to give me in my daily life.

RESPOND My Jesus, let me meditate over and over again on this beautiful and inspiring image of Your heavenly Father. You know Him as no one else can. May I frequently listen to You telling this story, and seeing in it not the God I dread, but the Father who constantly asks me for my love. Amen.

109. THE UNJUST STEWARD

READ "There was a certain rich man who had a steward, who was reported to him as squandering his possessions. And he called him and said to him, 'What is this that I hear of thee? Make an accounting of thy stewardship, for thou canst be steward no longer.' And the steward said within himself, 'What shall I do, seeing that my master is taking away the stewardship from me? To dig I am not able; to beg I am ashamed. I know what I shall do, that when I am removed from my stewardship, they may receive me into their houses.' And he summoned each of his master's debtors and said to the first, 'How much dost thou owe my master?' And he said, 'A hundred jars of oil.' He said to him, 'Take thy bond and sit down at once and write fifty.' . . . (Luke 16:1–8)

REFLECT The unjust steward sought his own satisfaction and contentment without regard for the laws of honesty and justice. He misused his master's goods and thereby forced his master to dismiss him. Nor did he learn his lesson from this dismissal. He was so fearful of being unable to provide for himself, that he sought to regain his security, peace, and welfare by intensifying his dishonesty and injustice.

REVIEW Having shown me the fatherliness of God, Jesus now cautions me against an immature concept of the heavenly Father. Though God understands my natural limitations and human weaknesses, He can never tolerate outright presumption and bad will. He expects me to prove the sincerity of my sorrow for past sins by a whole-hearted effort in the present. He will judge the quality of my love by my daily endeavor to follow the principles and example of His divine Son.

Like the steward in this gospel, I, too, have received charge over some of God's possessions. He has placed a number of talents, graces, and earthly opportunities at my disposal. He has sent Jesus not only to make reparation for my sins, but also to guide and strengthen me in my daily use of His gifts. Through the virtue of wisdom, I must learn to see God in His gifts. Through the virtue of prudence I must learn to use my gifts for God's glory and my own eternal welfare. With these two virtues I shall more easily fight against my natural tendency to seek my welfare and contentment without regard for the laws of God.

RESPOND Heavenly Father, it is only right that I prove my love for You by action rather than by words alone. Help me become more aware of Your presence in my life, and of the eternal happiness and glory You have reserved for me in heaven. In this way, I hope to gain the strength necessary to correct my unreasonable attitudes, desires and actions. Amen.

110. THE VALUES OF GOD AND THOSE OF MEN

READ Now the Pharisees, who were fond of money, were listening to all these things, and they began to sneer at him. And he said to them, "You are they who declare yourselves just in the sight of men but God knows your heart; for that which is exalted in the sight of men is an abomination before God." (Luke 16:14–15)

REFLECT These men were following the traditional belief that God's favor is shown through earthly prosperity. But Jesus tells them that, even if God promised such prosperity in the past, they must now prepare themselves for the New Law of His Kingdom. Not material wealth, but spiritual wealth is to be preferred. Earthly goods derive their eternal value from their proper use in accordance with the laws of justice and charity.

REVIEW Jesus had just warned His audience to beware of being so concerned about their earthly welfare as to neglect their eternal well being. The gifts of God are bestowed on men to help them live with a reasonable security, comfort and dignity. Unless they strive to broaden their spiritual outlook, they will fail to see the wider value of these earthly gifts. If they are concerned only with their present contentment and satisfaction, they will be blind to the requirements of justice and charity. Jesus shows the folly of this spiritual condition through the parable of Dives, the rich man who lost his soul, and Lazarus, the beggar who went to heaven.

If I am to avoid the dangers of which Jesus speaks on this occasion, I must train myself to become eternity-minded. Through frequent meditation on the brevity of this earthly life and the eternal duration of heaven and hell, I shall gradually see my earthly gifts and possessions in their proper place. I shall not lament the gifts I lack, nor envy others for their greater gifts. Rather, I shall try to make the most of my earthly talents, possessions, and opportunities. I shall not be so eager for earthly advantages and benefits as to sin for them. I shall be more disposed to accept the limitations and privations which I cannot remedy, and to help others as far as my limited means will permit.

RESPOND   O Jesus, King of wisdom, and prudence, grant me the vision to see the eternal glory of my daily endeavors on earth. May I never lose sight of the reality of death, and the all-satisfying life which awaits those who try to live in accordance with Your truth. Fortified with this interior vision, I hope to use my gifts with the intention of pleasing You and thereby saving my soul. Amen.

111. THE DEATH OF LAZARUS

READ   Now a certain man was sick, Lazarus of Bethany, the village of Mary and her sister Martha. . . . The sisters, therefore, sent to him, saying, "Lord, behold he whom thou lovest is sick." But when Jesus heard this, he said to them, "This sickness is not unto death, but for the glory of

God, that through it the Son of God may be glorified."
Now Jesus loved Martha and her sister Mary, and Lazarus.
So when he heard that he was sick, he remained two more
days in the same place. . . . and after this he said . . .
"Lazarus is dead; and I rejoice on your account that I was
not there, that you may believe." (John 11:1–6, 11–15)

REFLECT Though Jesus loved Martha and her sister,
Mary, and their brother, Lazarus, He nevertheless permitted Lazarus to die. Through Lazarus He would work one
of His most astonishing miracles, and, thereby, strengthen
His disciples for the ordeal which they would have to face
in the near future, the ordeal of His own passion and death.

REVIEW My natural way of thinking is inspired and con-
ditioned by the spontaneous drives, acquired wants, and
developed emotions within me. I do not easily accept
adversities and hardships. Just as I am inclined to defend
myself against people who threaten or hurt me, so, too,
am I inclined to defend myself against God when I feel
afraid or uncertain of Him. I feel either distrustful, resentful, or rebellious toward Him. In so far as these inclinations are not voluntary, they are not sinful, and God does
not condemn me for them. Nevertheless, I need to correct
them so that they may never lead me into some deliberate
sin.

I must realize that, when compared to God's infinite
wisdom, my way of thinking is more limited than the intelligence of a child compared with that of an adult. God
never does anything without a good reason. Moreover, God
is absolute Master of all that I am and have. I can never
really exact any claims or demands from Him. God is
also my loving Father. In all that He does to me His greatest concern is my eternal welfare. The more I appreciate
these facts, the more easily shall I be disposed to prefer
His holy Will in all things. Some people make reservations in their service to God. They are willing to accept
many things of Him, but they keep hoping that He will

not require certain things of them. This is the result of
either a lack of knowledge, a lack of maturity, or a lack of
good will. If I knew God as He really is, I would be free of
all fears, doubts, and distrust of Him. I would gladly place
my life and all my dearest possessions in His hands, because I would be utterly convinced that only what is best
for me can come from His hands.

RESPOND   Take, O Lord, and receive all my liberty, my
memory, my understanding, and my entire will. Whatever I have or hold, Thou hast given me; I restore it all to
Thee and surrender it wholly, to be governed by Thy will.
Give me only Thy love and Thy grace, and I am rich
enough and ask for nothing more. Amen.

112.   JESUS, MY RESURRECTION AND LIFE

READ   When, therefore, Martha heard that Jesus was coming, she went to meet him. But Mary remained at home.
Martha therefore said to Jesus, "Lord, if thou hadst been
here, my brother would not have died. But even now I
know that whatever thou shalt ask of God, God will give
it to thee." Jesus said to her, "Thy brother shall rise."
Martha said to him, "I know that he will rise at the resurrection, on the last day." Jesus said to her, "I am the resurrection and the life; he who believes in me, even if he die,
shall live; and, whoever lives and believes in me, shall
never die." (John 11:20–26)

REFLECT   Jesus consoled this sorrowing sister of Lazarus
by assuring her that her brother would rise again. He then
proceeded to tell her that everyone who believes in Him
will rise into a new life which will never pass away.

REVIEW   Christian life is a resurrection in more ways

than one. Before Baptism I was spiritually dead because I did not have sanctifying grace. God had not yet made a supernatural dwelling for Himself within my soul. With Baptism He entered into me and granted me power to think, judge, and live beyond the natural limits of my spirit. In Baptism, my natural self went through a mysterious death. The purpose and power of Christ was born in me. I received a supernatural tendency to share His thoughts, desires, and life. God gave me power to look at this earthly life through Christ's eyes and to value it as a pathway to eternity.

I experience another resurrection as I advance in the knowledge of His truth, the use of His graces and sacraments, and the application of His principles to my daily life. Thus, do I die to self and live to Christ. If I died spiritually through mortal sin, I was able to rise again into supernatural life through contrition, sacramental pardon, and the restoration of God's grace. Though I must someday undergo the death of my body, I shall continue to live in the supernatural life which God has granted me through the merits of Christ. Lastly, I shall behold my final resurrection in a glorified body on the day of judgment, to live with God forever in a happiness and glory that is far beyond my powers of imagination or thought. All this I may obtain through my faith in Christ and my fidelity to His principles.

RESPOND   O Jesus, my resurrection and life, this is the vision I need, to overcome the fears that upset me, the doubts that confuse my mind, and the anxieties that wear down my nerves and weaken my will. May I always value the good things of this life in so far as they help me please You each day. Without neglecting the obligations of this life, let me be deeply impressed by the happiness and joy that You have reserved for me in the unending life of heaven. Amen.

113. THE SYMPATHY OF CHRIST

READ When, therefore, Mary came where Jesus was, and saw him, she fell at his feet, and said to him, "Lord, if thou hadst been here, my brother would not have died." When, therefore, Jesus saw her weeping, and the Jews who had come with her weeping, he groaned in spirit and was troubled, and said, "Where have you laid him?" They said to him, "Lord, come and see." And Jesus wept. The Jews therefore said, "See how he loved him." But some of them said, "Could not he who opened the eyes of the blind, have caused that this man should not die?" (John 11:32–37)

REFLECT In this scene Jesus shows how truly human He is. He could feel the sorrow of His friends and weep with them. As usual, some demanded to know why He had not prevented this sorrow.

REVIEW If I desire a lasting mental peace and moral strength in my present circumstances, I shall need a mature outlook on the nature of human life on earth. Some problems can be avoided, some pains can be prevented, and some sorrows can be alleviated. But after I have done my best to live in health, comfort, security, and peace, I shall still have my quota of problems, pains, and sorrows. This earthly life will never be a substitute for heaven. Therefore, Jesus permitted this sorrow to come into the lives of these dear friends. Instead of rebelling against Him or rejecting His company, they found comfort in His presence and strength in His sympathy.

I too must become so close a friend of Christ that I can feel His sympathy in my sorrows. Instead of looking upon my life with useless anxiety and facing my sufferings with fear, I must believe that my daily burdens, mental distress and bodily pains are shared by Christ. If a miracle is necessary for my true welfare or for the good of my dear ones, I need not hesitate to ask for it. But in any circumstance, I can be sure that God permits my sufferings for infinitely wise reasons. In one way or another, my real welfare sometimes requires that I bear a cross. I shall prove myself a true friend of Jesus if I can believe this when suffering and sorrow cast their shadow across my earthly path to heaven.

RESPOND   My Jesus, in so many of my daily difficulties, and sufferings, and sorrows, I am truly a child. I follow my inborn instinct to protect myself without the guidance of reason and faith. Help me do what I can to remedy my problems and sufferings. When it is better for me to bear my burden, strengthen me with a strong conviction that You are near and ready to help me as my true welfare may require. Amen.

114.   ON AVOIDING SCANDALS

READ   And he said to his disciples, "It is impossible that scandals should not come; but woe to him through whom they come! It were better for him if a millstone were hung about his neck and he were thrown into the sea, than that he should cause one of these little ones to sin. Take heed to yourselves. If thy brother sin, rebuke him; and if he repent, forgive him. And if seven times in the day he sin against thee, and seven times in the day turn back to thee, saying, 'I repent,' forgive him." (Luke 17:1–4)

REFLECT   Living in human society involves the interplay of individual drives, wants, emotions, and external behavior. The natural self-concern of each individual necessarily produces its quota of emotional stresses and strains both within himself and within those with whom he deals. Jesus warns us against letting our personal preferences and prejudices become an unnecessary occasion of sin to ourselves and to others. He advises us to do this by being more disposed to pardon than to punish.

REVIEW If I am to avoid being an occasion of sin to others, I must know myself as fully as possible, and understand others as far as I am able. I must be intelligently content to be myself, without unreasonable shame, blame, or self-disgust. My fears, sensitivity, envy, irritability, contempt, and hostility toward others, often proceed from my own deficient self-respect. If I have a proper sense of my individual value and personal dignity, I shall find it much easier to accept others as they are, and to deal with them with interior peace, emotional strength, and moral conviction. As long as I am not reasonably content to be myself, I shall be uneasy, distrustful, and antagonistic with others.

Though I shall always need some measure of acceptance, approval and good will, I must not be disturbed when I fail to receive these from some people. They may be so upset by their own problems, that they cannot treat me with consideration. In spite of my best intentions and sincerest efforts, I shall be unable to win them over. Since this is part of every human life, I must be ready to accept my share of it. Until I grow into a mature attitude toward myself and others, I shall often be an occasion of sin to others and shall find them an occasion of sin to me.

RESPOND My Jesus, help me be reasonably content with myself, and intelligently considerate of other people. Let me see all personal tensions and interpersonal frictions as a normal part of everyday living. With this mature understanding and adult attitude, I shall find it much easier to avoid hurting others or being hurt by them. Amen.

115. THE UNPROFITABLE SERVANTS

READ "But which of you is there, having a servant plowing or tending sheep, who will say to him on his return to the field, 'Come at once and recline at table!' But will he not say to him, 'Prepare my supper, and gird thyself and serve me till I have eaten and drunk; and afterwards thou thyself shalt eat and drink?' Does he thank that servant for doing what he commanded him? I do not think so. Even so you also, when you have done everything that was commanded you, say, 'We are unprofitable servants; we have done what it was our duty to do.'" (Luke 17:7–10)

REFLECT For the benefit of those who were reluctant to offer homage and obedience to God, Jesus drives home this basic truth. No matter how much God may love men, and offer them a share in His divine life, perfections, and heavenly joys, they could never change what they are by their very nature . . . creatures of God, absolutely dependent on Him in all things at all times.

REVIEW God called me forth from nothing by the creative power of His divine will. His support is so utterly necessary to my existence each moment, that if He withdrew it for a single instant I would cease to exist. This is the most basic fact of my existence. Nothing that I am, have, use, or enjoy, is truly mine, but God's. When I choose to offer Him something in the form of obedience or voluntary self-sacrifice, I do Him no favor that puts Him in my debt. I can make no real claim on Him on the basis of justice, since He owns all that exists and owes nothing to any creature.

True, God has raised me up to a supernatural level. By the grace of Christ, I received a share in the life, power, and glory of God. This made me a son of His in a real sense. However, my sonship is not a natural one, but an adoption. This adoption does not destroy what I am by my original nature, a created being, subject to the absolute and universal dominion which God has over me. Therefore whatever I offer Him, even through the grace of Christ, I must never feel that I have given Him something that is mine and mine alone. I merely offer Him what He has placed within my power. As He gave it to me, He could as easily take it from me, and I would have no just grounds for complaining. If truth and justice are considered, I can only express gratitude for the power He has given me to know, serve, and love Him, and for the personal interest, intimate concern, and boundless love with which He admits me into His heavenly home.

RESPOND   My loving Father in heaven, may I never forget my true nature. Every instant of my existence is an act of goodness and love from You. Make me humble enough to accept this truth and grateful enough to make the most of my gifts and opportunities. You owe me nothing, and I owe You all that I am and have. I shall do my best to prove my gratitude each day. Amen.

116.   THE KINGDOM WITHIN

READ   And on being asked by the Pharisees, "When is the kingdom of God coming?" he answered and said to them, "The kingdom of God comes unawares. Neither will they say, 'Behold, here it is,' or 'Behold, there it is.' For behold, the kingdom of God is within you." (Luke 17:20–21)

REFLECT   The Pharisees had the traditional notion of a new Hebrew kingdom, surpassing the military might of Rome, and resplendent in worldly glory. Jesus puts an end once and for all to these dreams. He would later tell Pilate that His kingdom is not of this world. He now tells the Pharisees that the kingdom of God is already among them, and if they do not see it, it is because they are looking for something entirely different from God's plan.

REVIEW   A number of people look to religion for the fulfillment of a dream that is built not on Christ's teachings, but on their own emotional wants, desires, and yearnings. They want to "feel" the nearness of God, face every situation with equanimity and wisdom, overcome every temptation with perfect control, behave among others without the least sign of hesitation, give the perfect answer to every question, and receive the acknowledgment and admiration of everyone they meet. They want religion to make up for all their limitations, weaknesses, and defects. In effect, they are expecting a miracle.

The kingdom of God is invisible. Like the growth of the mustard seed and the fermenting of the leaven, it works invisibly. One can see it only through faith, hold on to it only by hope and trust, and use it daily only through the power of supernatural love of God. It elevates my natural actions to a supernatural dignity and brings me not only a temporary visible satisfaction, but also an eternal glory in heaven. But in this earthly life I shall often feel little or nothing of this dignity and power.

Because of their false expectations and unreasonable demands on themselves, many lose heart in their daily efforts to come closer to God. Jesus asks that they live their daily lives without seeing or feeling the supernatural glory which they earn throughout the day, but simply believe, on His word, that this glory is theirs. As long as they are performing their daily duties and fulfilling their obligations with a desire to serve God, they are following their divine Savior and pleasing their heavenly Father.

RESPOND   O Jesus, my divine King, I hope to live each day with faith in Your truth and confidence in Your nearness to me. I shall neither strain beyond my strength nor become discouraged at my human shortcomings. May I always believe that whatever I do this day, is important to You because it is my part of my state in life. Amen.

117. THE SELF-RIGHTEOUS

READ But he spoke this parable also to some who trusted in themselves as being just, and despised others. "Two men went up to the temple to pray, the one a Pharisee and the other a publican. The Pharisee stood and began to pray thus within himself: 'O God, I thank thee that I am not like the rest of men, robbers, dishonest, adulterers, or even like this publican. I fast twice a week; I pay tithes of all that I possess.' But the publican, standing afar off, would not so much as lift up his eyes to heaven, but kept striking his breast, saying, 'O God, be merciful to me the sinner.' I tell you, this man went back to his home justified rather than the other; for everyone who exalts himself shall be humbled, and he who humbles himself shall be exalted." (Luke 18:9–14)

REFLECT Jesus presents two types of people: those who take a foolish pride in their religious performance and those who approach God with a deep sense of their unworthiness. Jesus says that the latter are much more pleasing to God than the former.

REVIEW Balance is the law of nature. It is also the law of the supernatural life. I can make the mistake of the Pharisee by using religious activities to prove myself better than others. I may unconsciously despise those who do not recite as many prayers or perform as many good works as I. This is a childish way of thinking and an immature manner of acting. My religious activities are of little value without a right intention. I must perform them primarily to thank God, praise Him, seek His pardon for my sins, and beg His help for my spiritual and material needs. Since I know little or nothing of the interior dispositions and emotional problems of others, I am in no position to make a judgment on their worth before God.

On the other hand I can go to the opposite extreme. I can approach God with such a sense of unworthiness as to feel too small for His notice or too guilty for His pardon. This unhealthy disposition can prevent me from being at ease with God and His Saints. It can make me reluctant to pray and unable to concentrate on religious thoughts and spiritual matters. This extreme is as unhealthy as the one mentioned above.

RESPOND Heavenly Father, teach me to approach You with a peaceful humility, a sincere sorrow for my sins, and a deep appreciation of Your numberless gifts and fatherly forgiveness. Let me center my attention more on You than on myself. With this positive outlook, I shall never exaggerate my self-esteem nor minimize the personal worth of others. Amen.

118. THE CHILDLIKE IN SPIRIT

READ And they were bringing little children to him that he might touch them; but the disciples rebuked those who brought them. But when Jesus saw them, he was indignant, and said to them, "Let the little children come to me and do not hinder them, for of such is the kingdom of God. Amen I say to you, whoever does not accept the kingdom of God as a little child will not enter into it." (Mark 10:13–15)

REFLECT Jesus advises us to develop a childlike spirit of faith and trust in our religious disposition. This spirit is not to be confused with childishness and immaturity. Rather it is a realistic view of our position as children of God.

REVIEW Some people are ashamed to appear devout in their religious practices, while others are reluctant to show any religious tendencies at all. There are different causes for this, causes that developed over the years. Some cannot tolerate a sense of dependency on others, not even on God. Some cannot admit that they are lacking in some virtue or guilty of some sin. Some cannot stand being told what to do. Some fear the "strain" of "being good," or the sadness and discouragement they feel when reminded of what they "ought to be." Some fear the disapproval of others. In all these cases, these people are constrained to hide their feelings of inferiority, guilt, or fear of punishment under a claim or pretense of having outgrown their religious practices. In their emotional need to feel independent or appear superior, they become childish in their attitudes and immature in their behavior. Like children, they are unable or unwilling to face distasteful reality.

Only a mature person can be wisely childlike with God, since he alone is able to face facts and adjust to reality. Knowing his utter dependence on God, he can humbly approach God as the Father He really is. Being aware of his daily mistakes, weaknesses and sins, he is disposed to rely on God's infinite knowledge to guide him in his ignorance and mental confusion; God's divine strength to protect him in his moments of temptation; and God's fatherly love to forgive his sins and assist him in his daily necessities. There is nothing childish about the truly childlike person, because he acts in accordance with the dictates of reason and God's revealed truth.

RESPOND Heavenly Father, in the light of this meditation I see the wisdom of being childlike in my religious attitude and moral behavior. I believe what Jesus taught and lived, and I hope to fulfill Your holy Will as best I can each day.

Let me never be childish in my thinking and immature in my actions, so that I may never cause people to misunderstand You or religion. Amen.

119. THE RICH YOUNG MAN

READ And behold, a certain man came to him and said, "Good Master, what good work shall I do to have eternal life?" . . . "If thou wilt enter into life, keep the commandments." He said to him, "Which?" And Jesus said, *"Thou shalt not kill, Thou shalt not commit adultery, Thou shalt not steal, Thou shalt not bear false witness, Honor thy father and mother, and, Thou shalt love thy neighbor as thyself."* The young man said to him, "All these I have kept; what is yet wanting to me?" Jesus said to him, "If thou wilt be perfect, go, sell what thou hast, and give to the poor, and thou shalt have treasure in heaven; and come, follow me." But when the young man heard the saying, he went away sad, for he had great possessions. (Matt. 19:16–22)

REFLECT We see here a man who was living an exemplary life. Though he was faithful to the commandments, he felt a strong desire to do more for God. On hearing what would be the next step in his self-offering, he turned away sad, because he was unwilling to take this step.

REVIEW Regardless of my sincerity and good will, there is a limit to what I would actually do at this moment for love of God. I am willing to keep the commandments, since they are necessary for my salvation. I may even be willing to do more than this for God. But I must acknowledge the fact that there are some things which I would not be willing to do for God unless He gave me more graces than I now have.

I have learned to treasure certain things in this life. I find in them a sense of security, comfort, peace, and happiness. As long as they do not lead me into sin, God does not demand that I sacrifice these things.

I must not feel obliged to do more for God than keep His commandments. He permits me to enjoy the good things at my disposal within the bounds of moderation and justice. However, it is wise to practice occasional self-denial, so that if circumstances ever deprive me of the things I enjoy and value, I may not sin through rebellion against God, or undue hostility toward men.

RESPOND Dearest Lord, teach me to be generous. Teach me to serve Thee as Thou deservest; to give and not to count the cost; to fight and not to heed the wounds; to toil and not to seek for rest; to labor and not to ask for reward, save that of knowing that I am doing Thy will. Amen.

120. LEAVING ALL FOR CHRIST

READ Then Peter addressed him, saying, "Behold, we have left all and followed thee; what then shall we have?" And Jesus said to them . . . "And everyone who has left house, or brothers, or sisters, or father, or mother, or wife, or children, or lands, for my name's sake, shall receive a hundredfold and shall possess life everlasting." (Matt. 19:27–28, 29–30)

REFLECT Jesus had just watched the rich young man sadly walking away from Him, and had warned His disciples against attachment to worldly wealth. Peter expressed the thoughts which Jesus' words brought to his mind.

REVIEW Every man is obliged to serve God in his daily use or privation of earthly goods. The commandments do not oblige me to prove my love of God by leaving all things and entering into a religious community. My only strict obligation is to observe the laws of justice and charity in my daily attitudes and behavior. If I observe God's commandments, I shall one day enter into the eternal happiness and glory of heaven.

However, the possibility of performing more than the minimum requirement is open to a number of people. Some are like the rich young man. They do not feel strong enough to live without the material comforts and satisfactions they now enjoy. They commit no sin by preferring to serve God through their earthly achievements and natural satisfactions.

Then there are those who feel a sincere desire to give themselves to God as fully as possible. They leave their dear ones, earthly possessions, comforts, and opportunities, and enter into the religious state of poverty, chastity, and obedience. Jesus says that even before they leave this world, they will receive possessions, comforts, and opportunities that are far superior to those they left for His sake. In spite of the opposition and persecution they may have to endure for His name, they will know a peace of mind, contentment of heart, and strength of soul that will be a foretaste of the all-satisfying life of heaven.

RESPOND My Jesus, make me mature and generous in my religious outlook and daily conduct. Teach me to enjoy intelligently the earthly goods and legitimate pleasures You have placed at my disposal. May I never feel guilty where no commandment is broken. On the other hand, let me never be so dependent on these earthly comforts and pleasures as to reject Your invitation to come closer to You through a religious vocation. Make me wise and strong enough to let You direct and control my life. In any fears or doubts, I shall not hesitate to consult a spiritual director. Amen.

121. WORKERS IN THE VINEYARD

READ "For the kingdom of heaven is like a householder who went out early in the morning to hire laborers for his vineyard. And having agreed with the laborers for a denarius a day, he sent them into his vineyard. And about the third hour, he went out and saw others standing in the market place idle; and he said to them, 'Go you also into the vineyard, and I will give you whatever is just.' So they went. And again he went out about the sixth, and about the ninth hour, and did as before. But about the eleventh hour he went out and found others standing about, and he said to them, 'Why do you stand here all day idle?' They said to him, 'Because no man has hired us.' He said to them, 'Go you also into the vineyard.'" (Matt. 20:1-7)

REFLECT Jesus compares His earthly kingdom to a vineyard, into which He invites many laborers at different times and in different circumstances. Though He seems to favor some over others, no man can claim that he has been treated unfairly. The reward of our labors will never fall short of their just merits.

REVIEW I have been invited to live my daily life as a member of Christ's Church. This membership is intended to influence my outlook, attitudes, intentions, thinking, and external behavior. However, my daily service of God is not so easily computed that I can make a sure estimate of my merits before God. So many unknown factors are active in my daily prayers, efforts, and good works, that I cannot validly compare my merits with those of others. Had God placed me in similar circumstances, I might well have fallen lower than the people I despise, or failed in

215

the place of those I envy. Therefore I must leave all judgments and comparisons to God.

In view of my human ignorance, fears, and doubts, I might do well to consider whether I do not sometimes question God's dealings with me or others. Indirectly, I may claim to deserve more than I have, or resent the more desirable circumstances of others. Implicitly, I may demand for myself the peace, prosperity, or success of people who seem to deserve less than I.

Jesus advises me to consider the basic facts of my existence. God owes me nothing. It is I who owe Him everything I am and have. Nevertheless, He will grant me a reward that will be just. If He seems to favor others, I ought to remember that He is God. He does not act blindly on emotional impulse, but with the wisdom of the ages and a love that is infinite.

RESPOND My God, let me never forget the most central truth of all my life. I depend on You for every instant of my existence, for every good thing I enjoy, and for every defense against harm. The only attitude I can intelligently have toward You is gratitude, and the only sentiment is love. Do with me whatever You will, and I shall be content. Amen.

122. STRIVING FOR SUPERIORITY

READ And James and John, the sons of Zebedee, came to him saying, "Master, we want thee to do for us whatever we ask." But he said to them, "What do you want me to do for you?" And they said, "Grant to us that we may sit, one at thy right hand and the other at thy left hand, in thy glory." . . . And when the ten heard this, they were at first indignant at James and John. But Jesus called them and said to them, "You know that those who are regarded as rulers among the Gentiles lord it over them, and their great men exercise authority over them. But it is not so among you. On the contrary, whoever wishes to become great shall become your servant; and whoever wishes to be first among you shall be the slave of all; for the Son of Man also has not come to be served but to serve, and to give his life as a ransom for many." (Mark 10:35–37, 41–45)

REFLECT There was a good deal of concern among the disciples as to who was most influential with their Master. John and James felt that this was an opportune time to settle this question to their own satisfaction. With understanding and patience, Jesus tries once again to make them understand the lesson of true Christian greatness. As He would make Himself the servant of all, so must they find their true glory in being of service to others.

REVIEW A sense of superiority is naturally desirable to any man. It destroys most or all of one's anxiety, uneasiness, and tension. It makes one feel more content with himself, more relaxed, generous, and tolerant toward others, and more at ease with the problems and situations of everyday life. Interpersonal competition appears in countless forms all through life. Not even children are free from it. As we grow older, however, we learn to express our desire for superiority through admirable ideals, outstanding achievements, and praiseworthy conduct.

Actually I am obliged to strive for superiority, but not in the childish manner shown by the disciples. Instead of trying to prove myself better than others, Jesus wants me to be more at peace with myself, more helpful toward others, and more generous in my imitation of Him in my daily life. In striving for this mental, emotional, and spiritual development, I attain a greater superiority over what I am today. I shall then look on the faults of others with more regret than contentment. I shall help others, not with a condescending attitude, but with a conviction that

Jesus is doing me a favor by granting me the opportunity to imitate Him.

RESPOND My Jesus, let me not strive for the passing superiority of this earthly life, but for the eternal superiority of heavenly glory. Take such possession of my thinking, my attitudes, and my dispositions that I may be another Jesus to those with whom I deal. Grant me a share in Your understanding, Your patience, Your good will and sincere concern for the welfare of others. May they see in me no longer the small-minded, self-asserting human being I am, but the out-going, self-giving Christ Who enlightens my mind and rules my heart. Amen.

123. ZACCHAEUS

READ And behold there was a man named Zacchaeus; and he was a leading publican, and he was rich. And he was trying to see Jesus, who he was, but could not, on account of the crowd, because he was small of stature. So he ran on ahead and climbed into a sycamore tree to see him, for he was going to pass that way. And when Jesus came to the place, he looked up and saw him, and said to him, "Zacchaeus, make haste and come down; for I must stay in thy house today." And he made haste and came down, and welcomed him joyfully. And upon seeing it, all began to murmur, saying, "He has gone to be the guest of a man who is a sinner." But Zacchaeus stood and said to the Lord, "Behold, Lord, I give one half of my possessions to the poor, and if I have defrauded anyone of anything, I restore it fourfold." Jesus said to him, "Today salvation has come to this house . . . For the Son of Man came to seek and save what was lost." (Luke 19:2–10)

REFLECT Zacchaeus is an example to every sinner who

desires to draw close to Christ, and does something about his desires. Because he worked to overcome his internal obstacles and external hindrances, he received the privilege of having Jesus as his guest. In gratitude, Zacchaeus took steps to amend his past sins.

REVIEW Every man receives moments of grace, when he feels a desire to come closer to Christ. Too often he lets himself become afraid of the obstacles within himself or those created by others. Like Zacchaeus, I must disregard both my personal limitations and the objections or resentments of others, and follow the inspirations of God's grace. My sins are not so black that Christ cannot forgive them, nor are my habits so strong that I cannot do something about them with time, grace, patience, and persistent effort.

People may refuse to let me forget my past, but Christ is all too willing to help me make a new start. He does not expect me to make such a sudden change, nor does He demand that the transformation be perfect. In His understanding of my nature and His appreciation of my sincerity, He only asks me to see what changes are necessary, make an intelligent effort, and keep trying in spite of difficulties, relapses, and criticism from others. My efforts may show meager results at first, but with time and persevering determination, these results will increase and my failures will decrease.

RESPOND My Jesus, teach me to make my daily efforts without straining beyond my strength, without surprise at my failures, and with gratitude for whatever improvement I may achieve. With this attitude, I hope to prove that I do love You and hate my sins. Amen.

124. THE NOBLEMAN'S GOLD

READ Now as they were listening . . . he went on to speak a parable, because he was near Jerusalem, and because they thought that the kingdom of God was going to appear immediately. He said therefore, "A certain nobleman went into a far country . . . and then returned. And having summoned ten of his servants, he gave them ten gold pieces and said to them, 'Trade till I come.' . . . And it came to pass when he had returned . . . that he ordered the servants to whom he had given the money to be called to him in order that he might learn how much each one had made by trading. And the first came, saying, 'Lord, thy gold piece has earned ten gold pieces.' And he said to him, 'Well done, good servant; because thou hast been faithful in a very little, thou shalt have authority over ten towns.' Then the second came, saying, 'Lord, thy gold piece has made five gold pieces.' And he said to him, 'Be thou also over five towns.'" (Luke 19:11–19)

REFLECT Jesus paints earthly life as a service to God. There are gifts given by the Lord, and opportunities to employ these gifts according to His wishes. Each will be rewarded in proportion to his industry and zeal in his Master's service.

REVIEW This message of Christ can give me great vision and enthusiasm to make the most of my earthly life. I must respect my person and appreciate my gifts and opportunities as part of God's eternal plan. Though my talents, graces, and circumstances differ from those of everyone else, there is a certain individual quality in all of us. Like the gold coin received by each servant in this gospel, my lesser talents are as satisfactory to God as the greater talents of others. I was fitted for the particular task which

He has prepared for me. As I go about my daily routine, I can be of service to a number of people who cannot be reached by those with greater talents or higher social position. Though I may not see my value to these people, they will derive comfort or strength from the way I think, live, and deal with them. Through me they will be reached by God, and in turn reach out for Him.

RESPOND   My Jesus, in Your Father's eternal plan, Joseph was to be a carpenter, Mary a housewife, and You Yourself would live most of Your earthly life as a carpenter's son. Help me to see the dignity, merits, and power of my own God-given assignment on earth. Let me not waste time regretting lost opportunities, but make the most of my present circumstances. Grant me contentment with the gifts I have, and in my efforts to improve myself, let me not do so by reaching constantly for the impossible. Help me to be grateful for the good I can achieve, and thankful for the task You have assigned to me in my present state of life. Amen.

125. HIDDEN MOTIVES

READ   Jesus therefore, six days before the Passover, came to Bethany where Lazarus, whom Jesus had raised to life, had died. And they made him a supper there; and Martha served, while Lazarus was one of those reclining at table with him.

Mary therefore took a pound of ointment, genuine nard of great value, and anointed the feet of Jesus, and with her hair wiped his feet dry. And the house was filled with the odor of the ointment. Then one of his disciples, Judas Iscariot, he who was about to betray him, said, "Why was this ointment not sold for three hundred denarii, and given to the poor?" Now he said this, not that he cared for the poor, but because he was a thief, and holding the purse, used to take what was put in it. Jesus therefore said, "Let her be—that she may keep it for the day of my burial. For the poor you have always with you, but you do not always have me." (John 12:1–8)

REFLECT   In this scene we see two different types of followers of Christ; Those who serve with attention centered entirely on Him, and those who serve with personal motives that move them away from Him.

REVIEW   This scene is one of the most interesting in the earthly life of Jesus. Amid the group about Him were two outstanding persons, Mary and Judas. Mary found in Jesus her greatest peace, contentment and joy. She simply could not do enough for Him. Even in following the Jewish custom of washing the guest's feet, she was not content to use ordinary water. She used this jar of expensive ointment, as if to express her desire to pour out her very heart at His feet.

Judas, on the other hand, had other thoughts on his mind. His hopes also lay in Jesus, but as a means of obtaining the worldly comforts and power which he might gain as keeper of Christ's purse. The many discourses and lessons of his divine Master were tolerated as a necessary evil. Judas awaited the day when he might be treasurer in the new kingdom of God on earth. His assertion that Mary should have considered the needs of the poor, may have aroused the admiration of most of his hearers, but Jesus knew the heart from which those words flowed. There was far more virtue in Mary's apparent waste than in Judas' superficial concern for the poor.

RESPOND   My Jesus, save me from self-deception and from the natural human motives that can draw my heart away from You. Let no drive, desire, or emotion within me so govern my thinking or control my will, that I may eventually betray You by sin. Like Mary, I want to hear Your words, watch Your actions, and see You as the divine Treasure that You really are to me. Only then will my concern for earthly good works be directed with the self-forgetfulness that made Mary see You and You alone in her expression of generosity and love. Amen.

126. TRIUMPHAL ENTRY INTO JERUSALEM

READ   And when they drew near to Jerusalem . . . He sent two of his disciples, and said to them, "Go into the village opposite you, and immediately on entering it, you will find a colt tied, upon which no man has yet sat; loose it and bring it. . . . And they brought the colt to Jesus, and threw their cloaks over it, and he sat upon it. And many spread their cloaks upon the road, while others were cutting branches from the trees, and strewing them on the road. And those who went before him, and those who followed, kept crying out, saying, *"Hosanna! Blessed is he who comes in the name of the Lord!"* (Mark 11:1–10)

REFLECT   On this occasion Jesus was fulfilling a messianic prophecy (Isaias 62:11). Nevertheless, we cannot be sure just how much of the people's enthusiasm was aroused by God's grace and how much by the natural emotional impact of the occasion. We do know, however, that few in this crowd would stand by Jesus later in the same week, when He would be unjustly tortured and condemned to die.

REVIEW   My spiritual life will be balanced and vigorous only in so far as I can do what the disciples failed to do during that last week of Christ's earthly life. They were so eager to taste the glory of their divine Master that they forgot His predictions about His impending sufferings and death. Though they may have sensed that He was now fulfilling the words of the prophets, they failed to see the rest of the week as a further fulfillment of the messianic prophecies.

In His plans for me, Jesus intended that every part of my daily life should be a companionship with Him. He wants me to believe in His nearness not only when all goes well, but also when difficulties, pains, and sorrows confuse and weaken me. I cannot attain my share of Christ's glory unless I proceed along the same path He walked, namely, the path of daily human living. In my particular circumstances I must see His supernatural presence. In my human situations I must perceive His divine association with me. In the drab details of my daily routine, I must behold the glorious goal which He presents to me, eternal victory with Him after having endured the earthly trials of daily human living.

RESPOND O Christ, my King and Companion through life, I desire to follow You, wherever You may lead me each day of my earthly life. I believe that Your divine providence has foreseen and planned the particular circumstances, situations, and human events that lie before me. While I thank You for the consoling moments when I feel Your nearness, I also beg for a strong faith to enlighten me when my mind is darkened by doubts and fears; strength to keep me loyal to Your principles when I am tired and weakened by my daily efforts; and confidence in Your divine understanding and love when I am discouraged by my mistakes and failures. As I rejoice over Your triumph over evil, so let me embrace my share of daily burdens for Your sake. Amen.

127. WEEPING OVER JERUSALEM

READ And when he drew near and saw the city, he wept over it, saying, "If thou hadst known, in this thy day, even thou, the things that are for thy peace! But now they are hidden from thy eyes. For days will come upon thee when thy enemies will throw up a rampart about thee, and surround thee and shut thee in on every side, and will dash thee to the ground and thy children within thee, and will not leave in thee one stone upon another, because thou hast not known the time of thy visitation." (Luke 19:41–44)

REFLECT The Jewish leaders refused to acknowledge Christ's message because He did not agree with their notion of the Messias. In His love for His own people, Jesus could not hold back His tears, as He foresaw the disaster which they would bring upon themselves through their rejection of Him.

REVIEW Do I find Jesus hard to take? Is it distasteful for me to speak to Him in prayer or even to think of Him? Am I quick to turn away from Him through my earthly concerns or interests? Perhaps I am somehow disappointed in Him. I may have expected an easy fulfillment of my religious ideals, or a greater sense of satisfaction from my religious activities. Whether through malice, weakness, or sheer ignorance, I may be setting a deliberate limit to my acceptance of Christ's leadership over my life.

If this is true of me, Jesus has reason to weep over me as He wept over Jerusalem. In my own way, I am following the bad example of the Jewish leaders and turning my back upon my divine Savior. Without Him, I am exposed to moral dangers which can sooner or later destroy me. Jesus asks me to come to Him because I need Him. He accepts me as I am, and desires to help me make the most of what I have. He requires no impossible changes, but only patient, persevering efforts to live my daily life in accordance with His teachings. He does not want me to be constantly apologizing for my unintended failures and unwanted limitations. Neither does He wish me to be weighed down by the fear that I may be deceiving myself. He asks me to prove my good intentions by a daily effort to know Him and imitate Him as far as I am able.

RESPOND   Jesus, my divine Savior, let me not expect an earthly satisfaction or a worldly reward for my religious activities. I accept Your invitation to come closer to You through prayer, sacraments, and daily practice. In my moments of impatience, unkindness, or self-seeking, I hope to accuse myself when I have sinned and to make due allowance when I was momentarily unthinking or weak. Through a better understanding of You and of myself, I hope to live in close union with You, my divine Savior and my King. Amen.

128.   FEAR OF CHRIST

READ   And they came to Jerusalem. And he entered the temple, and began to cast out those who were selling and buying in the temple; and he overturned the tables of the money-changers and the seats of those who sold the doves. He would not allow anyone to carry a vessel through the temple. And he began to teach, saying to them, "Is it not written, *'My house shall be called a house of prayer for all the nations'*? But you have made it a den of thieves."

And the chief priests and the Scribes heard it, and they sought a way to destroy him; for they were afraid of him, because all the crowd were astonished at his teaching. (Mark 11:15–18)

REFLECT In their mistaken thinking, the Jewish leaders saw Jesus as a dangerous radical who was trying to ruin them. So anxious did they become about His growing popularity, that they hated Him for disturbing their sense of security, contentment, and authority. They finally determined to destroy Him.

REVIEW In one way or another, and in varying degrees, this sad condition can happen to me. I too can have mistaken ideas about God, Christ, morality, and religion. Though I be unaware of my errors, they can produce harmful effects in my religious attitudes, feelings, and practices. There are times when I am ill at ease with Christ. I may have little or no feeling in His presence, and my mind may be drowsy, blank, or bored as I perform some religious activity. I may even be reluctant, strained, and eager to finish quickly, so as to ease the tension aroused by my religious performance.

When there is no evident cause for these inclinations and feelings, I may rightly suspect my mistaken thinking or some deep anxiety, fear, or hate aroused by such thinking. For instance, I may feel too unimportant, guilty, or unworthy of Christ's attention. I may feel some guilt for the spontaneous inclinations, imaginations, or feelings of my human nature. I may feel obliged to perform my religious activities so perfectly that they have become repulsive to my limited human nature. Like the Jewish leaders, I may have a deep fear of Christ, and even some measure of hatred for the demands I believe He has placed on me.

RESPOND My Jesus, King of Truth and Justice, how can I think so wrongly of You when You have proven Yourself the very soul of understanding, acceptance, and reasonableness? Help me to see how often I live not according to Your loving message and wise commandments, but according to my childish distortions and misinformed notions of Your divine teachings. Help me correct my errors and strengthen my weaknesses through prayer, sacraments, knowledge, and daily practice. Amen.

129. THE GRAIN OF WHEAT

READ "The hour has come for the Son of Man to be glorified. Amen, amen, I say to you, unless the grain of wheat falls into the ground and dies, it remains alone. But if it dies, it brings forth much fruit. He who loves his life, loses it; and he who hates his life in this world, keeps it unto life everlasting. If anyone serves me, let him follow me; and where I am there also shall my servant be. . . . Now my soul is troubled. And what shall I say? Father, save me from this hour! No, this is why I came to this hour. Father, glorify thy name!" (John 12:23–28)

REFLECT In these words Jesus presents the great challenge of daily Christian living. He points out the wisdom of living for eternity, and calls on all men to follow His example. He declares that His own human nature is, at that very moment, enduring the same inner conflict that all men experience when they strive to prefer the divine will to their own human inclinations. He then proceeds to choose His Father's will.

REVIEW I was created to share in God's wisdom and holiness by learning His divine will for me, and fulfilling my part in His eternal plan. Through the necessary circumstances in my life, the personal graces God grants me, and the guidance of duly constituted authority, I am to find my place in this world. However, being human, I shall often experience some measure of conflict within myself. In spite of my best intentions, I shall be divided between my knowledge and my doubts, my desires and my fears, my decisions and my dislikes. Though I may decide in favor of God's holy Will, I shall often find myself leaning toward attractive satisfactions or away from disagreeable duties. If I permit my emotions to do my thinking and make my decisions, I may lose far more than the passing satisfaction I gain.

Like the grain of wheat that dies to bring forth a more abundant life, I shall find a greater self-fulfillment by rising above my unthinking emotions. Jesus urges me to follow His example by embracing the heavenly Father's will. Knowing the boundless goodness, wisdom, and love of His Father, Jesus refuses to pray for a release from His plan of redemption. Jesus fixes His attention on the greater good that will come from His Self-sacrifice, and thereby overcomes all contrary human inclinations.

RESPOND   O Christ my King, You offered Yourself not only as my Savior, but also as my Ideal in daily life. Like You, I need not be ashamed that my nature shrinks from what is disagreeable, difficult, or painful. This repugnance is natural to man, and it does not affect the purity of my good intentions. My true greatness lies in trying, with Your help, to rise above my natural feelings and to accept the responsibilities of my state in life. You will not expect me to achieve more than I am able, as I face the inevitable situations and tolerate the necessary circumstances of my daily life. Let me not fear the human judgments of others, but with eyes on Your shining example, let me do my reasonable best and accept the results as the Father's will. Amen.

130.   TWO SONS

READ   "A man had two sons; and he came to the first and said, 'Son, go and work today in my vineyard.' But he answered and said, 'I will not'; but afterwards he regretted it and went. And he came to the other and spoke in the same manner. And this one answered, 'I go, sir'; but he did not go. Which of the two did the father's will?" They said, "The first." Jesus said to them, "Amen I say to you, the publicans and harlots are entering the kingdom of God before you. For John came to you in the way of justice, and you did not believe him. But the publicans and the harlots believed him; whereas you, seeing it, did not even repent afterwards, that you might believe him." (Matt. 21:28–32)

REFLECT This parable might be compared to the preceding as the other side of the same coin. Jesus is still considering men's relationship with God, and their reluctance to fulfill His holy Will. However, Jesus distinguishes between spontaneous acceptance or rejection of God's commands and a deliberate decision to obey or disobey.

REVIEW Once again Jesus shows me that my human nature's tendency to rebel against God's will is no norm of my moral goodness or badness. Indeed, many of my actual sins may proceed more from the ignorance, inadvertence, or weakness of the moment than from deliberation and malice. However, when I have had time to reflect upon the objective wrongness of my attitude, and the harm which my error brings to me or others, God expects me to show my good will by amending my ways.

The difference between a child and an adult is that the child is dominated by his emotions. He is easily swayed by present needs and feelings, and morally hindered by the prevailing emotions of the moment. Everyone is subject to such immature thinking and behaving at some time or another, regardless of chronological age. Many a venial sin is committed under the influence of these passing childish attitudes and momentary whims. However, everyone has his adult moments, when he is able to perceive the moral nature of his attitude, inclination, or action. If one then makes a free decision to remain in his wrong situation, he makes a moral decision to sin. If the matter is serious enough and the person involved is aware and free enough, he commits a grave sin. True, even after having given much consideration to their probable guilt, some people find it practically impossible to arrive at any definite conclusion. The normal person expresses his honest judgment in prayer or confession, and leaves the matter in God's hands.

RESPOND My Jesus, desires and words are but the first steps toward a mature following of You. The surest proof of my sincerity is shown when I make definite plans to meet the actual situations of my daily life. As I try to put Your principles into practice, I show a still greater sincerity. Then comes the most difficult proof of all. I must expect setbacks and occasional failures, and still be determined to continue my efforts to be loyal to You. If I can renew my intention and resume my efforts again and again, I can be sure that my desires and words are sincere. Amen.

131. THE MASTER'S SON

READ And he began to speak to them in parables. "A man planted a vineyard, and put a hedge about it, and dug a wine vat, and built a tower; then he let it out to vine-dressers, and went abroad. And at the proper time he sent a servant to the vine-dressers to receive from the vine-dressers some of the fruit of the vineyard; but they seized him, and beat him, and sent him away empty-handed. And again he sent another servant to them; but this one they wounded in the head and treated shamefully. And again he sent another, and him they killed, and many others; beating some, and killing some. Now he still had one left, a beloved son; and him he sent to them last of all, saying, 'They will respect my son.'

"But the vine-dressers said to one another, 'This is the heir; come, let us kill him, and the inheritance will be ours.' So they seized him and killed him, and cast him out of the vineyard. What therefore will the owner of the vineyard do? He will come and destroy the vine-dressers, and will give the vineyard to others." (Mark 12:1–9)

REFLECT   In this parable Jesus tells about the Jews' repeated rejection of God through His prophets, and of their final rejection through the murder of His divine Son.

REVIEW   Though I hope never to reject God by serious sin, I must understand that there are other ways of rejecting Him. Many good people find it difficult to pray at any length, or to dwell too long on religious thoughts, or to reflect on the moral quality of their daily lives. When they hear or read of God's goodness, mercy, love, or providence, they feel no particular attraction toward Him, they simply feel an aloofness, indifference, or lack of warmth toward Him. Though they have no deliberate intention or desire to offend Him by sin, they feel no inclination to show Him any more than the barest minimum of honor and service.

Though this condition is a form of spiritual tepidity, it is not necessarily the culpable tepidity of which God complains in the Scripture. In many cases, it is an emotional condition that dominates one's outlook, attitude, feelings, thinking, and external behavior. These people are the victims, rather than the masters of their dispositions and conduct. Over the years, they learned to judge themselves without due consideration for their good will and limitations. They gradually believed that their narrow and harsh view of themselves was God's way of judging them. This made them overly afraid of making a mistake or committing some possible sins. In time, their nature spontaneously sought relief from the intolerable strain created by their inner anxiety. They now find it repugnant to think too much along religious lines. They have no feeling or attraction for religious considerations or practices. Even without intending to do so, they easily forget or neglect God.

RESPOND Lord, may I never turn against You or neglect You because of my mistaken notions about You. May I look upon myself with some of Your fatherly understanding and treat myself with some of Your divine love, patience, and mercy. With this attitude and disposition, I shall never be tempted to neglect You in my daily life. Amen.

132. THE ROYAL MARRIAGE

READ "The kingdom of heaven is like a king who made a marriage feast for his son. And he sent his servants to call in those invited to the marriage feast, but they would not come. . . . But they made light of it and went off, one to his farm, another to his business; and the rest laid hold of his servants, treated them shamefully, and killed them. But when the king heard of it, he was angry; and he sent his armies, destroyed those murderers, and burnt their city. Then he said to his servants, 'The marriage feast indeed is ready, but those who were invited were not worthy; go therefore to the crossroads and invite whomever you shall find.' And his servants went out into the roads and gathered all whom they found, both good and bad; and the marriage feast was filled with guests. Now the king went in to see the guests, and he saw there a man who had not on a wedding garment. . . . Then the king said to the attendants, 'Bind his hands and feet and cast him forth into the darkness outside . . .'" (Matt. 22:2–13)

REFLECT This parable represents man's earthly life as a

mixture of duty and pleasure. Those who fulfill their duty shall receive honor and joy at the table of their king. Those who fail to offer the obedience and honor due to their sovereign, will be punished for their unbecoming behavior.

REVIEW In order to live a balanced life on earth, I must live in accordance with facts. No matter how I may feel about God, the following is true of Him. He is the essence of understanding and the soul of acceptance. In His commands and counsels, He is most reasonable. He does not expect of me what is beyond my strength. He is truly a father in His concern for my lasting welfare. He is ever ready to grant me whatever help I need for my best interests. However, He will not permit me to live a lie. He cannot allow me to live as though I had no need of Him, nor to enjoy the good things of this life as though they were mine to use as I please, without regard for His wisdom and justice.

I am, by my very nature, dependent on God for each moment of life, and for every satisfaction and enjoyment. When He commands anything of me, He does not do it for the mere pleasure of commanding, but because reality and reason require it. My obedience is more than an arbitrary acceptance of His authority. It is a fulfillment of justice, an acknowledgment of facts, an acceptance of reality. I cannot knowingly and freely disagree with His judgment and object to His will without doing harm to myself. The citizens in the above parable might have been able to move to another country but I cannot remove myself from the authority of God without destroying myself.

RESPOND My God and my All, my very nature demands that I not only obey Your holy Will, but that I obey it in the manner You prescribe. Help me understand how ignorant, blind, and weak I am amid my human limitations, confusion and emotions. May I always see my true, lasting, and greatest welfare and advantage in the fulfillment of Your holy Will. Amen.

133. CAESAR AND GOD

READ Then the Pharisees went and took counsel how they might trap him in his talk. And they sent to him their disciples with the Herodians, saying, "Master, we know that thou art truthful, and that thou teachest the way of God in truth and that thou carest naught for any man; for thou dost not regard the person of men. Tell us, therefore, what dost thou think: Is it lawful to give tribute to Caesar, or not?" But Jesus, knowing their wickedness, said, "Why do you test me, you hypocrites? Show me the coin of the tribute." So they offered him a denarius. Then Jesus said to them, "Whose are this image and the inscription?" They said to him, "Caesar's." Then he said to them, "Render, therefore, to Caesar the things that are Caesar's and to God the things that are God's." (Matt. 22:15–21)

REFLECT Christ's enemies try to lead Him into a trap. If He advocates nonpayment, He will be in trouble with the Roman authorities; if He allows payment, He will lose His messianic standing with the people, since they conceive the Messias as their liberator from the foreign yoke. Christ's answer is irrefutable in its clarity and simplicity. He shows them that there is no inevitable clash between these civic transactions and the true service of God.

REVIEW These men claimed to see a vital opposition between their civic duties, as vassals of Rome, and their position as the chosen people. Actually, many of their countrymen were seriously concerned with the question which was presented to Jesus. They attached some religious significance to it. Jesus tried to show them that they must not live by false religious principles. As long as they were loyal to God's commandments, and realistic in facing their present situation as a conquered people, they could still be serving God in their daily life.

In different ways, many people create their own personal "religious" standards, by which they hold themselves accountable for more than God requires of them. They resent having to fulfill the normal requirements of their state in life. They often wonder whether they are "doing enough" to please God. In their good works, they needlessly question the purity of their motives. They believe that they are "wasting time" unless they are doing something that has a formal "religious" value. Actually, these sincere people would overtax their strength if they added more prayers or good deeds to those they already perform. I must pray for and develop the wisdom and prudence that will keep me emotionally stable and mentally at peace as I perform the duties and enjoy the legitimate pleasures that form part of my daily life.

RESPOND   My Jesus, let me strike a mature balance between my Caesar and my God. I would prefer to die rather than compromise Your principles. On the other hand, let me not imagine an unreal opposition between my normal daily activities and my religious ideals, but see in all my prayers, works, joys and sufferings a service to God and men. Amen.

134.   THE SADDUCEES' CHALLENGE

READ   Now there came to him certain of the Sadducees, who say that there is no resurrection, and they questioned him, saying, "Master, Moses has written for us: 'If a man's brother die, having a wife, and he be childless, his brother shall take the widow and raise up issue to his brother.' Now there were seven brothers. And the first took a wife and died childless. And the next took her and he also died childless. Then the third took her; and in like manner all seven, and they died without leaving children. Last of all the woman also died. At the resurrection, therefore, of which of them will she be wife? For the seven had her as wife."

And Jesus said to them, "The children of this world marry and are given in marriage. But those who shall be accounted worthy of that world and of the resurrection from the dead, neither marry nor take wives. For neither shall they be able to die any more, for they are equal to the angels, and are sons of God, being sons of the resurrection." (Luke 20:27–36)

REFLECT   These men thought of heaven as a fiction. They conceived it as a mere extension of earthly life, with the same imperfect relationships and human limitations it endures in this world. Jesus briefly states the error of their concept.

REVIEW   In this incident I see the danger of reading the Scripture without the guidance of a reliable interpreter. I can think of heaven only in terms of what I have learned, known, and experienced here on earth. The thought of eternity may frighten me beyond words simply because I know not what to expect. I may dread being lost in the immense crowd of God's Blessed, or becoming bored with the sameness of heaven. Like the Sadducees, I have ideas of the next life, based on my limited earthly knowledge and experience, and my misguided imagination and emotions.

It is important to recall that Jesus did not try to describe heaven except in the very barest of descriptions and briefest of terms. All that I can understand of life in heaven is that it will be stripped of the imperfections which are now part of my human nature. I shall be known, understood, accepted, and approved, not only by God, but also by each and all of His Blessed. I shall experience no want, no privation, no misunderstandings, no conflict, neither with myself nor others. So full, so rich, so all-satisfying will this heavenly life be, that I cannot exhaust it, though I live forever.

RESPOND My Jesus, let me not think of heaven in terms of my earthly life. All I can be sure of is that it will be an all-satisfying life whose happiness can never be diminished, and whose joys cannot fade in the slightest degree. It will be the perfection of family life and the most lovable of homes. I shall enjoy the security of God's fatherhood, and the intimate companionship of His Blessed. Though I continue to study about heaven until the day I die, whatever I learn is but the faintest of reflections, and the barest of ideas. Only the experience of it can teach me what heaven is really like. Amen.

135. THE GREATEST COMMANDMENT

READ And one of the Scribes came forward who had heard them disputing together; and seeing that he had answered them well, he asked him which was the first commandment of all. But Jesus answered him, "The first commandment of all is, *'Hear, O Israel! The Lord our God is one God; and thou shalt love the Lord thy God with thy whole heart, and with thy whole soul, and with thy whole mind, and with thy whole strength.'* This is the first commandment. And the second is like it, *'Thou shalt love thy neighbor as thyself.'* There is no other commandment greater than these." (Mark 12:28–31)

REFLECT Jesus names the law of charity as the first and highest of all God's commandments. By this commandment, man is obliged to show reverence and obedience to God, and good will to men. God wants man to develop his charity so fully that he may be able to make his entire life an expression of love and loyalty to God.

REVIEW   To those who do not have a true appreciation of God, this commandment seems too demanding. They feel that they are being asked to forget their own needs, wants, and rights, and to concern themselves only with serving others. They find such a demand unattractive and even repulsive. By their very nature, they want to feel safe from the anxieties and strains caused by the difficulties, problems, and burdens of daily living. This law of charity would seem to increase such anxieties and strains.

   The truth of the matter is that charity comes easily only in proportion as I know and appreciate God. God is the center of my being, the fountain of my life, and the source of my well-being, contentment, satisfaction, and enjoyment. In loving God, I love myself most wisely, most fully, and most purely. As I understand His boundless goodness, wisdom, power, and love for me, I can more easily prefer His will to mine. I shall gradually be more at peace with myself and less uneasy about my personal dignity on earth and my salvation in eternity. As my appreciation of God deepens, my heart will overflow with gratitude, and I shall have a stronger desire to express my love through prayers, good will, and service to my fellow men. I shall be more disposed to rise above the human smallness of men, and to deal with them with some of God's own "bigness."

RESPOND   My God and my All! I hope to become a little better acquainted with You each day, so that I may eventually see in You my highest good and most desirable happiness. I need no imagination, but only Your grace, to achieve this supernatural vision and understanding. Then shall I know why Your saints were content with so little in this earthly life. They really had more than the most prosperous worldly man. Though they seemed strange or foolish to the worldly minded, they proved themselves the wisest of all. Help me imitate them on earth and rejoice with them in heaven. Amen.

136. BAD EXAMPLE OF THE RULERS

READ   Then Jesus spoke to the crowds and to his disciples, saying, "The Scribes and the Pharisees have sat on the chair of Moses. All things, therefore, that they command you, observe and do. But do not act according to their works; for they talk but do nothing. And they bind together heavy and oppressive burdens, and lay them on men's shoulders; but not with one finger of their own do they choose to move them. In fact, all their works they do in order to be seen by men; for they widen their phylacteries and enlarge their tassels, and love the first places at suppers and the front seats in the synagogues, and greetings in the market place, and to be called by men 'Rabbi.' . . . He who is the greatest among you shall be your servant. . . ." (Matt. 23:1–11)

REFLECT   We owe obedience to superiors as long as they command us within the boundaries of their authority. The wise superior is one who sees himself as the servant of his subjects. Even in commanding, he does so as a fulfillment of duty to God and his subjects rather than as a proof of his superiority over others.

REVIEW   I need never be afraid of those who have authority over me. They are human beings like me, with their own quota of human limitations and failings. They are not necessarily the wisest in their community, and at times they can even show less maturity and self-control than their subjects. They may, without justification, consider themselves exempt from the obligations common to all, and may even have their favorites and their prejudices.

They may not have the depth of understanding and breadth of acceptance to permit their subjects to be themselves within the boundaries of due external order. And yet, in spite of all this, Jesus commands me to show them reverence and obedience in view of their position as superiors. At the same time, I must obey them with respect for my own human dignity, and with a mature understanding of my position as a subject.

On the other hand, I must beware of taking undue advantage of those who are placed under my authority. I must not deny them the right to be themselves, as long as they do not show open disregard for the authority vested in me. May I never look upon my position as proof that I am better than my subjects; nor permit myself privileges I would not grant to others who have the same reasons as I. I must be the servant of my subjects, the friend of all, and an understanding, accepting parent to those who need my support and assistance. As superior, teacher, counselor, or companion, I can give others a slight glimpse of the goodness of God and the self-giving of Christ. If they feel free and willing to come to me in their needs, anxieties, and troubles, I am the kind of superior that Jesus would have me be.

RESPOND My Jesus, may I be ever ready to dispense Your gifts of love, good will, self-giving, and material assistance whenever my position requires it of me, and my situation makes it possible. Whatever my state of life, I shall always have opportunities to help others, at least by my respect for their human dignity and consideration for their personal feelings. Make me so full of love for You that I may be a small reflection of You to all with whom I deal in my daily life. Amen.

137. TRIFLES VERSUS IMPORTANT DUTIES

READ "Woe to you, Scribes and Pharisees, hypocrites! because you pay tithes on mint and anise and cummin, and have left undone the weightier matters of the Law, right judgment and mercy and faith. These things you ought to have done, while not leaving the others undone. Blind guides, who strain out the gnat but swallow the camel!" (Matt. 23:23–24)

REFLECT Jesus tells the Scribes and Pharisees that in spite of their fidelity to the smallest external duties, they lack the proper religious attitude and disposition which make these exterior practices pleasing to God. Since they are unwilling to remedy this undesirable situation, Jesus warns them of God's disapproval.

REVIEW A number of people are considered religious because of their fidelity to external religious duties and practices. They omit nothing that is expected of them, whether it be to contribute to some worthy cause or to attend a very early Mass before undertaking a journey on Sunday. And yet, in their words or actions they have an utter disregard for the human dignity, the respect due, or even the justice owed, to others. I, too, have my share of this human failing.

It takes a long time to grow up in the mentality of Christ. It requires knowledge of God, myself, and my neighbor; a daily effort to apply this knowledge in daily life; a constant consideration of my efforts and failures; and an unwavering determination to develop within myself the outlook, attitude, and disposition of Christ. As it takes time to grow a tree, to build a home, or to enter upon a professional career, so does it require time to achieve this growth of my interior spirit. Though the natural rewards of my earthly achievements must end with death, the supernatural rewards of my spiritual growth will endure forever. The eternal worth of my external religious activities depends upon the interior spirit with which they are performed.

RESPOND Lord, make me sensitive not merely to the responsibility of external performances, but also to the interior spirit which gives these performances their supernatural value. Help me see You in every man I meet, every action I perform, and every waking moment I spend on this earth. Make me conscious of the eternal value of all I do, and eager for the heavenly joy that You have prepared for those who do their good for love of You. Amen.

138. THE WIDOW'S MITE

READ And Jesus sat down opposite the treasury, and observed how the crowd were putting money into the treasury; and many rich people were putting in large sums. And there came one poor widow, and she put in two mites, which make a quadrans. And he called his disciples together, and said to them, "Amen I say to you, this poor widow has put in more than all those who have been putting money into the treasury. For they all have put in out of their abundance; but she out of her want has put in all that she had—all that she had to live on." (Mark 12:41–44)

REFLECT This statement of Jesus must have surprised His disciples. They were more impressed by the visible quantity of the donations, but Jesus saw the inner value, the greater self-sacrifice involved in each gift. She who seemed to have given least of all, was proclaimed the greatest donor in that crowd.

REVIEW When shall I cease feeling inferior to those who are more gifted than I, or envious of those who attract more attention and win more admiration? God dispenses His gifts in accordance with His divine plan. The talents, graces, and circumstances of my life are granted to me for His own good reasons. My eternal greatness and personal worth are not to be measured by these, but by the love with which I use my personal gifts and daily opportunities.

I am what I am because God chose to make me such. In proportion as I understand my God-given value, and appreciate the importance of my personal gifts and daily activities, I shall find satisfaction and joy in offering every hour of my day to Him. Whatever my limitations, no matter how small my daily occupations may seem, God will judge my worth by the amount of love I express through my attitude, disposition, and daily conduct. Be my heart large or small, if I fill it with love for Him, I shall be giving Him as much as is possible to my nature. And what precisely does this love consist in? It consists in fidelity to His holy Will, and good will toward my fellow men. My effort to live with this disposition and effort, is proof enough that I love God.

RESPOND My God, You ask only that I be myself for love of You, and perform my daily activities with the intention of satisfying my legitimate needs and desires in accordance with Your holy commandments. Though my knowledge be less than that of others, my talents be inferior to those of others, and my accomplishments be less spectacular than those of others, You will never compare me to others. You will judge my worth by the appreciation and love of You that inspires my fidelity to Your holy Will. Help me see more of You and less of human judgments and standards in what I do for Your sake. Though I have little to give You, I shall consider it a privilege to offer it to You with all the love in my heart. Amen.

139. DESTRUCTION OF THE TEMPLE

READ   And as he was going out of the temple, one of his disciples said to him, "Master, look, what wonderful stones and building!" And Jesus answered and said to him, "Dost thou see all these great buildings? There will not be left one stone upon another that will not be thrown down." (Mark 13:1–2)

REFLECT   Jesus uses this occasion to impress His disciples with the transitory nature of earthly satisfactions and worldly glories. Admirable as all this beauty and grandeur are, His followers must never allow themselves to forget that the good things of this world are but a means to the full and lasting joys of heaven.

REVIEW   God does not wish me to become so entangled in the satisfactions and achievements of this earthly life that I lose sight of the unending satisfaction and glory for which I was created. This does not mean that I am to fear the good things of this world as though they were harmful, or despise them as though they were evil. God made them for good reasons. They can help me to achieve the development, satisfaction and accomplishments, by which I may give glory to God, bring assistance to my neighbors, and obtain eternal happiness and glory for myself.

However, in my use of the good things of this world, God desires me to be realistic. I depend on a certain number of earthly necessities and satisfactions for my health of body, peace of mind, and moral strength. In my endeavor to attain religious perfection, I must not attempt to live as though I had no need of earthly things. Neither, on the other hand, must I be so immature as to look on these things as my only means of security, peace, and contentment. God desires that I enjoy the beautiful things of this world. He wants me to use the good things at my disposal in so far as they help me be more contented in the fulfillment of my daily duties and more self-controlled in resisting temptation. At all times, however, I must not forget that these earthly satisfactions are imperfect and short-lived. They are but shadows of the full and enduring satisfactions and joys of heaven.

RESPOND   My Jesus, make me wise in my daily use and enjoyment of the good things of this life. Let me not unduly minimize them nor foolishly overestimate them. Rather, help me see them for their real value, namely, as means to improve myself, and as aids to a better fulfillment of Your holy Will. May I never demand of these earthly things more than they can give me, nor seek them as though they alone were important to me. May I always view the satisfactions and joys of this earthly life in the light of that all-satisfying life which You have promised to those who love You. Amen.

140.   FALSE PROPHETS

READ   "And many false prophets will arise, and will lead many astray. And because iniquity will abound, the charity of the many will grow cold. But whoever perseveres to the end, he will be saved. And this gospel of the kingdom shall be preached in the whole world, for a witness to all nations; and then will come the end." (Matt. 24:11–14)

REFLECT   In this discourse Jesus speaks of the destruction of Jerusalem and the end of the world. He stressed the difficulty of holding on to religious principles amid the disorder and confusion which would mark both events. He exhorts His hearers to persevere in the practice of His teachings, that they might not be lost in their fight for earthly survival.

REVIEW   In the daily struggle for existence there is always some measure of insecurity, anxiety, confusion, and doubt. In such an atmosphere, each man is inclined to be on guard against the possible intrigues and injustices arising from the unprincipled self-concern of others. In my urge to defend myself, I may become indiscriminately suspicious, cynical, resentful, and inclined to get the better of others. Under the pressure of these natural tendencies, my religious ideals may fade and my principles may be weakened. Charity will become more difficult as my self-concern absorbs more of my attention and energy.

Jesus urges me to persevere in the good will which He taught me by word and example. He does not expect me to neglect my own welfare, but only to be disposed to do what little I can to help others. To maintain my fidelity to Christ amid the difficulties and problems of my daily life, I must strengthen my interior vision of God and foster my moral strength. By daily contact with God through prayer, intimacy with Jesus through some reading and reflection each day, understanding of myself through a daily review of my behavior, and examination of my dispositions and intentions, I can learn to look above the present human emotions, beyond the momentary conflicts, and through the passing confusion into the light of eternal day and the joy of heavenly peace and happiness.

RESPOND   Lord, let me not go through life with my eyes closed to the difficulties and problems that arise along my daily path. Help me apply Your truth and prove my loyalty to You in the real life situations that develop each day. Though confusion and disorder may make me uneasy and anxious at times, teach me to turn quickly to You for guidance and strength. May my love for You be as strong in those difficult moments as in my moments of prayerful union with You. Amen.

141. THE END OF THE WORLD

READ "And there will be signs in the sun and moon and stars, and upon the earth distress of nations bewildered by the roaring of sea and waves; men fainting for fear and for expectation of the things that are coming on the world; for the powers of heaven will be shaken. And then they will see the Son of Man coming upon a cloud with great power and majesty. But when these things begin to come to pass, look up, and lift up your heads, because your redemption is at hand." (Luke 21:25–28)

REFLECT In this brief but graphic description of the end of the world, Jesus impresses on us the fact that this earthly existence must crumble and pass away. Amid the terrifying details He assures us of His nearness and His personal concern.

REVIEW The question that almost forces itself into the awareness of many people is this: "Why should God end the world in so terrifying a manner? Why should He permit the sincere, well-intentioned people and those innocent of any crime, to undergo this dreadful experience along with the malicious and the guilty?" God has not chosen to explain His divine purpose in this revelation. Perhaps we will understand the answer to this mystery only when we stand before Him in eternity.

At any rate, this revelation of the world's destruction has shocked many into a serious re-evaluation of their earthly benefits, worldly advantages, and daily conduct. It can make me wiser in my attitudes toward the satisfactions and hardships of my daily life, and more prudent in my use of the good things at my disposal. It can help me show greater justice and charity toward those with whom I deal each day. The more I am impressed by the limited existence of this world, the less shall I be blinded by the passing glory of earthly achievements, and drawn to disorderly satisfactions of the moment. In spite of the human limitations or weaknesses that shame or humiliate me, the emotional conflicts that set me at odds with myself and with others, and the mental confusion caused by my anxieties, fears, and doubts, I shall be less tempted to sin. I shall find my conscience clear and my will strong in proportion to my deep supernatural realization that all this must pass away all too soon.

RESPOND My Jesus, teach me to meditate on this discourse of Yours without morbid fears or foolish worries. Help me understand that You are always near me and concerned for my true and lasting welfare. Grant me so deep a conviction of Your love, that I may face the future with confidence and trust in You. Amen.

142. A HEALTHY CONCERN FOR ETERNITY

READ "But of that day and hour no one knows, not even the angels of heaven, but the Father only. And as it was in the days of Noe, even so will be the coming of the Son of Man. For as in the days before the flood they were eating and drinking, marrying and giving in marriage until the day when Noe entered the ark, and they did not understand until the flood came and swept them all away; even so will be the coming of the Son of Man.

"Then two men will be in the field; one will be taken, and one will be left. Two women will be grinding at the millstone; one will be taken, and one will be left.

"Watch therefore, for you do not know at what hour your Lord is to come. But of this be assured, that if the householder had known at what hour the thief was coming, he would certainly have watched, and not have let his house be broken into. Therefore you also must be ready, because at an hour that you do not expect, the Son of Man will come." (Matt. 24:36–44)

REFLECT   Jesus warns us of the power which earthly pleasures and cares have of distracting our minds from our eternal welfare. He advises us to live in such a manner that we may always be ready to answer His summons into eternity.

REVIEW   It is quite normal for me to feel some measure of fear, uncertainty, and hope as I consider this warning of Christ. However, I must beware of the tendency to let fear and doubt dominate my religious thinking and behavior. Some people live under the influence of a vague, indefinite, and persistent uneasiness. In their religious exercises, they are overeager for a perfect performance. They wonder whether the good they are doing is good enough, or whether they might not be doing something better than what they are doing. They feel undeserving of the necessities they use, and in their legitimate rest, leisure, or recreation they feel guilty. While performing one activity, they may wonder whether they did the previous one well enough, or feel obliged to hurry on to the following one. Though they are full of good will, they lack the peace of a good conscience. They look on their natural limitations and normal weaknesses with the same shame, humiliation, self-accusation, and dread of punishment as they would feel toward their worst sins. They are more easily impressed by unfavorable remarks about themselves than by encouragement or praise.

I must beware of this unhealthy emotional approach to God and religion. Basically, it is not a religious problem as such. It is the result of past unhappy experiences and present emotional habits. It gradually develops into an unwarranted low self-opinion which makes one ill at ease with others, even God. It can gradually induce me to think of God as little as possible. Unless I respect my personal sincerity and individual limitations, I shall be unable to receive the above discourse as Christ intended it. He meant His words to be friendly advice. And He would prove His friendship by dying for my sins.

RESPOND My Jesus, let me not receive Your words as a threat, but as an instruction in wise living. I desire to please You because I love You. When, however, my love becomes too weak to keep me from sin, let me recall this friendly warning of Yours. Though I prefer to follow You with my deepest love, I would rather hold on to You through fear of Your justice than to lose You through sin. At the same time I intend to fight any tendency in me that inclines me to serve You through fear alone. Amen.

143. TWO SERVANTS

READ "Who, dost thou think, is the faithful and prudent servant whom his master has set over his household to give them their food in due time? Blessed is that servant whom his master, when he comes, shall find so doing. Amen I say to you, he will set him over all his goods. But if that wicked servant says to himself, 'My master delays his coming,' and begins to beat his fellow-servants, and to eat and drink with drunkards, the master of that servant will come on a day he does not expect, and in an hour he does not know, and will cut him asunder, and make him share the lot of the hypocrites." (Matt. 24:45–51)

REFLECT My life is a service of God for which I am accountable at all times. God is not obliged to give me time to prepare for His coming, since I am obliged to be ready at all times.

REVIEW A number of people become so accustomed to

the gifts, circumstances, and opportunities which fill their lives, that they forget that all that they are, and have, and enjoy, is not truly their own, but God's. Once a man loses his sense of indebtedness to God, he tends to become careless in his daily use of the good things at his disposal. Like the wicked servant in this gospel, they become tired of being servants, and begin to act as though they were the master of the household.

On the other hand, the good servant lives his life in accordance with the facts. He fulfills his daily duties as faithfully as though his master were visibly present. At no time has he reason to fear his master's return, since he is always performing his duty. I can imitate this wise and faithful servant or the unfaithful servant who was finally cast out for his injustices to his master and his fellow-servants.

My daily life is truly a service to God. Through the various circumstances which have led to my present state of life, God prepared me for my present duties and obligations. Instead of despising my limitations, hating my weaknesses, or rebelling against unpleasant circumstances, I shall be more mature, more virtuous, and more content if I try to make the most of the opportunities within my grasp. As Jesus did not consider it a disgrace to be the carpenter of Nazareth, so should I never look upon my limited circumstances as a cause for shame.

RESPOND   O Jesus, my divine Master, I am so utterly dependent upon You that I have nothing I can call my very own. Therefore I desire to make my life one constant act of sincere gratitude. Of the many gifts You have granted me, let me treasure most of all the genuine friendship which You offer to me every moment of my life. Amen.

144. THE LAST JUDGMENT

READ "But when the Son of Man shall come in his majesty, and all the angels with him, then he will sit on the throne of his glory; and before him will be gathered all the nations, and he will separate them from one another, as the shepherd separates the sheep from the goats; and he will set the sheep on his right hand, but the goats on the left. Then the king will say to those on his right hand, 'Come, blessed of my Father, take possession of the kingdom prepared for you from the foundation of the world; for I was hungry and you gave me to eat; I was thirsty and you gave me to drink . . . Amen I say to you, as long as you did it for one of these, the least of my brethren, you did it for me." (Matt. 25:31–40)

REFLECT Jesus continues His discourse on the four last things: death, judgment, heaven, and hell. With clarity and brevity, He impresses us with the finality of that last judgment. He will base His judgment on our supernatural vision of faith and our daily practice of charity. He even says that what we do to others, we do to Him.

REVIEW As Jesus has indicated in a number of ways, my great problem is that of seeing my present circumstances and experiences in their relationship to eternity. To an ant, a puddle is a lake and a pool is an ocean. To a mature man, a puddle is just a puddle and a pool is simply a pool. I must grow up in the thinking of Christ and the viewpoint of God. I am too easily affected by the small-mindedness of some and the emotional exaggerations of others. Most of the crises of my past are now forgotten, and even those I recall have lost the terror they once aroused in me.

Jesus shows me the shortest way to emotional maturity

and supernatural moral strength. He advises me to recall the judgment often, and to remember that He will approach me in my neighbor. If I am eternity-minded in my interior dispositions, and Christ-conscious in my interpersonal relations, I shall be able to free myself from my unreasonable self-disgust and my immature fears of human disapproval. I shall see my daily life as a striving for eternal glory and a proof of sincere love for Christ.

The just will rejoice at the sight of their Judge, and exult in His loving invitation. I need not center my attention on my unwanted defects and my unintended failures. Jesus will judge me by my deliberate intention and my sincere efforts. He does not demand that my effort be strained, but just a simple human effort, which will often be imperfect, even though inspired and sustained by His grace. He is so reasonable in His demand and so understanding of my limited results. If I try to live with this attitude and disposition today, I am living for heaven.

RESPOND   Jesus, my Judge, may I love You enough to try each day, in spite of repeated failures, and regardless of human judgments concerning my personal worth. I hope to live with eyes on the last judgment and heaven's all-satisfying happiness. Amen.

145. THE PLOT OF JUDAS

READ   But Satan entered into Judas, surnamed Iscariot, one of the Twelve. And he went away and discussed with the chief priests and the captains, how he might betray him to them. And they were glad, and agreed to give him money. He accordingly promised, and sought out an opportunity to betray him without a disturbance. (Luke 22: 3–6)

REFLECT We have already seen (on pages 221—22) how Judas resented Mary's anointing of Jesus with an expensive ointment. In spite of his pretended concern for the poor, his real reason was a worldly love of money, which had gradually turned him into a thief. We now see the final results of this sad transformation. As he realized that the proposed kingdom of God on earth would not involve the wealth and grandeur he had expected, he became bitter against his Master. He became an easy prey to temptation, and finally decided to get whatever gain he could by betraying Jesus.

REVIEW One of my daily problems is that of becoming too attached to the good things of this world. Through experience, I have learned to value some things over others. Hence I have my preferences and my prejudices, which may easily incline me to sin. Though I may still profess to seek God's will, I may be doing so with reservations in my heart.

Consciously or unconsciously, I value things in proportion as they bring me a sense of security, satisfaction, and contentment. Unless I keep my thinking clear and my will strong, I am always in danger of being unduly dominated by my emotional preferences and prejudices. Through reading, meditation, and prayer, I can gradually find my greatest security, highest satisfaction, and deepest contentment in God. Through an intelligent practice of self-denial, I can strengthen my preference of God and slowly obtain freedom from my sinful preferences and prejudices. However, I must beware of the clever deceits of Satan. When he sees me resolving to draw closer to God, he tempts me to immature extremes. I must never have such a disregard for my real needs and legitimate wants that my nature is forced to rebel against my unreasonable demands on myself.

RESPOND My Jesus, may I never seek to satisfy my wants by betraying You. Help me see my greatest gain and high-

est advantages in Your kind of wealth. You offer me the
treasures of Your divine wisdom and supernatural strength.
You urge me to seek not only the temporary satisfaction
of my earthly needs, but also the eternal satisfaction of
heaven. Amen.

146. THE LAST SUPPER BEGINS

READ   And when the hour had come, he reclined at table,
and the twelve apostles with him. And he said to them, "I
have greatly desired to eat this passover with you before I
suffer; for I say to you that I will eat of it no more, until it
has been fulfilled in the kingdom of God." . . . Now there
arose also a dispute among them, which of them was reputed to be the greatest. But he said to them, ". . . let
him who is greatest among you become as the youngest,
and him who is the chief as the servant." (Luke 22:14–16,
24–26)

REFLECT   In the behavior and words of their divine Master, the apostles could sense the solemnity of this particular
occasion. Yet as they proceeded through the evening, one
of them brought up a subject which seems to have been
a frequent cause of dispute. In their eagerness to dispel
the inner discomfort aroused by the superiority claims of
others, each pronounced himself better than the others.

REVIEW   As I meditate on this sacred occasion in the
life of Jesus, I may react with a bit of disgust or shock at
the childish conduct of the apostles. How could they think
of themselves at the very moment when their beloved
Master was reminding them of the sufferings He would
undergo for them and for the world? The more I understand myself and my fellow man, the less will I be in-

clined to look upon the apostles with surprise, disgust, or shock.

Every man is self-centered by his very nature. I shall have to contend all through my earthly life with my ever vigilant self-concern, and with the self-interest of those around me. In the practical situations of daily life, my mind will be distracted from God by my anxieties, fears, anger, or hostility. The self-interest of others will momentarily blind me to my supernatural desires, intentions, and efforts, as I spontaneously rise to defend myself from the threats I feel or the dangers I see. Even when I try to help or please others, I shall sometimes be the victim of their self-centered nature in a number of ways.

Through an intelligent, patient, persevering effort to understand the bigness of Christ and the smallness of human nature, I shall be more inclined to imitate Him in my dealings with others. As I come to appreciate His divine wisdom and goodness, I shall strive more earnestly to develop within myself the maturity and charity which He taught by word and example. If I am willing to take the time, face repeated failures, and accept slow improvement, I shall someday know the peace of mind and joy of soul which Jesus promised to those who prove their love for Him.

RESPOND Lord, at times life seems so complicated and difficult. I am tempted to trust nobody, and to think only of my own interests. Yet, You urge me to serve You by being considerate and helpful to others. Show me how to fulfill this divine request without neglecting my own necessary rights and obligations. Amen.

147. CHRIST WASHES THE FEET OF THE APOSTLES

READ And during the supper . . . Jesus . . . rose from the supper and laid aside his garments, and, taking a towel, girded himself. Then he poured water into the basin and began to wash the feet of the disciples, and to dry them with the towel with which he was girded. . . . Now after he had washed their feet and put on his garments, when he had reclined again, he said to them, "Do you know what I have done to you? You call me Master and Lord, and you say well, for so I am. If, therefore, I the Lord and Master have washed your feet, you also ought to wash the feet of one another. For I have given you an example, that as I have done to you, so you also should do. Amen, amen, I say to you, no servant is greater than his master . . . If you know these things, blessed shall you be if you do them." (John 13:2–5, 12–17)

REFLECT In order to drive His lesson home, Jesus acted as a servant to His apostles. They would never forget this lesson. If they were ever again tempted to raise themselves above the others, they would overcome the temptation with the recollection of their divine Master, washing and wiping their feet.

REVIEW I must often meditate on this beautiful scene. Jesus, King of Love, shows me the meaning of true love. As He did on this occasion, I must show concern for the honor and welfare of others. This does not mean that I am to neglect my own needs, rights, and obligations, but that I am to include my neighbor's welfare among my own interests and concerns. As far as my strength and material means will allow, I am to find a supernatural satisfaction in helping others.

With this disposition, I shall never be oversensitive about my rights nor overeager to prove myself above others. When compelled to defend my rights against those who are inconsiderate or unjust, I shall be disposed to do so with justice and moderation rather than exercise an unreasonable cruelty toward the offenders. Whenever possible, I shall try to help others feel accepted, respected, and welcome. All this can I do if I obtain, increase, and strengthen my personal love of Jesus. It will not happen in a single day. I shall have to reflect often on Who He is, What He means to me, and What He desires of me. As I persevere in my effort to become more like Him, I shall grow in the power to follow His example more fully.

RESPOND My Jesus, though I am capable of very little just now, I do hope to increase my imitation of You with time, grace, and practice. Let me find a happy balance in my spiritual efforts, so that I may not be foolish in my personal endeavors, nor unreasonable in my demands on others. Amen.

148. JUDAS LEAVES JESUS

READ Now when evening arrived, he reclined at table with the twelve disciples. And while they were eating, he said, "Amen I say to you, one of you will betray me." And being very much saddened they began each to say, "Is it I, Lord?" But he answered and said, "He who dips his hand into the dish with me, he will betray me. The Son of Man indeed goes his way, as it is written of him; but woe to that man by whom the Son of Man is betrayed! It were better for that man if he had not been born." And Judas who betrayed him answered and said, "Is it I, Rabbi?" He said to him, "Thou hast said it." (Matt. 26:20–25)

REFLECT Without addressing Judas personally, Jesus points out the enormity of his sin by hinting at the fearfulness of his punishment. As He handed the morsel to Judas, their eyes must have met. But Judas had ceased seeing the real Christ some time ago. He was so unaffected by his Master's appeal, that he could ask along with the rest, "Is it I?" Even when Jesus told him frankly that He knew, Judas felt nothing. Jesus then tells him to get it over with.

REVIEW There is no sadder sight than that of a person who has lost interest in Christ. Some lose it because of conscious and malicious attachment to sin. They have made a free decision, and then endeavor to enjoy it fully by shutting out the "disagreeable" truth of God. Others, on the other hand, feel cut off from God for purely emotional reasons. They may have a deep desire to achieve a close union with God, but feel shut out of His attention and love.

Some feel unable to free themselves of habits which are objectively wrong. They have tried for some time to overcome these habits, but have gradually given up their effort. Either they demanded a sudden, complete mastery over themselves, or they strained too hard in their effort, or they were overwhelmed by feelings of self-disgust or guilt each time their habit recurred. They finally felt compelled to turn their attention from the entire effort. Even without deliberately intending to do so, they lost interest in all religious exercises, and this diminished the unbearable anxiety and tension which their religious awareness aroused in them.

The third group in this category consists of people who feel so obliged to maintain a flawless conduct that they become unduly annoyed or disturbed by normal, unintended, unwanted, and often inevitable human defects. Their constant conviction that they "should" be able to correct these human limitations, makes them feel some measure of guilt and rejection by God. Since it is difficult, and even repulsive, to live in the presence of God Who is seen through these immature emotional distortions, a number of these innocent people remain aloof from Him in fear or discouragement.

RESPOND My Jesus, teach me to hope in You so firmly that I may never turn away from You. Whatever my real sins, and regardless of my human defects, I shall never deliberately walk away from You as Judas did. Because I need You more than I need any other person or thing on earth, I shall hold on to You by hope and trust. Amen.

149. THE HOLY EUCHARIST

READ And while they were at supper, Jesus took bread, and blessed and broke, and gave it to his disciples, and said, "Take and eat; this is my body." And taking a cup, he gave thanks and gave it to them, saying, "All of you drink of this; for this is my blood of the new covenant, which is being shed for many unto the forgiveness of sins. But I say to you, I will not drink henceforth of this fruit of the vine, until that day when I shall drink it new with you in the kingdom of my Father." . . . "A new commandment I give you, that you love one another. By this will all men know that you are my disciples, if you have love for one another." (Matt. 26:26–29; John 13:34–35)

REFLECT This is a timeless moment; a moment of importance to me, which cannot adequately be described or explained by all the books in the world. Jesus institutes His sacrifice and sacrament of love, and He issues His supreme commandment that His followers love one another as He has loved them.

REVIEW Having lived every moment of His earthly life as

an act of reparation and redemption, Jesus now prepares for the sufferings and death He will freely embrace for my sake on the next day. As though unable to do enough for me, He now institutes a lasting remembrance of His earthly life and death. He instituted the Mass as a visible bridge between His earthly life and mine, His death and my sins, His resurrection and my supernatural life of grace. In the frequent repetition of the Mass throughout the world, He will express His endless desire to give Himself for my sake, and His repeated wish that I show my love for Him in action.

By showing forth His body and blood under the appearance of bread and wine, He reminds His Father and me of the infinite reparation He has made for my sins, and the boundless graces He has placed at my disposal. In Holy Communion, He offers me a greater share in His supernatural life with the total self-giving of food, which must undergo its own destruction to sustain the life of its consumer. My daily life is to be my Mass, my self-offering and self-sacrifice for His sake. My concern, consideration and assistance of others will be my proof of love for Christ.

RESPOND My Jesus, words can never say what I would like to tell You, as I consider the unbounded generosity which You are constantly showing me in every Mass and Holy Communion. Let me express my gratitude in the manner You desire, namely, by a greater generosity and concern for those who are involved in my daily life. Amen.

150. PETER'S GOOD WILL

READ Simon Peter said to him, "Lord, where art thou going?" Jesus answered, "Where I am going thou canst not follow me now, but thou shalt follow later." Peter said to him, "Why can I not follow thee now? I will lay down my life for thee." Jesus answered him, "Wilt thou lay down thy life for me? Amen, amen, I say to thee, the cock will not crow before thou dost deny me thrice." (John 13:36–38)

REFLECT The denial of Peter was not caused by a loss of faith in Christ, but by his fear and discouragement at seeing his Master captured by His enemies. In his claim to be stronger than the rest, Peter was sincere but presumptuous. He was actually offended by Jesus' assertion that he would deny Him. He really expected to stand by His Master in any eventuality.

REVIEW Too many people fail to take their human limitations into account when they make their good resolutions. They do not realize that in spite of their present sincerity and determination, they will still have to face their difficult moods, and their moments of forgetfulness or weakness. Due to this immature attitude, they are easily upset by unexpected failures and unintended lapses into old defects. Without regard for their sincerity or consideration for their human frailty, they demand of themselves a perfect performance.

These people and I can learn a precious lesson from this gospel scene. Peter confused his sincerity with strength. He forgot to pray for the grace to help him stand by his Master. I must ask for God's support in all my good desires and hopes. At the same time, I must understand that there will be times when my energies are low, my self-control is diminished, and my cooperation with grace is more difficult. In spite of my best efforts, and my intention never to offend God, I shall be influenced by my immature attitudes, thoughts, or desires. Like Peter, I may fall when I least expect it.

RESPOND My Jesus, I acknowledge my human limitations and weaknesses. Grant me grace never to offend You again. If, however, I do, grant me humility to confess my fault, sorrow for offending You, and determination to keep trying for Your sake. Amen.

151. SEEING GOD IN JESUS

READ "Let not your heart be troubled. You believe in God, believe also in me. In my Father's house there are many mansions. Were it not so, I should have told you, because I go to prepare a place for you. And if I go and prepare a place for you, I am coming again, and I will take you to myself; that where I am, there you also may be. And where I go you know, and the way you know. . . . I am the way, and the truth, and the life. No one comes to the Father but through me. . . . he who sees me sees also the Father." (John 14:1–4, 6, 9)

REFLECT For some time now Jesus has been preparing His disciples for the shock they would experience at His capture, condemnation, and death. As He looks upon them now, overwhelmed by sadness and uncertainty as to what might befall them, He offers them reassurance and encouragement. They are to trust in God and in His own personal concern for them. They need only remain faithful to Him, and they will be introduced into their eternal reward.

REVIEW These words of Jesus apply not only to the apostles present in the upper room, but to every Christian down through the ages. In every human life there are moments of insecurity, uncertainty, fear, doubt, disappointment, pain, sorrow, and discouragement. To each and every individual, Jesus addresses these same words of reassurance and encouragement. They apply to me as personally as they did to His sorrowful apostles.

In my personal difficulties, problems, and hardships, do I turn easily to Jesus for the supernatural understanding and strength I need? Is His word powerful enough to bolster my faith and restore my confidence, or am I held back from Him by my fears, doubts, guilt-feelings, and sense of unworthiness? In Jesus I must see the heavenly Father's concern for me. In the words of Christ, I hear the assurance of God and the promises which He has made to me through His divine Son.

I shall never be alone in my troubles. My personal limitations and human weaknesses will be more than compensated by the infinite wisdom, divine strength, and personal companionship of Jesus. If I doubt His reassuring promises, I shall find only mental confusion, unsettling fears, and moral weakness in my moments of earthly sorrows, sufferings, and troubles.

RESPOND My Jesus, in all my difficulties, problems, and sufferings of mind and body, I shall never turn from You in doubt or offend You by voluntary rebellion. In spite of any spontaneous fear of You, unwanted doubt of You, or unintended resentments against You, I shall rely upon Your proven love for me and Your promised help. I shall make a willful act of trust in Your interest and confidence in Your nearness. With this attitude, I shall place my problems, sufferings and life in Your hands. Amen.

152. INDWELLING OF THE BLESSED TRINITY

READ "If you love me, keep my commandments. And I will ask the Father and he will give you another Advocate to dwell with you forever; the Spirit of truth whom the world cannot receive, because it neither sees him nor knows him. But you shall know him, because he will dwell with you and be in you. I will not leave you orphans; I will come to you. Yet a little while and the world no longer sees me. But you see me, for I live and you shall live. In that day you will know that I am in my Father, and you in me, and I in you. . . . If anyone love me, he will keep my word, and my Father will love him, and we will come to him and make our abode with him." (John 14:15-21, 23)

REFLECT   Jesus asks His apostles to stand by Him, and follow His commands, in spite of their natural inclinations and feelings. He then promises them a companionship with God, far beyond their fondest dreams. Father, Son, and Holy Spirit would dwell within them, and they would be aware of this divine indwelling by a faith that would stand firm against all earthly hardships and trials.

REVIEW   In baptism I too became a living temple of God. The Holy Trinity came into my soul, in a union more intimate than any earthly companionship. The moods, feelings, attitudes, and tendencies which I cannot even put into words, are openly seen, wisely understood, deeply appreciated, and lovingly accepted and directed aright by my closest Companion, truest Friend, most untiring Assistant, and most encouraging of all Fathers.

Alone, I have reason to feel inadequate to many of life's daily situations. Alone, I am limited and weak in so many ways. Alone, I am just one of numberless millions created by God. My sense of littleness, insignificance, guilt, and unworthiness might be justified if I were alone. But I am not alone. By the word of Christ Himself, I am a living temple of God and a member of His Mystical Body, which is the Church. I am personally joined to the Holy Trinity within me, and to Jesus, the living Head of His Church. I can rightfully feel superior to the natural human self I was before baptism, because I now live by the grace of the Son of God.

RESPOND   Most holy Father, I thank You for having given me the privilege of being redeemed by Your beloved Son. My Jesus, I thank You for having proven in so human a way Your divine love, which surpasses all human words. Holy Spirit, I thank You for being my constant Guide, Support, and Companion in my daily activities, experiences, and situations. May I express my thanks in the best language of all, the language of desire, intention, and effort to be loyal to Your holy Will. Amen.

153. THE VINE AND THE BRANCHES

READ "I am the vine, you are the branches. He who abides in me, and I in him, he bears much fruit; for without me you can do nothing. . . . If you keep my commandments you will abide in my love, as I also have kept my Father's commandments, and abide in his love. . . . This is my commandment, that you love one another as I have loved you. . . . You are my friends if you do the things I command you. No longer do I call you servants, because the servant does not know what his master does. But I have called you friends, because all things that I have heard from my Father I have made known to you. You have not chosen me, but I have chosen you, and have appointed you that you should go and bear fruit, and that your fruit should remain . . . These things I command you, that you love one another." (John 15:5, 10, 12, 14–17)

REFLECT Jesus continues to develop His revelation of the Christian life. As a vine is joined to its branches, so intimately are we united to God through Christ. We are to exercise this new supernatural life by a daily imitation of His earthly example. His commandments will guide us to a life of love—love of God by fidelity to our daily duties and obligations, and love of men by a generous exercise of personal respect and concern for them.

REVIEW In virtue of this union with Jesus, I bear Him about in my person. Where I walk, Jesus walks with me. What I do, Jesus does in me, sin alone excepted. My thinking is overshadowed by His, and is often a reflection of His. My vision of this earthly life is extended to the life beyond. My desires are like rays proceeding from His divine intention, and my daily activities bear the stamp of Christ, to Whom I am joined by the grace of baptism. Though I am usually unaware of this unity with Christ, He declares it to be a fact. It depends not upon my moods or feelings, but upon His plan of redemption. Once received, this union with Him can be enriched by a growing knowledge of His truth and a persevering effort to apply that knowledge to my daily living.

RESPOND My Jesus, help me become ever more conscious of this supernatural vocation. I am now duty bound to become as much like You as my knowledge, strength, and graces will permit. Help me see how I may be another Christ to those around me, without putting undue strain upon myself or unnecessary pressures upon them. Amen.

154. IN HATRED OF CHRIST

READ "If the world hates you, know that it has hated me before you. If you were of the world, the world would love what is its own, but because you are not of the world, but I have chosen you out of the world, therefore the world hates you. Remember the word that I have spoken to you: No servant is greater than his master. If they have persecuted me, they will persecute you also; . . . But all these things they will do to you for my name's sake, because they do not know him who sent me." (John 15:18–21)

REFLECT One of the necessary consequences of our being

united to Christ and faithful to His holy example, is the aversion and hatred of those who lack good will. When we meet this hatred and hostility, we must remember that we are merely undergoing what Jesus experienced in His own earthly life. Even though we have to defend our rights for the glory of God, we shall do so with a sense of joy at sharing something of Christ's sufferings.

REVIEW   Jesus is realistic in His teachings. He does not want me to live in a dream world. He tells me that I shall have to suffer for my union with Him. My fidelity to His principles and holy example will offend and antagonize the worldly minded. Those who reject Him, will reject me, and those who have turned against Him may easily turn against me. This is part of the price I must pay for my union and friendship with Jesus.

In the emotional atmosphere of the moment, my natural inclination will be to return hate for hate and to repay hostility with hostility. Jesus does not expect me to let these people trample me underfoot, nor to permit them to take unfair advantage of me. However, He does expect me to rise above my limited natural outlook, and to defend my necessary rights without childish extremes or a malicious readiness to overstep the bounds of justice in my self-defense. In loyalty to Him I am to desire the welfare of these people, and to pray for it. I can rise to this Christ-like attitude by frequent association with Jesus through reading, meditation, and prayer. As I develop within me the mind of Christ, I shall grow in His divine understanding, patience, and good will, and enjoy a greater share in His supernatural peace.

RESPOND   My Jesus, I hope for a gradual transformation of the small-minded person I now am, into an understanding, self-giving reflection of You. Through daily practice in little things, I shall endeavor to show forth the strength of Your meekness, the power of Your love, and the peace of Your personal friendship. Amen.

155. THE SORROWS OF LIFE

READ "Amen, amen, I say to you, that you shall weep and lament, but the world shall rejoice; and you shall be sorrowful, but your sorrow shall be turned into joy. A woman about to give birth has sorrow, because her hour has come. But when she has brought forth the child, she no longer remembers the anguish, for her joy that a man is born into the world. And you therefore have sorrow now; but I will see you again, and your heart shall rejoice, and your joy no one shall take from you." (John 16:20–22)

REFLECT Jesus continues to prepare His followers for the future. He tells them to expect suffering and sorrow, and He advises them to look beyond their passing earthly difficulties and pains to the all-satisfying joy which He intends to bestow on them.

REVIEW As Jesus points out so well, human life on earth has its sorrows and its joys, its labors and its rewards. People are quick to forget their hardships when they have achieved the success and satisfaction for which they labored and suffered. How much more ought I to endure whatever difficulty, burden, or suffering is necessary in my own daily life? After all, this life is all too short and incomplete. Once the early years of training are over, the rest of life races by so quickly that I can hardly account for the vanished years. Were there no eternal life, this world would be very frustrating and aggravating to most people.

And yet, in my troubles, pains, and sorrows, I am easily tempted to forget the all-satisfying life which Jesus has promised to me. My nature reaches blindly for the immediate relief, the quick solution, the present satisfaction. In spite of my belief in the wisdom, mercy, and love of God, I sometimes feel so unsure of myself and of others, so alone against life, so abandoned by God. At times I may feel that He is angry at me for my shortcomings and sins, or that He is unjust in His demands on me, or that He finds satisfaction in my sufferings. In my confusion I may even wonder whether He exists at all.

In this frame of mind, I may easily envy those who seem content in the enjoyment of this present life without too much concern for the next. Jesus urges me to fix my intelligence on facts. Worldly people are ready to labor and sacrifice for the passing satisfactions of this brief life. How much more should I be willing to labor and sacrifice for the eternal joy which He has promised me?

RESPOND My Jesus, the wisdom You teach and the strength You offer me, are to be developed by a daily application to real life. Show me how to live this day wisely, peacefully, and contentedly for the glory of God and for my own all-satisfying joy in heaven. Amen.

156. MY SOURCE OF STRENGTH

READ His disciples said to him, "Behold, now thou speakest plainly, and utterest no parable. Now we know that thou knowest all things, and dost not need that anyone should question thee. For this reason we believe that thou camest forth from God." Jesus answered them, "Do you now believe? Behold, the hour is coming and has already come, for you to be scattered, each one to his own house, and to leave me alone. But I am not alone, because the Father is with me. These things I have spoken to you that in me you may have peace. In the world you will have affliction. But take courage, I have overcome the world." (John 16:29–33)

REFLECT As the apostles listened to their beloved Master, their enthusiasm rose, and they made this public profession of faith. Once again, however, Jesus keeps His eyes on reality and predicts their fear and desertion. He foretells His human aloneness in His trial, but asserts that He will not really be alone, but in the company of His Father. He declares that His trial and example will give them inspiration and courage in their own sufferings.

REVIEW   Just as my human nature is constantly subject to conflicting emotions and changing moods, so does Jesus constantly remind me of the unchanging facts of my spiritual life. As He was abandoned by His closest friends and followers, so at times shall I feel very much alone in my troubles and sorrows. As He sought the company of His heavenly Father in His mental torment, bodily tortures, and spiritual agony, so too must I seek the Father with eyes of faith, lean on Him with trust and confidence, and hold His fatherly hand by my fidelity to His divine will. As Jesus overcame the folly and malice of this world by His teachings and personal example, so must I find peace of mind and strength of soul in the truth of His words and the holiness of His life.

Jesus promises me no heaven on earth. He tells me to expect external opposition and internal weakness. Instead of looking for perfect answers to my questions, and complete earthly solutions to my problems, I am to see my personal troubles and hardships as a continuation of His. In proportion as I perceive my union with Christ and His devotedness to me, I shall find courage to face my earthly life and strength to overcome my daily conflicts.

RESPOND   My Jesus, help me understand the emotions that confuse my mind, and resist the tendencies that weaken my will, so that I may find You in every problem and see You behind every burden. May I never abandon You through fear of earthly sufferings or through a desire for the brief satisfactions of this world. Amen.

157. TRUTH AND HOLINESS

READ "Holy Father, keep in thy name those whom thou hast given me, that they may be one even as we are. . . . I have given them thy word; and the world has hated them because they are not of the world, even as I am not of the world. I do not pray that thou take them out of the world, but that thou keep them from evil. . . . Sanctify them in the truth. Thy word is truth. . . . Yet not for those only do I pray, but for those also who through their word are to believe in me, that all may be one, even as thou Father, in me and I in thee; that they also may be one in us, that the world may believe that thou hast sent me." (John 17:11, 14–15, 17, 20–21)

REFLECT Though Jesus prays as a human being, He still retains His dignity as the Son of God. Therefore His prayer merited the perfect attention and approval of His heavenly Father. He prayed that His followers might always live their lives in accordance with the facts and reality which He had revealed to them. In this way they would achieve a supernatural union with Him and His Father and thereby inspire others to draw closer to God.

REVIEW To be a true follower of Christ, I must be a man of truth, that is, one who is mature enough to acknowledge facts and respect reality. No one blames a child for living in a dream world, pretending that he is master of all things and above all others. When, however, he reaches the age of reason, he is expected to live in accordance with facts. If he insists on behaving as a child, he is either immature or proud, since he claims more than his right or pretends to be what he is not.

Since the truth alone can help me find my real worth with God and men, I must learn to love the truth. Instead of demanding that life adjust to my needs and wants, I must try to adjust myself to life. Though I may try to take full advantage of my personal gifts and circumstances, I must know how to accept the inevitable limitations and necessary disappointments of my daily life. This maturity and honesty with facts will dispose me to be loyal to Jesus, united with God, and an inspiration to those who know me.

RESPOND   My Jesus, may I know the peace that You have promised to Your true followers. Grant me an adult attitude and a mature outlook on the facts that govern my daily life. With this grace I shall find joy in Your companionship, strength in my union with God, and contentment in the good I do for those who are well disposed. Amen.

158. A NIGHT OF AGONY

READ   Then Jesus came with them to a country place called Gethsemani, and he said to his disciples, "Sit down here, while I go over yonder and pray." And he took with him Peter and the two sons of Zebedee, and he began to be saddened and exceedingly troubled. Then he said to them, "My soul is sad, even unto death. Wait here and watch with me." And going forward a little, he fell prostrate and prayed, saying, "Father, if it is possible, let this cup pass away from me; yet not as I will, but as thou willest."

Then he came to the disciples and found them sleeping. And he said to Peter, "Could you not, then, watch one hour with me? Watch and pray, that you may not enter into temptation. The spirit indeed is willing, but the flesh is weak." Again a second time he went away and prayed, saying, "My Father, if this cup cannot pass away unless I drink it, thy will be done." And he came again and found them sleeping, for their eyes were heavy. And leaving them he went back again, and prayed a third time, saying the same words over. . . . And there appeared to him an angel from heaven to strengthen him. And falling into an agony he prayed the more earnestly.

And his sweat became as drops of blood running down upon the ground. And rising from prayer he came to the disciples, and found them sleeping for sorrow. And he said to them, "Why do you sleep? Rise and pray, that you may not enter into temptation." (Matt. 26:36–45; Luke 22:43–46)

REFLECT For the benefit of all His followers through the ages, Jesus undergoes the emotional conflict, mental turmoil, and bodily disturbances of a fallen human nature overwhelmed by the indescribable crisis that now faced Him.

REVIEW In all my anxieties, fears, and troubles of spirit and body, I shall find my most inspiring vision and power in this timeless experience of Christ my King. I shall more easily rise above myself as I consider that my burdens and trials are but a small part of what He bore for my sake. He became so afraid and upset that He could have died from the emotional pressure and mental shock that rocked His human nature to its very core. His human drive to self-preservation urged Him to run away from the harrowing tortures of mind, body, and soul that pressed in on all sides. Instead of surrendering to this natural urge, He acted as a man of supernatural vision. He resorted to prayer for deliverance from His anguish, or strength to bear it if He must. His apostles were so exhausted by their sympathy and their sense of helplessness, that they could not resist sleep. Jesus was alone. So great was the emotional pressure within Him, that blood was intermingled with His sweat.

RESPOND My disturbed and suffering Jesus, may I never forget this mental torment, and bodily agony which you experienced for my sake. When anxiety, fears, doubts, confusion, and conflicting emotions oppress my mind, crush my spirit, and torture my body, may I have the faith to roll back the centuries and join You, so alone and anguished for my sake. May I accept with You whatever the Father may decide for me. Amen.

159. THE BETRAYAL

READ And while he was yet speaking, behold Judas, one of the Twelve, came and with him a great crowd with swords and clubs, from the chief priests and elders of the people. Now his betrayer had given them a sign, saying, "Whomever I kiss, that is he; lay hold of him." And he went straight up to Jesus and said, "Hail, Rabbi!" and kissed him. And Jesus said to him, "Friend, for what purpose hast thou come?" . . . Jesus therefore knowing all that was to come upon him, went forth and said to them, "Whom do you seek?" They answered him, "Jesus of Nazareth." Jesus said to them, "I am he." Now Judas, who betrayed him, was also standing with them. When, therefore, he said to them, "I am he," they drew back and fell to the ground. (Matt. 26:47–50; John 18:4–6)

REFLECT Most of this rabble were too ignorant and excited to appreciate the eternal significance of this moment. The eyes of Christ were fixed on the leader of this mob. Judas was enjoying his brief moment of worldly power and glory. With a greeting and a sign of a friendship that was dead, Judas directed the mob toward his Master. In this very moment of treachery, Jesus made a very personal appeal to win back this lost soul that had once enjoyed graces and privileges granted only to the chosen few. Jesus called Judas "friend," and looked for the least sign of repentance, the smallest excuse to forgive him. Judas remained in his self-made deafness and blindness. Then Jesus resorted to one last effort to redeem Judas. Fear might succeed where love had failed. With a simple statement He struck Judas and the mob to the ground. Judas rejected this grace and disregarded this final miracle which Jesus worked for his sake.

REVIEW Whatever my deliberate sins and human failings, I can be heartily grateful to Jesus for the numberless graces and infinite love by which He has held on to me up to now. As He did with Judas, so does He beg me not to walk away from Him to my own destruction. As on this unforgettable night, He disregards the price which my sins cost Him in agony of mind, torment of soul, and torture of body. His only concern is that I may never use my freedom so foolishly as to make it impossible for Him to save me.

RESPOND My Jesus, when earthly cares and worldly yearnings threaten to separate me from You by sin, I beg You to prevent me by whatever means You can. If I will not avoid sin for Your sake, let me at least do so for my own eternal welfare. Even then, You will be glad to grant me eternal life. You proved this in Your last efforts to save Judas. I hope to heed Your warnings and hear Your loving appeal. Amen.

160. JESUS SURRENDERS HIMSELF

READ And behold, one of those who were with Jesus reached out his hand, drew his sword, and struck the servant of the high priest, cutting off his ear. Then Jesus said to him, "Put back thy sword into its place; for all those who take the sword will perish by the sword. Or dost thou suppose that I cannot entreat my Father, and he will even now furnish me with more than twelve legions of angels? How then are the Scriptures to be fulfilled, that thus it must take place?"

In that hour Jesus said to the crowds, "As against a robber you have come out, with swords and clubs, to seize me. I sat daily with you in the temple teaching, and you did not lay hands on me." Now all this was done that the Scriptures of the prophets might be fulfilled. Then all the disciples left him and fled. (Matt. 26:51–56)

REFLECT Jesus assures Peter that He has no need of physical protection now. He is willingly surrendering Himself in accordance with the divine plan of redemption. Overcome by their mental confusion and fear for their own safety, the apostles fled.

REVIEW Confusing and upsetting as this moment appeared to the frightened apostles, the situation was not so far out of hand as it seemed. What was happening tonight was foreseen and decreed by God from all eternity. It was foretold to the human race by the prophets, and predicted by Jesus Himself a number of times to His disciples and to the Jews. The conditions and circumstances of the redemption were being fulfilled. By His utter acceptance of the toils, troubles, and burdens of His earthly life, Jesus was making full reparation for the sins of men, and regaining the eternal glory that had been lost to them. Though the disciples fled in terror and confusion, Jesus remained amid His enemies with complete presence of mind and strength of soul.

In my earthly life, there will always be some unwanted situations which are unavoidable. Most of my problems can be solved entirely or in part. When, however, I meet difficulties that are beyond all human help, I can try to escape them by abandoning Christ, or I can stand by Him and face them with His support. A number of people are overwhelmed by their emotions in time of adversity. They pray feverishly to God as though they must advise or convince Him to grant His help. Or again, they may feel so alone and helpless that they question God's wisdom, goodness, love, or even His existence. I shall find my strength at the side of Jesus standing before this disorderly mob with a clear appreciation of what He is doing and why He must do it.

RESPOND My Jesus, help me see the Father's wise and loving hand in my earthly troubles, as You saw it amid this confused rabble. Let me find peace in Your companionship and strength in Your support. Grant me a firm loyalty to You, my King, and a deep gratitude for the personal love You showed me on this night. Amen.

161. JESUS DECLARES HIS DIVINITY

READ Then the high priest, standing up, said to him, "Dost thou make no answer to the things that these men prefer against thee?" But Jesus kept silence. And the high priest said to him, "I adjure thee by the living God that thou tell us whether thou art the Christ, the Son of God." Jesus said to him, "Thou hast said it. Nevertheless, I say to you, hereafter you shall see the Son of Man sitting at the right hand of the Power and coming upon the clouds of heaven." (Matt. 26:62–64)

REFLECT The fact that many false witnesses disagreed among themselves in their charges against Jesus, meant nothing to the high priest. He was intent only on finding a reason to condemn Christ. The question he asked Jesus would either obtain this condemnation or publicly discredit Him, since He had already made this claim on several occasions. Jesus knew that a truthful answer would mean torture and death. Nevertheless, He told the truth.

REVIEW   Jesus came down not only to redeem me by making reparation for my sins, but also to show me how to be a man of principle. He preferred humiliations, injustices, indignities, tortures, and agonizing death to the telling of a lie. He will never ask me to endure as much as He did, but He does require that I love truth and right order to the conveniences, advantages, and benefits which might be gained by falsehood and dishonesty.

In my daily life I am required to be a man of truth. This means that I must acknowledge the facts about myself. I am human and therefore limited in my talents, graces, and personal circumstances. I am human and therefore imperfect in my efforts and accomplishments. I am human and therefore I have sinned in the past and, in spite of my best intentions and efforts, I shall sin again in the future. Instead of being unduly ashamed or humiliated by these facts I must endeavor to acknowledge them humbly not only by my interior attitudes, but also by my external behavior with others.

This humility and love of truth will make me more understanding and patient with others. By accepting what I am and making the most of it, I shall find contentment within myself and a willingness to let others be themselves. I shall no longer need to prove myself better than others, nor fear that others might put me to shame by their superior qualities. I shall seek no earthly advantage or convenience at the expense of truth and honesty. I shall be following the example of Jesus, Who died for me rather than tell a lie.

RESPOND   My Jesus, King of truth, implant in my heart such a love of truth that I may always be at peace with myself. Instead of trying to hide my limitations, imperfections, and sins from myself, teach me to live with them and make the most of them without straining beyond my powers. Amen.

162. PETER IN THE COURTYARD

READ Now Peter was sitting outside in the courtyard; and a maidservant came up to him and said, "Thou also wast with Jesus the Galilean." But he denied it before them all, saying, "I do not know what thou art saying." And when he had gone out to the gateway, another maid saw him, and said to those who were there, "This man also was with Jesus of Nazareth." And again he denied it with an oath, "I do not know the man!" And after a little while the bystanders came up and said to Peter, "Surely thou also art one of them, for even thy speech betrays thee." Then he began to curse and to swear that he did not know the man. And at that moment a cock crowed. And Peter remembered the word that Jesus had said, "Before a cock crows, thou wilt deny me three times." And he went out and wept bitterly. (Matt. 26:69–75)

REFLECT When Peter saw his divine Master being bound by his enemies, he was seized by fear, and fled. Confused and upset, he followed the mob from a distance. Without Jesus, Peter had no one to counsel and reassure him. It was this lack of self-assurance that made him afraid and weak in the presence of this group of servants.

REVIEW I too have my measure of inner insecurity and anxiety with my fellow men. So accustomed am I to this emotional state, that I am usually unaware of its meaning. Many of my likes and dislikes stem from my lack of self-assurance with others. In my need to calm my inner uneasiness, I may strive for their acceptance and approval; or I may feel contrary, critical, and hostile; or again, I may simply be superficial or passive in my interpersonal relations.

If I am to avoid Peter's weakness, I must achieve an intelligent self-contentment and self-assurance, and a firm confidence in God's assistance. I must know my strength and my limitations, and accept myself as I am. With this mature self-regard, I shall be more disposed to believe that God is not disgusted with me. Having faith in my personal worth, and trust in Christ's personal concern for me, I shall be able to tolerate the numberless forms and countless degrees of disapproval which others may feel toward me. Being free of undue anxiety, I shall more easily understand that others are subject to their own inner anxieties, fears, self-doubts, and defensive hostility. Believing in my own God-given value, I shall not feel alone when exposed to the unfavorable attitudes or behavior of others. I shall be able to defend myself, when necessary, without the frantic thoughtlessness of Peter.

RESPOND My Jesus, help me be mature in my dealings with others. I do not wish to be inconsiderate of their reasonable expectations of me. Neither, on the other hand, must I disregard my own legitimate needs. May I never be so foolishly displeased with myself or insecure with You, as to have a childish need for the approval of others. Help me please others without displeasing You or unduly neglecting my own basic rights. Amen.

163. PETER'S DENIAL

READ Now Peter was sitting outside in the courtyard; and a maidservant came up to him and said, "Thou also wast with Jesus the Galilean." But he denied it before them all, saying, "I do not know what thou art saying." And when he had gone out to the gateway, another maid saw him, and said to those who were there, "This man also was with Jesus of Nazareth." And again he denied it with an oath, "I do not know the man." And after a little while the bystanders came up and said to Peter, "Surely thou also art one of them, for even thy speech betrays thee." Then he began to curse and to swear that he did not know the man. And at that moment a cock crowed. And Peter remembered the word that Jesus had said. "Before a cock crows, thou wilt deny me three times." And he went out and wept bitterly. (Matt. 26:69–75)

REFLECT   Peter is an image of every sincere follower of Jesus. He really meant it when he affirmed that he would accompany his Master to prison or to death. He had nobly drawn a sword in defense of Jesus in the garden. Only when he saw his Master seized and led away did he lose his self-confidence. He now felt so alone and afraid that his emotions dominated his thinking and his conduct. God alone can estimate how seriously he sinned in denying his divine Master.

REVIEW   My emotions can be helpful or hurtful to me in my daily life. As long as they are under the influence of God's truth and grace, they can help me serve God with contentment and enthusiasm. Once I lose sight of Jesus, I shall be dominated by varying degrees of inner insecurity and anxiety. In a number of ways I shall deny my friendship with Christ. I must daily pray and strive to become ever more aware of Christ's presence, support, and love for me.

Nevertheless, in spite of good intentions and sincere efforts to please Jesus in all things, I shall have my emotional moments, my moments of forgetfulness, and my moments of weakness. At such times I shall use any natural means to defend myself from my inner insecurity, anxieties, and fears. Only after I have fallen from my ideals, shall I realize that I have followed Jesus from a distance or denied Him outright by my attitude, words, or conduct. If

I am as wise as the repentant Peter, I shall return to Christ with sorrow for my infidelity and confidence in His understanding, forgiveness and encouragement.

RESPOND My Jesus, You showed neither disgust for the shortcomings of Your apostles nor contempt for their sins. After Your resurrection, You came to them without reproach and continued to instruct them for their approaching ministry. May I remember this when I fail You, and return quickly, sorrowfully, and sincerely to You. Amen.

164. DEATH OF JUDAS

READ Then Judas, who betrayed him, when he saw that he was condemned, repented and brought back the thirty pieces of silver to the chief priests and the elders, saying, "I have sinned in betraying innocent blood." . . . And he flung the pieces of silver into the temple, and withdrew; and went away and hanged himself with a halter. (Matt. 27:3–5)

REFLECT After his betrayal, Judas' excitement gradually simmered down. His mind began to review the events of the previous evening. As he recalled his refusal to heed Christ's warning, consider His appeal, and accept His forgiveness, Judas was overwhelmed by the most destructive force in human nature, namely, self-hatred. He could neither face himself nor forgive himself. He finally sought relief from this intolerable situation through suicide.

REVIEW In my religious endeavors, I must beware of mistaken ideas and misunderstandings. The "self-contempt" mentioned by spiritual writers, and the "self-hatred" recommended by the Scriptures are far removed from what Judas felt within himself. God urges me to a holy anger against whatever inclines me toward sin. On the other hand, He commands that I love myself. Even when I sin, I must hate the sin, but not the sinner.

Without an intelligent self-love, I cannot offer a mature love to either God or men. In order to give any part of my attention or service gladly to others, I must believe that both my person and my services are worth giving. Without this conviction, I shall be afraid of possible rejection. Consequently, I may either strain for approval or give up all hope of being accepted. I must reflect often on the fact that God has made me worthy of Himself by the grace which His divine Son merited for me.

A spiritual life which is built upon the principle of self-hate, divides me against myself. By my very nature I strive for love. My natural drives to self-preservation, self-expression, and self-defense are expressions of the self-love which God implanted in my human nature. With the light of faith and the strength of charity, I am to guide this natural self-love toward my eternal welfare and everlasting happiness. I am to love God by offering Him whatever good I have and achieve in my daily life. If I attempt to stifle this holy self-interest, I may either destroy my generosity with God or upset my emotional balance.

RESPOND My Jesus, may I never believe that I am too little for Your attention or too sinful for Your forgiveness. Impress me with the fact that You bore every inconvenience, discomfort, pain, and sorrow on earth for my sake. By these You tell me what words alone can never fully express, namely, that I am worth loving, worth saving, and worth living with, forever in heaven. Amen.

165. PILATE QUESTIONS JESUS

READ Pilate therefore said to him, "Thou art then a king?" Jesus answered, "Thou sayest it; I am a king. This is why I was born, and why I have come into the world, to bear witness to the truth. Everyone who is of the truth hears my voice." Pilate said to him, "What is truth?" And when he had said this, he went outside to the Jews again, and said to them, "I find no guilt in Him." (John 18: 37–38)

REFLECT Jesus asserts that He is the King of Truth. Only those who love the truth can hear and understand Him. Pilate is not particularly interested in truth or idealism except in so far as they involve his worldly authority and earthly security. He therefore sees no threat or crime in Jesus.

REVIEW Little did Pilate dream that he was standing face to face with his divine Redeemer and his final Judge. Had he understood the brief message of Christ, and appreciated the goodness and spiritual power that radiated from His person, Pilate would have knelt reverently before his eternal King and risen to His defense at any cost to himself. Unfortunately, Pilate was interested only in his earthly advantages. He could not see beyond the security and comforts of this life.

Am I more impressed by the material conveniences and tangible enjoyments of this earthly life, than by the truth and rewards of Christ? Is my interest held so firmly by the pleasures of this earthly life, that I have no feeling for the supernatural realities within my soul and the all-satisfying joys of heaven? If so I shall expect Christ's truth to make my earthly life more satisfying. I shall perform

my religious activities for the sake of immediate blessings
and worldly advantages.

Jesus stands before Pilate with eyes on the eternal values that will flow from His work of redemption. Though
He does not despise the good things of this life, He insists that I place them in their proper place, namely, second to the truth for which He is about to die and the
eternal life which will flow forth from His sacrifice.

RESPOND Jesus, Eternal King of Truth, may I love Your
teachings and prefer Your truth above all else in my life.
Grant me the grace to live my daily life as an act of personal love and loyalty to You. Let me not strive for any
earthly advantage or worldly benefit at the expense of sin.
I hope to treasure Your friendship above all the other
good things in my life. Amen.

166. JESUS MOCKED BY HEROD

READ Now when Herod saw Jesus, he was exceedingly
glad; for he had been a long time desirous to see him, because he had heard so much about him. Now he put many
questions to him, but he made no answer. Now the chief
priests and Scribes were standing by, vehemently accusing
him. But Herod, with his soldiery, treated him with contempt and mocked him, arraying him in a bright robe,
and sent him back to Pilate. (Luke 23:8–11)

REFLECT Jesus was actually in command of this situation at all times. He had willingly embraced all this to
bring the grace of salvation to each and every man here
present. There was no need to speak, because He had no
need of self-defense.

REVIEW Living in human society can be quite confusing

and disturbing at times. Each person has his own emotional needs, mental habits, and personal behavior. No matter how interested I may be in others and how sincerely I may wish them well, a large measure of their attitudes and behavior toward me are beyond my control. At some time or other, I shall be misunderstood, misrepresented, and mistreated. Though I may sometimes bring the misunderstanding and mistreatment upon myself with or without my fault, in many cases, I shall be innocent.

Many times the interpersonal feelings will be so intangible, so indefinite and vague, so delicate that I can make no specific accusation, and others can make no particular charge against me. There will simply be a feeling of uneasiness and dislike between us. I shall be tempted to treat people with some measure of hidden resentment or some subtle retaliation for the discomfort they arouse in me. At such times I must strive to imitate the conduct of Jesus. As He stood before Herod's court, He saw some who were unaware of the truth, others who were too weak to behave differently, and others who were malicious and guilty of sin. In my interpersonal relations, I shall be wise to leave all judgment to God, and do my best to imitate the prayerful self-possession of Christ before Herod's court.

RESPOND   My Jesus, though You were humiliated by the mockery of these worldly men, You also have an unshakable peace of soul. In Your knowledge of the Father's plan of redemption, You found strength to endure this ordeal. Help me appreciate the eternal value of what I must bear from others, and let me join my inevitable interpersonal frictions and tensions to the sufferings You endured on this occasion. Amen.

167. PILATE'S DECISION

READ Now at festival time the procurator used to release to the crowd a prisoner, whomever they would. Now he had at that time a notorious prisoner called Barabbas. Therefore, when they had gathered together, Pilate said, "Whom do you wish that I release to you? Barabbas, or Jesus who is called Christ?" For he knew that they had delivered him up out of envy. . . . But the chief priests and the elders persuaded the crowds to ask for Barabbas and to destroy Jesus. But the procurator addressed them, and said to them, "Which of the two do you wish that I release to you?" And they said, "Barabbas." Pilate said to them, "What then am I to do with Jesus who is called Christ?" They all said, "Let him be crucified!" The procurator said to them, "Why, what evil has he done?" But they kept crying out the more, saying, "Let him be crucified!" (Matt. 27:15–23)

REFLECT Though Pilate had a desire to be just in his judgment of Jesus, he was not willing to suffer the annoyance of a public disturbance. He therefore took the convenient way out. He publicly renounced all personal approval of the sentence, and then sacrificed the King of truth and justice on the altar of falsehood and injustice.

REVIEW Every man is faced with occasional situations that require him to act in accordance with truth and justice. As a man becomes more worldly minded, he seeks more freedom from the restrictions of right reason and God's revelation. In his desire to satisfy his personal feelings and emotional wants, he creates reasons that will enable him to follow his personal preferences, fears, prejudices, and aversions without arousing his inner shame or external humiliation. Herod's excuse for surrendering Jesus

to the mob was that one man was not worth the trouble
that might develop if he insisted on justice.

I must beware of my own emotional tendencies. They
can incline me to be more concerned with my own convenience or satisfaction than with the requirements of
truth and justice. Many people feel a vague uneasiness
with God because they suspect themselves of self-deception and insincerity with Him. Though their self-deception may be largely unconscious, their conscience keeps
unsettling their peace of mind. Though I cannot achieve
perfect self-knowledge, I must make the daily effort to
know myself as well as I can. In this way I may diminish
my degree of self-deception and injustice in my daily dealings with God and men.

RESPOND My Jesus, the least I can do is to try to give my
heart entirely to You by learning to apply Your truth to my
daily conduct. I shall never be entirely certain of my success in this effort, but I wish to achieve what I can. May I
prefer poverty, pain, or any earthly inconvenience to a
deliberate act of self-deception or injustice. Amen.

168. INSINCERITY OF THE JEWISH LEADERS

READ Pilate, then, took Jesus and had him scourged. And
the soldiers, plaiting a crown of thorns, put it upon his
head, and arrayed him in a purple cloak. And they kept
coming to him and saying, "Hail, King of the Jews!" and
striking him.

Pilate therefore again went outside and said to them,
"Behold, I bring him out to you, that you may know that
I find no guilt in him." Jesus therefore came forth, wearing the crown of thorns and the purple cloak. And he said
to them, "Behold, the man!" When, therefore, the chief
priests and the attendants saw him, they cried out, saying,

"Crucify him! Crucify him!" Pilate said to them, "Take him yourselves and crucify him, for I find no guilt in him." The Jews answered him, "We have a Law, and according to that Law he must die, because he has made himself Son of God." . . . Pilate said to them, "Shall I crucify your king?" The chief priests answered, "We have no king but Caesar." (John 19:1–7, 15)

REFLECT The present position of Pilate was not half so pathetic as that of the Jewish leaders. In his false reasoning, Pilate was somewhat confused by his pagan background and his sense of public duty to keep peace. The chief priests and Scribes, on the other hand, knew the Law of God and were quite aware of their determination to destroy Jesus at any cost. In their eagerness to make the most of the present opportunity, they were deliberately lying. For this reason Jesus said that theirs was the greater sin.

REVIEW As I grew up, I developed a number of likes and dislikes, preferences and prejudices, fears and aversions. With or without my awareness, these forces are constantly influencing my imagination, thoughts, feelings, decisions, and behavior. In spite of my supernatural graces and gifts of faith, hope, charity, etc., my spontaneous appetites and natural inclinations urge me toward my earthly conveniences without regard for the holy Will of God and the inspiring example of Christ. There is nothing shameful or sinful in this natural aversion to what is unpleasant or difficult. It is normal to every man.

In order to avoid the self-deception of Pilate, and the malice and hypocrisy of the Jewish leaders, I must learn to see Christ as my greatest advantage and my most lasting good. Without this deep conviction, I shall be tempted to give Him a minimum of service. I may even violate His principles when I do not feel like enduring the burdens, pains, and labors that face me. I may push Him aside or seek to forget Him as I reach out for false worldly solutions to my problems.

RESPOND My Jesus, may I never consider You an obstacle to my true welfare. The emotional forces that stir within me are like children who do not know what is truly good for them. They need the guidance of a loving mother and the restraining hand of a truly wise father. In You I can find the guidance and restraint which will help me walk more surely toward the all-satisfying life of heaven. Help me know You ever better and love You ever more fully, so that I may never turn away from You for any earthly advantage. Amen.

169. JESUS IS HANDED OVER TO THE MOB

READ Now Pilate, seeing that he was doing no good, but rather that a riot was breaking out, took water and washed his hands in sight of the crowd, saying, "I am innocent of the blood of this just man; see to it yourselves." And all the people answered and said, "His blood be on us and on our children." . . . Then he handed him over to them to be crucified. And so they took Jesus and led him away. (Matt. 27:24–25; John 19:16)

REFLECT In view of his office, Pilate could not legally lay aside his responsibility for the torture and death of Jesus, nor could the Jews legally assume the authority for it. They were all guilty of this gross injustice not only in the eyes of God, but also in the light of right reason. Having done His best to open the minds and hearts of all concerned, Jesus accepted the injustice as a reparation for all the sins committed against the virtue of justice.

REVIEW Much as I may express sympathy with the suffering Savior, my sympathy would be much more true if I could at least be resigned to those injustices which I am unable to correct in my own life. When I fail to rectify the wrong done me, through reasonable means and legitimate methods, I might consider bearing it patiently for Christ as He bore His injustices patiently for my sake. If I am lacking in a supernatural attitude and outlook, this notion of offering my experience to Jesus, Who bore the same experience for me, is just a vague theory and an unrealistic idea. It will not appeal to me as I chafe under my personal hurt and active resentment.

And yet, as Jesus chafed in mind, body, and soul under the lash, the crown of thorns, and the cross; under the sweat, spit, dust, blood, and tears on His holy face; amid the calumny, mockery, insults, and blasphemy of his enemies; He did not refuse to offer all this to the heavenly Father in reparation for my sins. Amid all this, I was as real to him as the thorns that dug into His temples and the cross that bit into His bruised shoulders. Not for a moment did He hesitate to offer it all as His act of love for me.

RESPOND My Jesus, if I practice this kind of thinking and living, I may someday learn to offer my own experiences to the Father as my act of appreciation for the indescribable labors, pains, and sufferings You bore for my sake. I hope for the day when this will be my ordinary way of seeing the problems, difficulties, and hardships which now incline me to resent God or hate my human enemies. Amen.

170. THE CRUCIFIXION

READ And when they had mocked him, they took the cloak off him and put his own garments on him, and led him away to crucify him. Now as they went out, they found a man of Cyrene named Simon; him they forced to take up his cross. And they came to the place called Golgotha, that is the Place of the Skull. And they gave him wine to drink mixed with gall; but when he had tasted it, he would not drink. . . . And Jesus said, "Father, forgive them, for they do not know what they are doing." (Matt. 27:31–34; Luke 23:34)

REFLECT Scripture scholars tell us that the drink Jesus refused was treated with a narcotic to dull the mind and deaden the pain of those who were being crucified. Jesus chose to make the fullest sacrifice possible for me. In the midst of unnumbered pains and untold sufferings, He shows us His attitude and disposition in this prayer for our forgiveness.

REVIEW If the last meditation seemed like the unrealistic dream of a strange idealist, what shall I say of this present consideration of Christ? Am I to join the ranks of those who say in word or action that it was quite proper, or even easy, for Christ to behave this way, but that it is asking too much of me? Will I claim that my life is more difficult than this experience of Jesus, or will I insist that I have more reason than Jesus to wish evil on those who offend or hurt me? I may think that, since He is divine as well as human, He could more easily bear His torments and more readily find it in His heart to express forgiveness. Since I am human, I may prefer to follow my human emotions and demand an equal or greater retribution for those who make my daily life difficult.

Though I am human, and easily governed by my basic drives and swayed by my emotions, I must not forget that Jesus has given me supernatural powers to rise above my human tendencies and to control my natural emotions. If these divine powers are not effective in my daily activities, it is because I have not taken the trouble to develop them into active habits. Instead of feeling guilty or unworthy because of this failure, I would please Jesus more by beginning at long last to develop the disposition and practice the virtues which He manifested upon the cross.

Slowly, patiently, and perseveringly, I can learn to shoulder my daily burdens, perform my daily duties, and accept my daily disappointments and interpersonal hurts with a larger vision and deeper spirit of self-sacrifice. In my own small way, I can gradually be joined in spirit with Christ upon the cross. Thus will my life be a dying to self and a living to Christ. I shall be losing my human self and gaining a new self, a glorious self that reflects and extends the self-offering of Jesus to His heavenly Father.

RESPOND   My crucified Savior, grant me Your divine vision to see the supernatural grandeur of my personal life, the eternal value of my earthly routine, and the everlasting glory of my daily activities. Upon the cross of daily life let me be as self-giving as You were upon Your cross. Amen.

171. THE GOOD AND THE BAD THIEF

READ   Now one of those robbers who were hanged was abusing him, saying, "If thou art the Christ, save thyself and us!" But the other in answer rebuked him and said, "Dost thou not even fear God, seeing that thou art under the same sentence? And we indeed justly, for we are receiving what our deeds deserved; but this man has done nothing wrong." And he said to Jesus, "Lord, remember me when thou comest into thy kingdom." And Jesus said to him, "Amen I say to thee, this day thou shalt be with me in paradise." (Luke 23:39–43)

REFLECT   It seems from the gospel accounts, that at first both thieves directed to Jesus the bitterness and hatred they felt toward their executioners. They could not help expressing the irony they saw in His reputed claims to power and His present helplessness. Gradually one of the thieves caught a glimpse of Christ's spiritual power and goodness. This revived in him a small spark of hope, hidden deep beneath the dead ashes of a sinful life. He felt an urge to acknowledge his own guilt, profess faith in the innocence and truthfulness of Jesus, and express a petition for help. Jesus reached out to this dying sinner with absolution and redemption.

REVIEW May I spend my earthly life in the light of this sacred moment! Too many people are frightened by the memory of their past faults and sins. They feel insecure with God and doubtful of His forgiveness. They make more acts of contrition than of hope, express more petitions for pardon than acts of love. They are not so sure of their love because it is undermined by their dread of His justice. Even as they consider this last hour of Jesus upon the cross, they are afraid that He might consider them unworthy of the mercy and pardon He granted to this dying thief. In their self-doubts, they are unable to see the true Christ.

Regardless of how I feel about myself, this is the true Christ, the Good Shepherd, the Seeker of the lost coin, the Father of the prodigal son, Doctor of the sick, Friend and Forgiver of sinners. When shall I learn to study this praying, crucified Savior, Who could excuse those who were, at that very moment, mocking, insulting, blaspheming, and torturing Him? Forgetting His own pain-wracked body, tormented mind, and agonized soul, He paused to give pardon and grace to this dying sinner beside Him. By His words and example here upon the cross, He speaks to me. He shows Himself to me to encourage me with hope and strengthen me with gratitude for His proven understanding, love, and pardon.

RESPOND My crucified Redeemer, I refuse to be more impressed by my childish fears and immature thinking than by the boundless love and pardon You showed upon the cross. Though I may sin a moment before I die, I pray for the grace to turn to You with my last breath and my final ounce of strength. If I ever again stand in need of Your forgiveness, I shall never again doubt Your love or fear Your condemnation. Amen.

172. AGONY ON THE CROSS

READ   Now from the sixth hour there was darkness over the whole land until the ninth hour. But about the ninth hour Jesus cried out with a loud voice, saying, "Eli, Eli, lema sabacthani," that is, "My God, my God, why hast thou forsaken me?" . . . After this Jesus, knowing that all things were now accomplished, that the Scripture might be fulfilled, said, "I thirst." Now there was standing there a vessel full of common wine; and having put a sponge soaked with the wine on a stalk of hyssop, they put it to his mouth. Therefore, when Jesus had taken the wine, he said, "It is consummated!" And bowing his head, he give up his spirit. (Matt. 27:45–46; John 19:28–30)

REFLECT   During His entire ordeal upon the cross, Jesus prayed. His present state of soul and actual experience is well reflected in Psalm 21. He suffered acutely from the actual abandonment of His beloved nation and of His closest friends. By a miracle He permitted His human nature to experience the sense of loneliness and desolation that is common to all men in time of great suffering. His human nature felt cut off from God.

REVIEW   It is difficult for the average person to appreciate the agony of Jesus upon the cross. Apart from extraordinary graces, Christ's agony is best understood by those who have experienced unbearable pains and overwhelming exhaustion of body, those who have been weighed down by mental depression, sadness, and protracted discouragement, those who have tasted the bitterness of rejected love, loneliness, and a sense of abandonment by God and men, those who yearn for the relief of sleep and feel a repulsion to facing another day. Those who have suffered can best appreciate the sufferings of Christ crucified.

Though I may never experience these extreme pains of body, sufferings of mind, and torments of soul, I can at least be willing to accept the small crosses and sufferings of everyday living. This willingness will increase with my frequent meditations on the story of Christ's passion and death. With this supernatural outlook, my mind will see through the superficial appearances of my human experience, and my soul will look beyond the narrow limits of my present difficulties and hardships. I shall find in each unpleasant experience a golden opportunity to unite my heart to the generous heart of Jesus crucified. Even when obliged by duty to avoid some burden or reject some suffering, I shall find myself doing it with a sense of loyalty to Christ, my King.

RESPOND My Jesus crucified, may I always desire to be nailed in spirit with You upon the cross. Let me not be unreasonable or foolish in this desire, but wise and prudent in accordance with my daily obligations and personal limitations. Amen.

173. THE BURIAL OF JESUS

READ Now when it was evening, there came a certain rich man of Arimathea, Joseph by name, who was himself a disciple of Jesus. He went to Pilate and asked for the body of Jesus. Then Pilate ordered the body to be given up. And Joseph taking the body, wrapped it in a clean linen cloth, and laid it in his new tomb, which he had hewn out in the rock. Then he rolled a large stone to the entrance of the tomb, and departed. But Mary Magdalene and the other Mary were there, sitting opposite the sepulchre. (Matt. 27:57–61)

REFLECT The redemption of mankind was now completed. Christ's earthly life had run its course. The final curtain had descended upon the stage, where the Redeemer had revealed in eloquent deeds His divine wisdom, understanding, acceptance, forgiveness, and personal love for every individual soul.

REVIEW How do I respond to this scene of Christ's burial? Does it arouse emotions in me that hold me back from Him, or am I induced to draw closer to the divine Savior Who chose to prove His love by dying for me? If my religious attitudes are centered upon myself, I may experience a bitter sense of self-accusation, a fear of God's punishment for my real or exaggerated ingratitude, or even an absence of thoughts or feelings. If, on the other hand, my concern is centered on the lifeless body of Christ, I shall feel some measure of sorrow for His sufferings and my sins, which caused them; gratitude for the personal love which induced Him to make this generous Self-sacrifice; and an intelligent desire to express my sincere appreciation by a life of daily loyalty to His principles.

The more maturely I respond to the grace and love of Christ, the less strained will my emotions be. With genuine sincerity, I shall calmly consider how I can offer Him a living expression of my appreciation and love. The less childish I am in my reverence toward God, my expectations in life, and my demands upon myself, the more easily and persistently will I strive through the years to live a life of humble self-acceptance and patient effort to prove my love for Jesus in word and action. The more informed I am about the mind and heart of Christ, the less will I permit my unreasoning emotions to depict Him as the critical, demanding, condemning Judge I sometimes feel He is. As I grow into a wholesome intimacy with my divine Savior, I shall lose that strained sense of duty that makes my religious performance a chore and a burden. The better I come to know Him, the more shall I experience that His yoke is truly sweet and His burden really light.

RESPOND My Jesus, in Your lifeless body I behold the greatest assurance of Your personal love for me. I shall never permit my inner insecurity, anxieties, fears, and doubts to demand further proof of Your concern for me. In my hours of mental confusion, nervous tension, bodily fatigue, mental depression, emotional discouragement, and spiritual weakness, I shall place my hope in Your personal love, and my trust in Your untiring assistance. Amen.

174. THE RESURRECTION

READ And when the Sabbath was past, Mary Magdalene, Mary the mother of James, and Salome, bought spices, that they might go and anoint him. And very early on the first day of the week, they came to the tomb, when the sun had just risen. And they were saying to one another, "Who will roll the stone back from the entrance of the tomb for us?" And looking up they saw that the stone had been rolled back, for it was very large. But on entering the tomb, they saw a young man sitting at the right side, clothed in a white robe, and they were amazed. He said to them, "Do not be terrified. You are looking for Jesus of Nazareth, who was crucified. He has risen, he is not here. Behold the place where they laid him. But go, tell his disciples and Peter that he goes before you into Galilee; there you shall see him, as he told you." (Mark 16:1–7)

REFLECT These women had been devoted to Jesus during His public life. They had also followed Him along the way to Calvary, and had kept prayerful watch through His crucifixion and slow death upon the cross. Having shared something of His labors, sufferings, and sorrows, they were now about to share something of His glorious resurrection.

REVIEW In a number of ways my earthly life resembles that of Jesus. I have my daily occupations, which require my personal attention and efforts. I am expected to live this life in union with God through the supernatural life granted to me in baptism. I am to develop within me the mind of Christ through the knowledge and sacraments He has bestowed on me in His Church. In all my activities, His principles are to guide me, and His example is to inspire me. My prayers, works, joys, and sufferings are but a continuation of His, and His divine intention moves my human desires to fulfill the will of His Father.

Nevertheless, I shall still have to contend with my blind human drives, immature emotions, fixed habits of thinking and behaving, and with the ever-present personal preferences, fears, and prejudices of the people around me. And yet, if I can imitate the holy women in their personal devotion to Christ, I shall find vision enough to look above and beyond my human obstacles, and strength enough to continue trying in spite of setbacks, shortcomings, and failures. As they assisted Jesus in His work, served Him in His needs, and stood by Him in His sufferings, so must I endeavor to see all the experiences of my daily life as a personal service to Him. Then I shall live with a strong hope of seeing Him in His glorious resurrection.

RESPOND My risen Savior, help me imitate these holy women. Even when it seemed that Your mission had failed, they continued to offer You what little service they could. Whatever my feelings, You have proven that You deserve my loyalty. By Your life and death, You have proven that You are God and that You care for me in a personal way. Grant me enough faith to believe that You see my good intentions, enough hope to trust that You appreciate my poor human efforts, and enough love to go on trying for Your sake. Amen.

175. THE SOLDIERS' REPORT

READ   And behold, there was a great earthquake; for an angel of the Lord came down from heaven, and drawing near rolled back the stone, and sat upon it. His countenance was like lightning, and his raiment like snow. And for fear of him the guards were terrified, and became like dead men. . . . some of the guards came into the city and reported to the chief priests all that had happened. And when they had assembled with the elders and had consulted together, they gave money to the soldiers, telling them, "Say, 'His disciples came by night and stole him while we were sleeping.' And if the procurator hears of this, we will persuade him and keep you out of trouble." And they took the money, and did as they were instructed. (Matt. 28:2–4, 11–15)

REFLECT   Torn between their stubborn refusal to believe in Christ and their present fear for themselves, these leaders of the people resolved to protect themselves by bribing the soldiers.

REVIEW   When a person compromises with his conscience, he is tormented from within. He feels within himself disgust, reproach, and a fear of punishment. If his compromise involves others, he is tormented even more by the fear of what they might think if he is discovered. In his need to escape his inner sense of shame, guilt, and external humiliation, his mind searches persistently for reasons to defend or excuse his error or malice. Whether he be emotionally immature or morally malicious, his nature will drive him to seek a release from his inner insecurity and anxiety. He may do it by striving to make reparation, or by presenting a real, or imagined, or malicious defense of his deed.

Just how guilty these Jewish leaders were, God alone can say. However, they do teach me a valuable lesson for my earthly and eternal welfare. Since no man is always correct in his thinking or right in his actions, I would be wise to take an occasional inventory of my spiritual assets and moral liabilities. Where I see my errors, I ought to be humble enough to acknowledge them, and honest enough to consider not only my degree of guilt, but also my sincerity, weakness, and innocence in the matter. This disposition will make it much easier for me to face myself and others, and less difficult to admit when I am wrong.

RESPOND   My Jesus, let me not be so immature as to claim that I am always right, nor so malicious as to deny it when I know I am wrong. Make me honest enough to admit that I am always open to error and occasionally guilty of sin. May this admission be reflected in my attitudes and conduct with God and the people I meet. Amen.

176. JESUS APPEARS TO MAGDALENE

READ   Now when he had risen from the dead early on the first day of the week, he appeared first to Mary Magdalene, out of whom he had cast seven devils. . . . Mary was standing outside weeping at the tomb. So, as she wept, she stooped down and looked into the tomb, and saw two angels in white sitting, one at the head and one at the feet, where the body of Jesus had been laid. They said to her, "Woman, why art thou weeping?" She said to them, "Because they have taken away my Lord, and I do not know where they have laid him."

When she had said this she turned round and beheld Jesus standing there, and she did not know that it was Jesus. Jesus said to her, "Woman, why art thou weeping? Whom dost thou seek?" She, thinking that he was the gardener, said to him, "Sir, if thou hast removed him, tell me where thou hast laid him and I will take him away." Jesus said to her, "Mary!" Turning, she said to him, "Rabboni!" (that is to say, Master). (Mark 16:9; John 20: 11–17)

REFLECT   On seeing the tomb open, Mary had run immediately to tell the apostles. Having followed Peter and John back to the tomb, she remained there when they departed. Overwhelmed by grief, she had but one desire, namely, to find the body of her beloved Master and to give it proper burial.

REVIEW   The full understanding and deep love which the Savior and this former sinner had for each other, may be imagined by their brief, but sufficient greeting. Magdalene had come to know the heart of Jesus as few people ever did. In turn, she also knew how well He understood her and how completely He accepted her. Only Jesus had been able to satisfy her tormenting hunger for peace, contentment, and unwavering love. He now came to her because she loved Him beyond words. She was concerned only with offering Him a last expression of her love. Her yearning to serve Him even in death, was like a shout in His ear and a cry in His heart. He gave her a different service to perform for Him. She was to bring hope and encouragement to the disciples by her eyewitness account of His resurrection.

When I am disturbed by the memory of my past sins, contempt for my present limitations and shortcomings, or disgust for my failure to fulfill my good intentions, I ought to contemplate this gospel scene. Jesus was as pleased by Magdalene's desire to serve Him as though she had fulfilled that desire. He did not mention her past sins, nor did He show disgust for her present helplessness. He was so glad that she cared so much, that He came to console her by His presence and strengthen her by His words. Jesus would gladly do the same for me, if only I could learn to think more of His love than of my personal limitations, failures, and sins.

RESPOND   My divine Savior, may I never be frightened by the memory of my past sins, nor discouraged by my present weaknesses. You are more interested in my desires and efforts than in my visible successes. Let me place my earthly life and eternal salvation in Your hands, and then proceed to prove my love for You as well as I can in my daily life. Though others or I may be inclined to judge my life by external achievements, let me never forget that You appreciate what I am trying to accomplish. Amen.

177.   THE ROAD TO EMMAUS

READ   And behold, two of them were going that very day to a village called Emmaus, which is sixty stadia from Jerusalem. . . . And it came to pass, while they were conversing and arguing together, that Jesus himself also drew near and went along with them; but their eyes were held, that they should not recognize him. And he said to them, "What words are these that you are exchanging as you walk and are sad?" . . . And they said to him, "Concerning Jesus of Nazareth, who was a prophet, mighty in work and word before God and all the people; and how our chief priests and rulers delivered him up to be sentenced to death, and crucified him." . . . But he said to them, "O foolish ones and slow of heart to believe in all that the prophets have spoken! Did not the Christ have to suffer these things before entering into his glory?" (Luke 24: 13–17, 19–21, 25–26)

REFLECT These two were Christ's very own disciples. They had seen many proofs of His wisdom and power during His public life. On a number of occasions, Jesus had tried to prepare them for the shock of His capture, trial, and execution. He had even foretold His triumphant resurrection. And yet, these disciples seemed unable to understand His sufferings when they actually occurred. In their emotional turmoil, they even forgot about His promise to see them again after His death. With divine patience and understanding, Jesus explained to them why it was necessary for Him to suffer as He did. He then revealed His identity and left them. Joyfully they returned to Jerusalem that same night.

REVIEW Life can be quite confusing at times. My desires, fears, and dislikes sometimes make it difficult for me to think clearly or to make wise decisions. Moreover, the attitudes, opinions, and emotional needs of others usually have some effect upon me, and may add to my interior problem. At such times, I am apt to forget my religious knowledge, or act against my better judgment. I may feel that Jesus has somehow failed me. What I had expected from Him, did not happen. I may wonder whether He is even interested in me, or whether He is displeased with me.

If I allow my emotions to do my thinking for me, I too may walk away from Jesus in my moment of greatest need. I may feel too disturbed to linger in His presence or to remain in the company of those who seem faithful and content with Him. In my momentary ignorance, I may feel excluded from His friendship. In my immaturity, I may feel a need to escape the sadness or discouragement that results from my emotional thinking. In my fear of His disapproval, I may try to achieve a perfect understanding of my innocence or my guilt, so as to be sure where I stand with Christ. Instead of tiring and confusing my mind with an endless search for the sure answer, I would do well to recall how Jesus came to the two discouraged disciples, and brought them knowledge, peace, and the courage to return to their place in life. In spite of my fears to the contrary, He will do the same to me, if I do not hinder Him through mistaken or emotional thinking.

RESPOND My divine Savior, grant me the wisdom to pause and listen to You when I am sad, discouraged, or confused by my troubles and problems. I hope to see You as You showed Yourself in this gospel. Help me remain with You in spite of a tendency to turn my attention to other thoughts. Amen.

178. JESUS APPEARS TO THE APOSTLES

READ Now while they were talking of these things, Jesus stood in their midst, and said to them, "Peace to you! It is I, do not be afraid." But they were startled and panic-stricken, and thought that they saw a spirit. And he said to them, "Why are you disturbed, and why do doubts arise in your hearts? See my hands and feet, that it is I myself. Feel me and see; for a spirit does not have flesh and bones, as you see I have." And having said this, he showed them his hands and his feet. But as they still disbelieved and marvelled for joy, he said, "Have you anything here to eat?" And they offered him a piece of broiled fish and a honeycomb. And when he had eaten in their presence, he took what remained and gave it to them. (Luke 24: 36–43)

REFLECT Jesus came to reassure His frightened and confused disciples. Though He scolded them for their weak faith and wavering trust, He also understood the overpowering emotions that had cast their minds into utter confusion. He therefore went to the trouble of satisfying their natural fears and doubts by giving them visible proof that He was truly their beloved Master, risen from the dead.

In spite of their hesitant belief, their desire for Him made them crowd around joyfully, like frightened, lost children who were being reunited to their parents.

REVIEW   In my daily life, there are moments when, like these disciples, I too am afraid. At such times I may find it difficult to be at ease with others, for fear of being unable to win their approval, gain their acceptance, hold their interest, or defend myself against their self-assurance, contradictions, criticism, or ridicule. Due to this lack of self-confidence, I may easily feel so inferior to others as to consider myself unworthy of anyone's esteem or friendship. I may then feel rejected by others or unworthy of their attention. In such a state of mind, I can easily feel that Jesus is far away from me. Even as I pray, He will appear vague and strange to me.

At such times Jesus desires to reveal His nearness to me and show His personal concern for me. He may gently scold me for not recalling His words and applying them to my present situation. Though my human emotions blind me to His presence, He bids me touch Him by my supernatural faith, gain peace and strength by my trust in His promises, and find my joy through confidence in His proven love. Having overcome my fears, sadness, and hopelessness, I shall once more feel reasonably content with myself, and able to face the people and situations that had frightened me.

RESPOND   My Jesus, may I never lose sight of You in my moments of mental confusion and moral weakness. With You at my side and Your grace in my soul, I shall be able to live at peace with myself and others. Amen.

179. THE POWER TO FORGIVE SINS

READ He therefore said to them again, "Peace be to you! As the Father has sent me, I also send you." When he had said this, he breathed upon them, and said to them, "Receive the Holy Spirit; whose sins you shall forgive, they are forgiven them; and whose sins you shall retain, they are retained." (John 20:21–23)

REFLECT Having settled the fears and doubts of His disciples, Jesus now grants them power to bring God's peace and certitude to many a fearful and doubtful soul. They are to judge and forgive the sins of men through the sacrament of penance. In this visible sign, men will have Christ's assurance of pardon and renewed grace.

REVIEW Jesus knew that I would need this holy sacrament in spite of my good will, in spite of my sorrow for past sins, in spite of my sincere desire to sin no more, and in spite of my firm determination to practice justice and charity toward God and men. He knew that my past habits would not vanish with a wish, nor my life change with a resolution. He knew that, with all my efforts to amend my faults, I would still have to return again and again for His pardon, confessing the same failures and repeating the same resolutions. For this reason, He gave me a visible sign by which I may be assured that He is willing to forgive me over and over again, as long as I am humble enough to confess my sins, sincere enough to renew my efforts, and determined enough to keep trying, regardless of discouragement, self-doubts, and fear of God's rejection.

Just as He understood the emotional conflicts, mental confusion, moral weakness, persistent fears, and stubborn doubts of His beloved disciples, so too does He understand my human limitations and personal defects. Just as

He appreciated the good will that made them repent their abandoning Him in His sufferings and doubting Him in His resurrection, so too does He appreciate the good will that brings me back to Him every time I fail Him by my sins. Though I consider myself unworthy of Him because I return for my own "selfish" reasons, He is glad that I return. Like the father of the prodigal son, He asks no questions and offers no criticism, but rejoices that I have come back to His house for forgiveness, assistance, and a chance to try again.

RESPOND My Jesus, when Peter asked You how often he should forgive others, You said "seventy times seven times," which is equivalent to our expression, "a million times." This is truly Your attitude toward me. You set no limit to Your pardon. Your heart is ever ready to receive me, forgive me, and help me begin again. If I do not tire of beginning again, You will never tire of forgiving again. Amen.

180. THOMAS DOUBTS

READ Now Thomas, one of the Twelve, called the Twin, was not with them when Jesus came. The other disciples therefore said to him, "We have seen the Lord." But he said to them, "Unless I see in his hands the print of the nails, and put my finger into the place of the nails, and put my hand into his side, I will not believe." And after eight days, his disciples were again inside, and Thomas with them. Jesus came, the doors being closed, and stood in their midst, and said, "Peace be to you." Then he said to Thomas, "Bring here thy finger, and see my hands; and bring forth thy hand, and put it into my side; and be not unbelieving, but believing." Thomas answered and said to him, "My Lord and my God!" Jesus said to him, "Because thou hast seen me, thou hast believed. Blessed are they who have not seen, and yet have believed." (John 20:24–29)

REFLECT It was quite a shock to the disciples to hear Thomas' refusal to accept their testimony. His demand to see and touch must have seemed blasphemous to them. In spite of their efforts to convince Thomas, he remained fixed in his attitude. Jesus returned a week later. With understanding, patience, and gentleness, He offered to satisfy Thomas' demands. At the same time, however, He declared the excellence of pure faith. Thomas should have recalled that Jesus had foretold His resurrection, and should have believed it on His word.

REVIEW What made Thomas doubt? Was he trying to overcome his disappointment at missing Jesus? Did his disappointment make him unwilling to support the joy of his more fortunate companions? Was he, perhaps, afraid that this news was too good to be true? Whatever his reasons, his emotions influenced his thinking and swayed his will toward a stubborn refusal to believe.

From this incident I can learn a precious lesson. My emotions enter into practically everything I think, judge, say, and do. My need to be at peace with myself can make me compete with others in a million hidden ways. My desire to feel equal or superior to others, can make me foolishly prejudiced, not only toward them as persons, but also toward what they say and accomplish. I may be so intent on looking for their human flaws and personal defects, that I may not hear the truth they speak or see the good they perform.

Jesus asks me to believe His truth on His word, even when it is brought to me by human messengers. He bids me hear His voice and see His presence with the ears and eyes of faith. His grace, however, can be hindered unless I learn to be reasonably content with myself and intelligently willing to accept others as they are. Free of immature competition with others, I shall find it easier to make use of Christ's gift of faith.

RESPOND   My Jesus, You speak to me through many channels. Let me not be blind to Your nearness or deaf to Your voice when You approach me through human agents. Help me raise my vision above these people and see You. In this way I shall avoid the mistake of Thomas. Amen.

181.   JESUS FEEDS HIS TIRED DISCIPLES

READ   After these things, Jesus manifested himself again at the sea of Tiberias. Now he manifested himself in this way. There were together Simon Peter and Thomas . . . Nathaniel . . . and the sons of Zebedee, and two others of his disciples. Simon Peter said to them, "I am going fishing." They said to him, "We also are going with thee." And they went out and got into the boat. And that night they caught nothing. But when day was breaking, Jesus stood on the beach; then Jesus said to them, "Young men, have you any fish?" They answered him, "No." He said to them, "Cast the net to the right of the boat, and you will find them." They cast therefore, and now they were unable to draw it for the great number of fishes. . . . When, therefore, they had landed, they saw a fire ready, and a fish laid upon it, and bread. Jesus said to them, "Bring here some of the fishes that you caught just now." . . . "Come and breakfast." . . . And Jesus came and took the bread and gave it to them, and likewise the fish. (John 21:1–6, 9–13)

REFLECT   This event is a striking example of Christ's personal concern for the natural needs of His disciples. Knowing how tired and hungry they were, He prepared breakfast for them. Though they did not recognize Him at first, they were convinced it was He when they made the large catch at His bidding. They sat down to eat, content to be with Him.

REVIEW In His plan of redemption, Jesus intends my daily life to be a close friendship with Him. It is not to be a one-sided friendship, which might simply require my loyalty to Him, but one in which He will be constantly working for my benefit and advantages. Just as He has given me supernatural power to help others by my prayers, example, and self-giving, so too has He taken it upon Himself to be my Helper in my difficulties, my Adviser in my problems, and my Support in my adversities and sorrows.

I am not expected to think little of this earthly life or to despise it. My earthly needs and wants are important not only to me, but also to Jesus. As He stood upon the shore watching His disciples labor all night in vain, He rewarded their labors by ministering to their bodily needs. I must become ever more Christ-conscious in my daily routine. He is near me in my home, my place of work, and in every place I visit. He is present in the circle of my family, among my friends, and in every person I meet. He approaches me in every human being, and draws near to them through me. In a very real sense, I can think of Jesus as my better half.

RESPOND My Jesus, help me drink deeply the truth of this meditation, so that it may enrich my daily life. As I draw closer to You in my desires and efforts, I shall know the joy of being accepted by You. I shall share with You my thoughts, worries, needs, and successes, and You will grant me that interior peace and contentment for which every heart yearns. Amen.

182. THE PRIMACY OF PETER

READ When, therefore, they had breakfasted, Jesus said to Simon Peter, "Simon, son of John, dost thou love me more than these do?" He said to him, "Yes, Lord, thou knowest that I love thee." He said to him, "Feed my lambs." He said to him a second time, "Simon, son of John, dost thou love me?" He said to him, "Yes, Lord, thou knowest that I love thee." He said to him, "Feed my lambs." A third time he said to him, "Simon, son of John, dost thou love me?" Peter was grieved because he said to him for the third time, "Dost thou love me?" And he said to him, "Lord, thou knowest all things, thou knowest that I love thee." He said to him, "Feed my sheep." (John 21:15–17)

REFLECT On this occasion Jesus showed what an understanding, accepting, and forgiving Savior He is. He probably had a twinkle in His eye as He asked Peter whether he had a greater love than the rest, as Peter had implied at the last supper. Jesus gently showed Peter that while he might be able to express his own love, only God could say whose love was greater. Peter understood the lesson only too well. However, he was hurt at the repetition of the question, since it seemed to imply that Christ doubted his love. That there was no doubt in the mind of Jesus is plain from the fact that He now confirmed the appointment which He had previously predicted. Peter was to be the visible foundation of Christ's Church and the chief pastor of His flock.

REVIEW This was a solemn and joyful moment, not only for Peter, but also for every sincere Christian who would ever fail Jesus in a moment of weakness. By his behavior Peter had admitted his shame and sorrow for denying and deserting his captured Master. At the same time, he refused to surrender to discouragement and morbid self-punishment. He would not destroy his mind, and heart, and life, as Judas had done. As he reflected on his present situation, he knew that Jesus would want him to come back to the confused and frightened disciples. Sure as Peter was now of his human weakness, he was just as sure of his desire to love and serve his divine Master. He therefore returned to the disciples and remained with them, awaiting some sign from heaven.

Like Peter, I too have my moments of confusion and weakness. Like him, I must refuse to let my failings and sins discourage me. Like him, I have a task to perform in life. The less I brood over my shortcomings, the more time, energy, and grace shall I have to perform my duties and obligations. I must quickly return to my proper place, where I shall find Jesus awaiting me. As He did with Peter, He will show me no disgust or condemnation, but only understanding, acceptance, mercy, and love. He will gladly accept my sorrow and forgive my sins, and then request that I take up where I left off in my resolutions and efforts to please Him in my daily life.

RESPOND   My Jesus, when shall I cease feeling that You think like me? You came to save, not condemn. Your greatest desire is to forgive and encourage, so that I may make the most of my life, in spite of my failures and sins. Help me trust at last in Your divine wisdom, goodness, and love. Let me look back only long enough to learn from my mistakes, understand my weaknesses, and prepare for future opportunities and temptations. Then, like Peter, I hope to take up where I left off, to offer You a more mature, intelligent, and faithful service. Amen.

183. THE DIVINE COMMISSION

READ But the eleven disciples went into Galilee, to the mountain where Jesus had directed them to go. And when they saw him they worshipped him; but some doubted. And Jesus drew near and spoke to them saying, "All power in heaven and on earth has been given to me. Go, therefore, and make disciples of all nations, baptizing them in the name of the Father, and of the Son, and of the Holy Spirit, teaching them to observe all that I have commanded you; and behold, I am with you all days, even unto the consummation of the world." (Matt. 28:16–20)

REFLECT Jesus now completes His work of redemption. He is about to ascend into heaven, and will henceforth remain invisible to his followers. He commissions them to teach the world in His name and promises His guarantee of orthodoxy. So truly will He guide His disciples in the truth and guard them against error, that those who hear them will be hearing Him, and those who reject them will be rejecting Him.

REVIEW Being human, I am open to many errors in my thinking and to many mistakes in my decisions. My sincerity is no guarantee against false ideas, and my good will is no defense against the deceptions of Satan and worldly men. This commission of Christ to His Church, grants me the guarantee and the defense I need. In listening to the teachings of His Church, I hear Him, and in applying these teachings to my daily life, I can be sure that I follow Him.

However, I shall better insure myself against misapplying Christ's teachings if I improve my understanding of human nature. I may then more easily avoid the misconceptions or immature idealism that compels some to make impossible demands on themselves or others; and I may better avert the inner anxiety, strain, fatigue, depression, and discouragement that often lead to tepidity and laxity in religious practice.

With an improved knowledge of Christ's truth and of human nature, I can make better use of God's graces. I can daily advance in my appreciation of His infinite goodness, Christ's personal love for me, my own individual worth, and an intelligent consideration for the needs and shortcomings of others. My interior peace will increase through my supernatural conviction of God's concern for me, my reasonable contentment with my real self, my mature desire for self-improvement, my humble acceptance of my natural limitations, my realistic patience with unintended mistakes, my sincere sorrow for my real sins, and my wholesome willingness to keep trying in spite of repeated failures. Being at peace with myself and with God, I shall be disposed to acknowledge the talents and virtues of others, understand their weaknesses, and leave their judgment to God when they appear to be guilty of sin.

RESPOND   My Jesus, may I never tire of improving my understanding of God, myself, and my neighbor. When, however, my natural knowledge fails me, may Your divine truth and personal example guide me through the dark hours and lighten the burden that weighs me down. With You I hope to walk daily toward eternal life, in spite of the blinding gloom and rocky paths that lie before me. Amen.

Image Books

... MAKING THE WORLD'S FINEST
CATHOLIC LITERATURE AVAILABLE TO ALL

I 6

Image Books

ON THE TRUTH OF THE CATHOLIC FAITH
Summa Contra Gentiles Book II: Creation. Newly translated, with an Introduction and notes by James F. Anderson D27—95¢

ON THE TRUTH OF THE CATHOLIC FAITH
Summa Contra Gentiles Book III: Providence. Newly translated, with an Introduction and notes by Vernon J. Bourke
D28a Book III, Part 1—95¢
D28b Book III, Part 2—95¢

ON THE TRUTH OF THE CATHOLIC FAITH
Summa Contra Gentiles Book IV: Salvation. Newly translated, with an Introduction and notes. By Charles J. O'Neill D29—95¢

THE WORLD'S FIRST LOVE
By Fulton J. Sheen D30—85¢

THE SIGN OF JONAS
By Thomas Merton D31—95¢

PARENTS, CHILDREN AND THE FACTS OF LIFE
Sattler, C.S.S.R. D32—75¢

LIGHT ON THE MOUNTAIN:
The Story of La Salette
By John S. Kennedy D33—75¢

EDMUND CAMPION
By Evelyn Waugh D34—75¢

HUMBLE POWERS
By Paul Horgan D35—75¢

SAINT THOMAS AQUINAS
By G. K. Chesterton D36—75¢

APOLOGIA PRO VITA SUA
By John Henry Cardinal Newman Introduction by Philip Hughes D37—95¢

A HANDBOOK OF THE CATHOLIC FAITH
By Dr. N. G. M. Van Doornik, Rev. S. Jelsma, Rev. A. Van De Lisdonk. Ed. Rev. John Greenwood D38—$1.55

THE NEW TESTAMENT
Official Catholic edition
D39—95¢

MARIA CHAPDELAINE
By Louis Hémon D40—65¢

SAINT AMONG THE HURONS
By Francis X. Talbot, S.J.
D41—95¢

THE PATH TO ROME
By Hilaire Belloc D42—85¢

SORROW BUILT A BRIDGE
By Katherine Burton D43—85¢

THE WISE MAN FROM THE WEST
By Vincent Cronin D44—85¢

EXISTENCE AND THE EXISTENT
By Jacques Maritain D45—75¢

THE STORY OF THE TRAPP FAMILY SINGERS
By Maria Augusta Trapp
D46—95¢

THE WORLD, THE FLESH AND FATHER SMITH
By Bruce Marshall D47—75¢

THE CHRIST OF CATHOLICISM
By Dom Aelred Graham
D48—95¢

SAINT FRANCIS XAVIER
By James Brodrick, S.J.
D49—95¢

SAINT FRANCIS OF ASSISI
By G. K. Chesterton D50—75¢

Image Books

*...making the world's finest
Catholic literature available to all*

VIPERS' TANGLE
by François Mauriac D51—75¢

THE MANNER IS ORDINARY
by John LaFarge, S.J. D52—95¢

MY LIFE FOR MY SHEEP
by Alfred Duggan D53—90¢

**THE CHURCH AND THE RECON-
STRUCTION OF THE MODERN
WORLD:** *The Social Encyclicals
of Pius XI.* Edited by T. P. Mc-
Laughlin, C.S.B. D54—$1.25

A GILSON READER: *Selections from
the Writings of Etienne Gilson.*
Edited by Anton C. Pegis.
D55—$1.25

**THE AUTOBIOGRAPHY OF
ST. THERESE OF LISIEUX:** *The Story
of a Soul. A new translation by*
John Beevers. D56—75¢

HELENA
by Evelyn Waugh D57—75¢

THE GREATEST BIBLE STORIES
A Catholic Anthology from
World Literature. Edited by Anne
Fremantle. D58—75¢

THE CITY OF GOD—St. Augustine.
Edited with Intro. by Vernon J.
Bourke. Foreword by Etienne
Gilson. D59—$1.55

SUPERSTITION CORNER
by Sheila Kaye-Smith D60—65¢

SAINTS AND OURSELVES
Ed. by Philip Caraman, S.J.
D61—95¢

CANA IS FOREVER
by Charles Hugo Doyle
D62—85¢

**ASCENT OF MOUNT CARMEL—
St. John of the Cross.** Translated
and Edited by E. Allison Peers.
D63—$1.25

**RELIGION AND THE RISE OF
WESTERN CULTURE**
by Christopher Dawson
D64—85¢

**PRINCE OF DARKNESS AND OTHER
STORIES**
by J. F. Powers D65—85¢

ST. THOMAS MORE
by E. E. Reynolds D66—95¢

JESUS AND HIS TIMES
2 Volumes D67A—95¢
by Daniel-Rops D67B—95¢

ST. BENEDICT
by Justin McCann, O.S.B.
D68—85¢

THE LITTLE FLOWERS OF ST. FRANCIS
Edited and Translated by
Raphael Brown. D69—95¢

THE QUIET LIGHT
by Louis de Wohl D70—95¢

CHARACTERS OF THE REFORMATION
by Hilaire Belloc D71—85¢

THE BELIEF OF CATHOLICS
by Ronald Knox D72—75¢

FAITH AND FREEDOM
by Barbara Ward D73—95¢

**GOD AND INTELLIGENCE IN
MODERN PHILOSOPHY**
by Fulton J. Sheen D74—$1.25

If your bookseller is unable to supply certain titles, write to Image
Books, Department MIB, Garden City, New York, stating the
titles you desire and enclosing the price of each book (plus 5¢
per book to cover cost of postage and handling). Prices are subject to change without notice.